Business and Public Policy

Series Editor:

ASEEM PRAKASH, University of Washington

Series Board:

Vinod K. Aggarwal, University of California, Berkeley
Tanja A. Börzel, Freie Universität Berlin
David Coen, University College London
Peter Gourevitch, University of California, San Diego
Neil Gunningham, The Australian National University
Witold J. Henisz, University of Pennsylvania
Adrienne Héritier, European University Institute
Chung-in Moon, Yonsei University
Sarah A. Soule, Stanford University
David Vogel, University of California, Berkeley

This series aims to play a pioneering role in shaping the emerging field of business and public policy. *Business and Public Policy* focuses on two central questions. First, how does public policy influence business strategy, operations, organization, and governance, and with what consequences for both business and society? Second, how do businesses themselves influence policy institutions, policy processes, and other policy actors, and with what outcomes?

Other books in the series:

TIMOTHY WERNER, *Public Forces and Private Politics in American Big Business*
HEVINA S. DASHWOOD, *The Rise of Global Corporate Social Responsibility: Mining and the Spread of Global Norms*
LLEWELYN HUGHES, *Globalizing Oil: Firms and Oil Market Governance in France, Japan, and the United States*
EDWARD T. WALKER, *Grassroots for Hire: Public Affairs Consultants in American Democracy*

The Managerial Sources of Corporate Social Responsibility

The Spread of Global Standards

CHRISTIAN R. THAUER
The Hebrew University of Jerusalem
Department of International Relations, Center
for German Studies

CAMBRIDGE
UNIVERSITY PRESS

University Printing House, Cambridge CB2 8BS, United Kingdom

Cambridge University Press is part of the University of Cambridge.

It furthers the University's mission by disseminating knowledge in the pursuit of education, learning and research at the highest international levels of excellence.

www.cambridge.org
Information on this title: www.cambridge.org/9781107066533

First published 2014

Printed in the United Kingdom by Clays, St Ives plc

A catalogue record for this publication is available from the British Library

Library of Congress Cataloguing in Publication data
Thauer, Christian
The managerial sources of corporate social responsibility: the spread of global standards / Christian R. Thauer.
    pages   cm. – (Business and public policy)
Includes bibliographical references and index.
ISBN 978-1-107-06653-3 (hardback)
1. Social responsibility of business.   2. Management – Moral and ethical aspects.   3. Management – Environmental aspects.   I. Title.
HD60.T466   2014
658.4'08–dc23   2014006058

ISBN 978-1-107-06653-3 Hardback

Contents

Figures

Tables

1 | *Introduction*

In Durban, South Africa, the textile firm Crossley Carpets provides HIV/AIDS-related health care services to employees and their families.[1] The firm produces hotel carpets for big chains such as the Hilton and Marriott. Its factory has an on-site clinic that employs specifically trained nurses and arranges for doctor visitations. It hands out immune boosters to employees who have contracted HIV and consults them on how to avoid the outbreak of AIDS. What is more, the clinic treats the so-called "secondary diseases" of HIV/AIDS such as tuberculosis, organizes sexual education training and awareness-raising campaigns, and distributes condoms and information pamphlets among employees. The firm also runs environmental programs high above the level of what would be legally required if environmental laws and regulations were strictly enforced in Durban. In China's Zhejiang province, Nike, the large multinational sportswear and apparel brand, demands that its suppliers apply the minimum labor standards of the International Labour Organization (ILO) (Locke *et al.* 2007; see Chapter 6 for details). The brand's workers benefit from relatively well-paying jobs with a regular five-day work week and eight-hour days, where overtime is subject to clear procedures and extra compensation.

These corporations stand out for their responsibility vis-à-vis their workers and the local environment. They particularly stand out in the context of South Africa and China, where the state often lacks the capacity, the competence, and at times also the willingness to set and enforce rules and regulations and to provide vital services. Moreover, these corporations stand out for defying common wisdom. Firms are profit-driven while social and environmental standards are costly. Common expectation would therefore have them behave more like the

---

[1] Interview with the Director of Human Resources, the Assistant to the Managing Director, the Chief Engineer, and the Environmental Manager of Crossley Carpets, September 28, 2007, Durban.

multinational high-end fashion and luxury goods brand, C.[2] Just like the sportswear and apparel company Nike, C has a number of suppliers in Zhejiang province. Among them is CL, a firm making leather products near the city of Tonglu. Unlike the suppliers of Nike, however, CL does not adhere to any standards of corporate social responsibility. CL is a "sweatshop" (see Chapter 6 for details). Production at CL involves chemical leather-treatment processes that expose workers to health-hazards such as fumes and gases. Working hours exceed the legal maximum and overtime is unpaid. Children as young as eight work and live in the factory far from their families, and suffer intimidation and mistreatment. The firm releases untreated chemical effluents into the river behind the factory building. C has a hands-on policy towards its suppliers. "Inspectors" (Héritier *et al.* 2009) of C are permanently present at CL, supervising the production process. As most firms with a brand name to protect, C has an official corporate social responsibility policy. In it, C demands from its suppliers to meet minimum labor, safety, and health standards, and to protect the environment. The conditions at CL violate this policy in every way. Yet the inspectors of C at CL take no action. As long as CL meets C's price and quality demands, they are satisfied and there is nothing to report.

The central question in this book is: *why do some firms care about the wellbeing of their workers and the natural environment while others remain indifferent and are even accomplices of social and environmental exploitation?* This book addresses this question by laying out a new transaction cost theory-based perspective on corporate social responsibility suggesting that *internal* drivers are important for our understanding of firm behavior in relation to social and environmental standards. The concept of corporate social responsibility is understood as companies caring for the wellbeing of their workers, for the natural environment, or for society in general by adhering to international standards.

What does this book mean by *internal* drivers? *Internal* – or *intraorganizational* – drivers are asset-specific investments within a firm. For example, when a company invests in employee skills which are otherwise hard to come by on the labor market, these skills are internal asset-specific investments. The firm is then motivated to provide social and

---

[2] Firm names are abbreviated to allow for anonymity. Most firm cases in the analyses in this book will be presented in this way.

health-related services to its employees in order to maintain their good health, thus enabling them to continue working. In South Africa, for instance, HIV/AIDS is heavily affecting the productivity of firms. Those companies that have made investments in rare skills run strong HIV/AIDS workplace programs in order to ensure they can reap the benefits of a workforce capable of fulfilling highly specific tasks. The textile firm Crossley Carpets is such a business, having invested in engineering skills specific to the processes and needs of its production. The Human Resources Director of Crossley Carpets explains: "the skills that we require here, most of them cannot be found or recruited from anywhere because we use specialized machines." Hence, "the difficulty with respect to a high prevalence rate of HIV/AIDS is that you will be losing some very good, experienced workers that have attained these unique skills. The HIV/AIDS program is one way of trying to retain these skills."[3]

This book makes four asset specificity-based arguments for internal drivers, which serve to explain four causal relationships:

(1) between a firm's investments in rare skills – and labor-related stand ards and workplace programs, as in the case of Crossley Carpets. The argument in relation to the first internal driver is that *asset-specific investments in unique skills motivate firms to adopt high social and labor standards (hypothesis 1)*;

(2) between long pay-off times of investments in production sites and technology – and environmental standards. The argument in relation to the second internal driver is that *asset-specific investments in plant sites incline firms to adopt strict environmental standards (hypothesis 2)*;

(3) between asset-specific investments that originate from a highly regulating "home" country and are made in production sites located in a weakly regulating "host" country – and the transfer of high environmental standards from "home" to "host" country operations. The argument in relation to the third internal driver is that *asset-specific investments originating from a highly regulating country cause a transfer of high standards to operations in a weakly regulating country (hypothesis 3)*;

---

[3] Interview with the Director of Human Resources of Crossley Carpets, September 28, 2007, Durban.

(4) between dependency on brand image – and corporate social responsibility. The argument in relation to the fourth internal driver is that
*asset-specific investments in marketing result in a general concern
for corporate social responsibility (hypothesis 4).*

Intra-organizational dynamics of business social conduct have so far
not been studied extensively.[4] Much of the literature concentrates on
external drivers of corporate social responsibility: it is the influx of
foreign direct investment originating from a home country with high
levels of self-regulation (Greenhill *et al.* 2010; Prakash and Potoski
2007; Zeng and Eastin 2007) and exports to a highly regulating country, which triggers the diffusion of high standards among firms in low-
regulating countries (Greenhill *et al.* 2009). This so-called "California
effect" (Vogel 1995) can also be unleashed by firms operating on high
voluntary standards that lobby governments to strengthen regulation in
order to keep foreign competitors operating on lower standards out of
the market (Börzel *et al.* 2011). Other studies point to the importance of
pressure from consumers (Auld *et al.* 2008; Epstein 2008; Smith 2008),
NGOs (Barry *et al.* 2012; Hendry 2006; Schepers 2006), associations
(Cutler *et al.* 1999; Hall and Bierstecker 2002; Ronit and Schneider
2000), and the reputation which standards provide (Abbott and Snidal
2009; Prakash and Potoski 2006).

These externally oriented explanations have significantly enhanced
our understanding of business behavior in relation to regulatory standards under conditions of economic globalization. Until recently, firms
investing in overseas markets were considered to do so exclusively for
the end of profiting from "pollution havens" and generally lax standards (Collingsworth *et al.* 1994; Mani and Wheeler 1998; Xing and
Kolstad 2002). They were thus presumed to drive states into a regulatory "race to the bottom" (Bohle 2008; Chan 2003; Singh and Zammit
2004): competitive downsizing of regulation or "regulatory freeze"
(Madsen 2009: 1298) with the intent to create comparative cost advantages. *External*-driver analyses showed that business does not always
and does not necessarily play such a destructive role in relation to the

---

[4] Notable exceptions are the works of Prakash (2000), Gunningham *et al.* (2003),
Howard-Grenville (2007), Dashwood (2012) and Thauer (2014). This book seeks
to complement and further develop this literature; also in econometric analyses
some internal factors have been featured as control variables (for example,
Khanna *et al.* 2007).

establishment of regulatory standards. On account of external drivers, firms voluntarily adhere to high international social and environmental standards in offshore production locations (Flohr *et al.* 2010; Mol 2001; Vogel and Kagan 2004), and sometimes even drive a regulatory "race to the top" in emerging markets – competitive upgrading of regulation or convergence of standards on the highest level (Blanton and Blanton 2009; Börzel and Thauer 2013; Prakash and Potoski 2006).

, However, external driver-oriented analyses have also limited our perspective, as they assume – not unlike the "race to the bottom" argument – that firms' profit-maximization and the establishment of social and environmental standards are generally incompatible. Indeed there are many examples illustrating this assumption. The luxury goods brand C, for instance, may serve as a case in point. As mentioned, C is a firm that ignores social and environmental standards for the sake of saving costs and maximizing profits. In such cases, only strong external pressure – exerted by NGOs, consumers, or states threatening to impose stricter regulation – can possibly bring about corporate social responsibility. This is what external-driver analyses point out. But is this the whole picture?

Crossley Carpets, to mention an example of a firm that feels responsible for its workers and the environment, shows that there is more to corporate social responsibility than external pressure on business. This textile company was not facing any external pressures when it decided to confront the problem of HIV/AIDS. Neither was the firm pushed by consumers, nor forced by government, NGOs, unions, or associations. It decided to fight the disease to protect the rare skills its production depends upon. The perspective of this book, focusing on internal drivers, draws our attention to cases of *intrinsic* motivation. It suggests that – under the conditions specified – it is *intra*-organizational *economic rationale* that determines the choice for corporate social responsibility. This means that, unlike previously assumed, profit-orientation and the establishment of standards are not mutually incompatible. Accordingly, the perspective on internal drivers in this book provides us with a more complete picture of how, why, and when firms engage in corporate social responsibility. It also helps understand the variation in the preferences firms have in this respect: even if external pressure factors (NGO-pressure, consumer demands, private regulation set by associations or other non-state bodies) are either constant or absent,

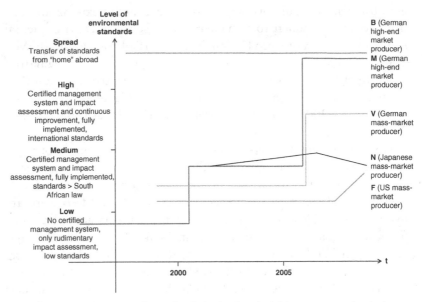

Figure 1.1 Environmental standards in the South African automotive industry over time

this book argues that we will see variation in the level and type of corporate social responsibility among firms on account of internal drivers.

By taking into account varying preferences of firms for corporate social responsibility, this book addresses and resolves some important empirical puzzles. The South African automotive industry and its concern for environmental standards is an example of such a puzzle, as illustrated by Figure 1.1. The five car firms – each represented by one line – are structurally very similar: they originate from Germany, Japan, and the US, where environmental regulations are stricter than in South Africa.[5] They are equally embedded in the web of global production and trade that characterizes the automotive industry in general. The production of these five firms in South Africa is also export-oriented to the same extent. In addition, the companies are under similar scrutiny and pressure by transnational, national, and

---

[5] Barnes and Black 2003; Black 2001; Lorentzen 2006; Lorentzen and Barnes 2004; Meyn 2004. See Chapter 5 for a detailed analysis.

local civil society groups and NGOs. From the perspective of external driver-based analyses of corporate social responsibility one would suspect these firms to operate on similar levels with regard to environmental standards. Yet they show remarkable differences when looked at over time. What explains these differences?

Internal drivers are the answer: the level of *intra*-organizational investments in production sites with long pay-off periods causes the different levels of environmental standards among these firms. Such investments are asset-specific and create a distinct "managerial dilemma" (Miller 1992). While they increase production output and, thus, potentially profits, they also bear some significant risks and hazards from the perspective of management. It will be increasingly difficult to control and to incentivize the production unit to make efficient use of resources once it has received the long-term investment. Inefficient use of resources, in turn, may result in a loss of profits, however. In addition, what makes investments with long pay-off periods risky is that profits will to a large extent be dependent on cost factors beyond the control of the firm. Costs for energy, water, waste management, and transportation may rise in the future and challenge the envisioned returns of the investments made.

These are typical concerns in the face of long-term, asset-specific investments. There are ways to deal with them. A manager of a car company in South Africa, for instance, points to the necessity that "we bring the house in order before we make any such long-term investments."[6] By this he means that management in the global headquarters in Stuttgart, Germany, requires the production plant in South Africa to implement strict quality, environmental, and health-related management systems. These systems structure and regulate processes at the production site in South Africa. They allow management in Stuttgart to control and verify that the production unit is following procedures. Such measures, in turn, help to assess and control any uncertainties that may arise from fluctuating costs in the investment's environment, such as a rise in energy, water, or waste management costs. It is for these reasons of organizational efficiency and control that the car firms in Figure 1.1 show different levels of environmental standards over time. Whenever one of the South African car firms represented in the graph

---

[6] Interview with the Manager: Quality and Integrated Management Systems of M South Africa, September 23, 2008, East London.

receives long-term investments from global operations head office management, the branch has to demonstrate beforehand that it has increased the strictness and level of standards of its rule-based systems of management. Environmental standards and management systems are at the very core of "bringing the house in order." They guarantee an efficient use of resources and minimize costs for utilities and services. Hence, the level of environmental standards rises each time before any such investment is made.

The empirical analysis in this book demonstrates that internal drivers solve a whole variety of such puzzles – and in very different contexts. The investigation will take the reader to automotive and textile factories in South Africa and textile manufacturers in China showing how internal drivers bring about corporate social responsibility in these distinct settings. Internal drivers explain labor, social, and health policies of firms. They also explain environmental standards, as in the puzzle of different levels of environmental policies in the South African car industry illustrated by Figure 1.1. While analytically important for our understanding of corporate social responsibility, the argument for internal drivers has some very important implications for policy-making inside and outside of firms as well: according to the arguments in this book, top managers gain rather than lose managerial freedoms when they force their companies to act in a socially responsible way following international standards. Corporate social responsibility is a means by which management can maintain its discretion and solve managerial dilemmas, for example when deciding to make long-term investments in production sites in offshore markets such as South Africa.

The findings in this book are also important for those who drive corporate social responsibility within firms, such as health, human resources, and environmental managers or union activists. Relating corporate social responsibility to economic risk minimization and efficiency concerns moves the issue closer to the center stage of intra-firm decision-making. In this way, demands for higher standards may receive greater support from top management. Beyond the firm, this book may provide external stakeholders, such as NGOs, representatives of development agencies, or government agencies, with a better understanding of what it is that drives firms in terms of corporate social responsibility. What will come to light is that not all firms are the same and thus require a varied approach in dealing with them. Firms that have internal drivers can be reliable allies in the context of joint health, social, or environmental governance projects, public–private partnerships or multi-stakeholder initiatives. However, firms that lack internal drivers will only behave responsibly if pressured to do so by external forces. These considerations should help policy-makers decide whether to pursue collaborative or conflict-oriented strategies vis-à-vis a firm. Finally, investors may wish to take note of the *economic rationale* for corporate social responsibility laid out in this book. It suggests that long-term investments in a company should be based on a priori proof of high social and environmental standards in relevant areas so as to guarantee that the "house is in order" and risks are minimized.

This book will first lay out in detail a theory of internal drivers. It will then demonstrate the plausibility, applicability, validity, and importance of the argument for internal drivers in different contexts and empirical settings. Chapter 2, *A theory of internal drivers of corporate social responsibility*, develops the key theoretical argument that *intra*-organizational asset-specific investments and the managerial dilemmas they give rise to cause corporate social responsibility. This chapter specifies four such dilemmas: the *human resources dilemma* (internal driver 1); the *foreign direct investment dilemma* (internal driver 2); the *technological specialization dilemma* (internal driver 3); and the *brand reputation dilemma* (internal driver 4). The theoretical analysis in this chapter specifies why and under which conditions they lead to corporate social responsibility. It also discusses the conditions under which the arguments for internal drivers apply and thus defines the limits of the theory suggested here.

Chapter 3, *Corporate social responsibility: an inside-view approach and perspective*, discusses the conceptual, methodological, and empirical foundations of the subsequent inquiry. It suggests looking *inside* the firm, but not only for the purpose of investigating internal drivers. The aim here is to observe corporate social responsibility in the behavior and practices of firms. In addition, the chapter lays out the organization of the empirical investigation and the logic according to which this book evaluates the theory of internal drivers, as well as the case selection. Moreover, it describes the institutional, policy, industry, and market contexts of the following case study analysis, which will take the reader to South African car and textile firms, as well as to textile firms in China.

Chapters 4–6 consider the theoretical arguments that have been previously construed empirically. They illustrate and test the arguments for internal drivers. Chapter 4 studies the responses of firms to the

HIV/AIDS pandemic in South Africa. Taking the example of nine firms in the auto and textile industries, the analysis shows that there is an emerging diffusion of HIV/AIDS workplace programs among firms in the country – where most of the population affected by the disease does not have access to health care. However, the nine cases also illustrate significant variation: while some firms run sophisticated HIV/AIDS programs, others show such activities only to a lesser extent or do not confront the problems resulting from this disease at all. What is it that may explain these differences? First, the chapter considers external drivers such as NGO pressure and other potential explanations for corporate social responsibility one can find in the literature. It emerges that none of the established factors can sufficiently explain the nine cases. For this, one must resort to internal driver 1, the *human resources dilemma*, as the subsequent analysis of the cases according to paired comparisons demonstrates. What is more, the investigation shows – through the application of process-tracing methods – that internal driver 1 is not only a valid predictor of HIV/AIDS programs. The analysis shows that the theorized logic and causal mechanisms unraveled by this driver are really the ones that motivate decision-making within the nine firms.

Chapter 5 is an inquiry into environmental policies of firms in South Africa, which are only weakly regulated and rarely enforced by the state. The chapter begins with a detailed discussion of the puzzle of environmental policies of multinational car firms, as illustrated in Figure 1.1. This discussion establishes the relevance of this puzzle and shows that external factors and other explanations for corporate social responsibility highlighted in the literature fail to explain it. The analysis then considers internal drivers 2 and 3, the *technological specialization and foreign direct investment dilemmas* in relation to the cases of the puzzle in paired comparisons in order to resolve it. Additional within-case, process-tracing analyses show that the theorized causal mechanism relating these internal drivers to environmental policies does not only lead to valid predictions, it is also empirically sound as it reflects the decision-making processes within the featured firms. The chapter then ventures beyond the car industry and investigates South African textile firms in order to establish the general validity of the relation between asset-specific investments in production technology and environmental policies. The analysis shows that this relation is not only valid in the context of the *foreign direct investment dilemma* – that is, when firms are based on investments originating from a highly regulating country – but also when they originate from a weakly regulating country such as South Africa.

Chapter 6 is an evaluation of internal driver 4, the *brand reputation dilemma*. It begins by presenting disconfirming evidence: the South African car industry, as well as the luxury fashion goods brand C and its relation to the supplier factory CL in China, offer no recognizable evidence that asset-specific investments in marketing have a bearing on the firms' engagement in corporate social responsibility. The chapter then turns to a consideration of cases in the South African textile industry where internal driver 4 has the expected effects, thus raising the question of what it is that accounts for this difference. An inductive investigation of cases suggests that internal driver 4 is valid only in combination with strong and recurrent NGO pressure and that, in turn, NGO pressure is only exerting effects on companies if they have internal driver 4. The remainder of the chapter assesses this inductively derived, internal–external driver nexus proposition by looking at the three US American brands Wal-Mart, Nike, and Gap and their sourcing practices in China and South Africa.

Finally, Chapter 7, *Conclusion: internal drivers, corporate social responsibility, and the spread of global standards*, summarizes the findings of this book and considers their importance in terms of their broader theoretical and practical implications. This discussion asks how far the arguments developed here travel, and relates these findings to debates concerned with the effects of globalization on regulation, the diffusion of policies and standards, comparative capitalism and welfare state policies, and governance in areas of limited statehood.

2 | A theory of internal drivers of corporate social responsibility

The perspective on *internal* drivers in this study alludes to a basic idea: if we wish to understand corporate social responsibility, we need to put ourselves in the position of those who decide for or against it. In corporations, decision-making power is in the hands of top management in head offices. What is it that makes these managers, whose task it is after all to run operations in the most cost-effective way, consider the welfare of employees and society in general and to this end voluntarily adopt costly standards? As explained in Chapter 1, previous analyses, particularly in political science, have focused on external pressure factors as drivers of corporate social responsibility. These often treated the firm as a "black box": NGO pressure, consumer pressure, self-regulation in the context of business associations, or market pressures for reputational gain, are external pressure factors that act on firms. They, in turn, react by adopting high business standards, irrespective of *intra*-organizational processes. In situations in which firms are, indeed, under strong external pressure, such an approach may suffice at times. However, it does not give us the full picture. Management decisions are usually determined by external *and* internal considerations. In terms of the latter, power struggles, rivalries, conflicts, and personal and organizational limitations as well as cognitive ones are factors that managers bear in mind when evaluating strategy options.[1] Two firms, if put in an identical external environment, may nevertheless

---

[1] Concerning this "political" perspective on the nature of *intra*-firm decision-making, see Alchian and Demsetz 1972; Dow 1985; Eccks 1985; Hart 2010; March 1962; Milgrom and Roberts 1988; Miller 1992; overview in Barney and Hesterly 2006. Approaches that have addressed *intra*-organizational dynamics for the analysis of voluntary standards and corporate social responsibility are: Dashwood (2012); Gunningham *et al.* (2003); Howard-Grenville (2007); Prakash (2000); and Thauer (2014).

behave differently on account of their distinct organizational features and *intra*-organizational dynamics. It will be argued here that such *intra*-organizational aspects are important for our understanding of firm behavior in relation to corporate social responsibility. Asset-specific investments are the *intra*-organizational features that, by giving rise to "managerial dilemmas" (Miller 1992), make decision-makers in firms opt for corporate social responsibility.

This chapter develops this argument in detail and thereby addresses the following questions: *what precisely are managerial dilemmas, how are they linked to asset-specific resource allocation, and in which dilemma situations does corporate social responsibility emerge? How does corporate social responsibility offer management a way out of these dilemma situations? What types of dilemmas will result in what kind of corporate social responsibility policies, and why?*

The chapter will first lay out the general theoretical assumptions of transaction cost economics and bargaining theory as the framework of analysis. In a next step, it will introduce asset specificity as the key concept of this study. The theoretically "new" turn suggested here is that of applying asset specificity – originally developed to explain the "make or buy" decision of market participants – *intra*-organizationally and to relate it to corporate social responsibility standards and policies. The subsequent sections specify this relation further by laying out distinct dilemma situations and the kind of corporate social responsibility they give rise to. The chapter concludes with a discussion of scope conditions, which define the limits within which these arguments apply, and a table that summarizes the main theoretical arguments and propositions.

Theoretical assumptions and framework of analysis

The argument for internal drivers of corporate social responsibility is based on transaction cost economics (Coase 1937; North 1990; Williamson 1975) and bargaining theory (Iklé 1964; Jönsson 2002; Lake and Powell 1999). It assumes bounded rationality: actors are "intendedly rational, but only limitedly so" (Simon 1961: xxxiv). They make purposive choices in light of the information and knowledge they have and, to the best of their ability, choose a strategy which meets their exogenously given, transitive interests. However, the information and knowledge they have, as well as their cognitive capacities, are limited. In an environment that is complex and/or uncertain, this implies that "approximation must replace exactness in reaching a decision" (Williamson 1975: 21). Uncertainty exists when decision problems are not deterministic. Neither a set of alternative paths, nor a rule for generating them is available. Complexity refers to the inability to ascertain the structure of the environment due to cognitive limitations. Approximation implies the possibility that actors make erroneous decisions (Ostrom 1999: 46) and try to exploit the lack of information of others by behaving opportunistically (Williamson 1975: 9). Opportunism is the making of false promises and the faking or misrepresentation of information in the attempt to influence the approximation of others. The acquisition of information reduces the risk of opportunism. The costs this involves are the costs specific to a transaction or interaction. The degree of complexity and uncertainty actors confront (hence the transaction costs) depend on the level of information of the involved actors and the institutional environment. Institutions are, from this perspective, condensed information. They are safeguards against opportunism and reduce transaction costs.

Based on these assumptions, this study explains corporate social responsibility as an outcome of implicit or explicit bargaining.[2] Bargaining is a mode of collective decision-making to be distinguished from choices that are made by numerical aggregation such as voting procedures (see Jönsson 2002: 217; Zartman 1977: 621). It is also different from hierarchical steering by means of a judge who aggregates conflicting interests into a single decision. In bargaining, the parties are left to themselves to solve their conflicts of interest and reach a single decision. Bargaining situations are characterized by three elements: interdependence, common interest, and conflict (see Iklé 1964: 2; Jönsson 2002: 218). Interdependence implies that the outcomes resulting from a given set of alternative actions depend on how others choose to behave.[3] An interdependently structured situation is therefore similar to a game in which each actor must take into account the choices of others when assessing his or her choice. Common interests are present

---

[2] Bargaining theory has been developed in the works of, among others, Brousseau and Fares 2000; Iklé 1964; Jönsson 2002; Lake and Powell 1999; Miller 1992, 2005; Sappington 1991; Zartman 1977.

[3] See the literature on cooperation, institutions, and bargaining: Levi 1997; Ostrom 1990; Scharpf 1997; Snidal 1986; Stein 1983; Zürn 1992.

when there is a need for cooperation, that is, when mutuality leads to superior outcomes than unilateralism. For example, a transaction is in the common interest of a fruit trader and a consumer intending to buy fruit. Conflict refers to diverging preferences over outcomes. The fruit trader may prefer to sell fruit at a high price, while the customer's preference is that of a low price. Processes of implicit or explicit bargaining set out to find a solution to the conflict, which is suboptimal for at least one of the parties – but still within the limits of the common interest. For example, if both parties to the transaction agreed on a medium price, this would constitute a suboptimal outcome for both, but nonetheless considered preferable to no transaction at all.

Bargaining is a mode of joint decision-making that can be found in different institutional settings. In (neo-)corporatist arrangements, bargaining is formally institutionalized within tripartite forums (Schmitter and Lehmbruch 1979), sometimes even officially named "bargaining councils," as in South Africa (Müller-Debus *et al.* 2009a). Bargaining also takes place in other institutional contexts, but often informally. In hierarchical organizations, management is often confronted with "managerial dilemmas" (Miller 1992) that necessitate joint decision-making through bargaining, as will be discussed in detail below. In a market context, bargaining over price takes place when market participants do not know the exact match of supply and demand and the costs of production. Also in hybrid forms of social order located between markets and hierarchies, as in a semi-integrated supply chain, bargaining is a mode of decision-making that actors rely on. The relation between a buyer and a supplier may be formalized by a contract. Conflicts over issues that are contractually regulated are therefore subject to hierarchical decision-making by means of a judge (i.e. court action). However, inevitably incomplete contracts, the possibility of unforeseen events, opportunism, and the costs of litigation often necessitate additional bargaining over governance (Héritier *et al.* 2009). Finally, in institutional contexts that prescribe decision-making through numerical aggregation and voting procedures, actors draw on bargaining when, for example, parliaments or executive councils have come to a deadlock regarding important decisions. "Issue linkage" or the suggestion of "package deals" are bargaining attempts that can effectively render voting behavior.

Potential outcomes of bargaining processes are threefold. First, bargaining can fail to reach an agreement. Bargaining failure implies a collectively suboptimal outcome.[4] Second and third, bargaining can be successful, but can result in either asymmetric payoffs or in a true compromise. Either outcome depends on the bargaining position and power of the actors. Bargaining positions and power, as well as the success and failure of bargaining processes, depend on the interests and level of information actors have and the strategic environment, i.e. the set of available alternative actions, the way events may unfold, the institutional context, and the information environment (see Lake and Powell 1999). Power, from a bargaining perspective, is thus the result of a complex social setting and not an absolute measure as, for example, "capabilities" in realism (Waltz 1954).[5]

In processes of bargaining, actors optimize their strategy on the understanding that others are equally bounded rational actors. Bargaining processes can be implicit and explicit. Explicit bargaining involves verbal communication and other signals informing the opponent of one's own preferences and bargaining position. Explicit bargaining increases the level of information on which an agreement is reached; this can prevent bargaining failure or a collectively suboptimal outcome. At the same time, opportunism is all-pervasive (Williamson 1975). However, opportunism can also be costly. Demanding too much can lead to bargaining failure (Miller 1992: 48). Lying can damage the reputation of a player when detected and thus may weaken his future bargaining position. Bargaining can also take on the form of non-verbal signals, such as "tit for tat" (Axelrod 1981) – or be entirely implicit. Non-communicative, single-shot game theory formalizes implicit bargaining processes. Thereby the "Nash equilibrium" is found "by calculating each player's best replies to each of the strategy combinations that might be played by others, and identifying those strategy combinations that are best replies to each other" (Hargreaves Heap and Hollis 1998: 101). This process of mutual adaptation,

---

[4] The "prisoner's dilemma" is an example of a situation in which implicit bargaining takes place, but does not lead to an outcome which is in the common interest of the two inmates (Luce and Raiffa 1957).

[5] To illustrate the point, bargaining theorists have pointed out that in interstate relations small states with more attractive action alternatives and, consequently, with lower losses associated with the failure of bargaining, are more likely to reach an outcome of bargaining processes that is close to their preferences than large states with fewer options (see Hopmann 1996: 119).

explicit or implicit, is the causal mechanism unfolded by bargaining situations (see Miller 1992: 48).

Asset specificity: concept and theory

Asset-specificity theory is a branch of transaction cost economics developed by Oliver Williamson and his followers.[6] The central concept of the theory, "asset specificity," refers to non-transferable investments in an exchange relationship. If market demand for goods, services, or know-how created by an investment in support of a transaction is absent, it cannot be transferred to another transaction and is therefore unique to the task (Williamson 2002: 175). However, non-transferability is rarely absolute. Another way to describe asset specificity is therefore that the investments made to support a particular transaction have a higher value in relation to that transaction than they would if they were redeployed for another purpose (McGuinness 1994). Asset specificity can take on various forms. For example, it can be in human skills ("human asset specificity"), specialized machine tools ("physical asset specificity") or natural resources that are linked to a certain location ("site specificity").[7]

Asset specificity can be one-sided or two-sided (Joskow 1988; Klein 1988; Williamson 1975). One-sided asset specificity implies that only one party to a transaction makes an investment so that it can produce something that is otherwise not attainable on the market or only hardly so. An example in this respect is a supplier's investment in tooling instruments specifically for the making of a component that one particular customer has ordered. Two-sided asset specificity refers to non-transferable investments made by both parties to the transaction, such as when buyer and supplier share the purchasing costs for the new tooling instruments (examples in Héritier *et al.* 2009).

Asset specificity transforms the bargaining situation between transaction partners. This transformation is "fundamental" (Williamson 1996: 16). The theory assumes an initial "large-n" situation. Large numbers of buyers (who demand goods) and a large number of providers (who supply

---

[6] Ben-Porath 1980; Héritier *et al.* 2009; Joskow 1988; Klein 1988; Malone *et al.* 1987; McGuiness 1994; Williamson 1975, 1985, 1996, 2000, 2002; Zaheer and Venkatraman 1994.

[7] Malone *et al.* 1987; Zaheer and Venkatraman 1994.

the demand) transact frequently and interchangeably. Immediate substi-
tutability of all exchanges renders potential information asymmetries
between the transaction partners and unforeseen events unimportant
on account of its disciplining effect on the parties. Hence, information
deficits are absent and the level of certainty is high.

Non-transferable investments change this. Buyers and suppliers "can
redeploy the specialized assets to their next best use ... only at a loss
of productive value" (Williamson 2002: 176). Transaction partners
become dependent on each other. A situation emerges in which small
numbers of buyers confront a small number of providers. In the extreme
case, buyer and supplier enter an exclusive exchange relation. Both
are vulnerable in this situation, as the disciplining effect of the market
is absent and because exchange contracts are inevitably incomplete.
Unforeseen events have to be dealt with jointly, thereby information
asymmetries persist and bear the risk of opportunism (Williamson
1975: 26). Both fear being cheated.[8] A collectively suboptimal outcome
could derive from the exchange. Consequently, both parties either
refrain from asset-specific transactions altogether or agree on devices
that help mitigate risks, discourage opportunism, and reduce uncertainty and complexity. "Governance" – institutional provisions sidelining the exchange contract – is the means by which the bargaining
partners can achieve this. Asset-specificity theory therefore posits
that, in bargaining situations characterized by non-transferable investments, a governance order will be the outcome of bargaining processes
between the transacting parties. In extreme cases, vertical integration is
predicted.

Governance rules define, for example, under which conditions the
exchange contract is fulfilled. They may also provide transaction
partners with positive incentives for the fulfillment of the contract or
impose penalties for premature termination. In addition, governance
can stipulate mechanisms for information disclosure and verification

---

[8] In this respect, an asset-specific exchange poses collective action problems similar
to those inherent in the "stag hunt" (Skyrms 2004). The involved players have a
strong self-interest to coordinate. However, in order to reach the desired outcome,
moves have to be coordinated throughout a sequence of events during which
actors may be offered rewards for defection. Even though these rewards are
smaller than the potential gains resulting from coordination, the risk-averseness of
the players tells them to defect and "cheat." The result is a collectively suboptimal
outcome.

as well as sanctioning mechanisms, how disputes are to be settled and what procedures are to be followed in the likely case of unforeseen events. A fundamental distinction with respect to the content of governance rules pertains to "product" versus "process regulation" (Vogel 1995, 2005).

Product regulation defines the physical attributes of the goods under exchange, such as quantity and size as well as quality-related aspects (see Vogel 1995: 18). Product regulation can be utilized for a number of purposes. First, in exchange relations, product regulation helps to establish whether an exchange contract is fulfilled or breached. Second, through high product standards, firms can keep foreign competitors operating on lower standards out of the market – if they succeed in lobbying government to raise the legal standards that regulate the product under exchange to their level (Börzel *et al.* 2011; Greenstein and Stango 2007). This strategy option exists, because product standards are exempt under the General Agreement on Tariffs and Trade (GATT)/World Trade Organization (WTO) regime. Strong regulatory states or markets, such as the European Union (EU) or the US, can therefore make use of high product standards, in effect turning them into a hidden form of import barrier. Most firm activities in the realm of product standards are consequently oriented towards anticipated or actual legislation in order to raise the legal standards and to keep external competitors out. Third, enhancing product quality standards allows firms to target a higher end of the market, promising higher margins. For these three reasons product regulation often follows "race to the top" dynamics, i.e. competition for higher standards (Abbott and Snidal 2009; Börzel and Thauer 2013; Vogel 1995, 2005).

This study concentrates exclusively on process regulation, however.[9] Process regulation formulates requirements for the production of goods. Management systems concerned with corporate social responsibility are just one example among many standards – such as minimum wage, energy consumption reduction in the production process, or recycling. Usually, process regulation is considered to be more prone to "race to the bottom" dynamics – i.e. regulatory downsizing for competitive cost advantages (Vogel 1995: 18). The reasons for this are

---

[9] See the section on scope conditions later in this chapter.

twofold: first, process regulation cannot be used as an import barrier under the WTO/GATT regime and is thus not a playing field for anti-competitive strategies of firms – i.e. for keeping competitors out of the market. Second, only in rare cases does process regulation add measureable value to the goods that are being produced in the eyes of end consumers. In fact, process regulation in most cases just increases production costs and has no direct marketable value. Hence, process standards are the unlikely case of corporate social responsibility.

However, why would transacting parties insist on process standards if their transactions involve asset-specific investments? It will be argued here that process regulation reduces uncertainty and information deficits and discourages defection and opportunism in the critical period between contract agreement and contract execution. Also, in the case of technologically complex products, the verification of product regulation can be very difficult and costly. It is for this reason that transaction partners will rely on process regulation. Therefore, it will be argued that, wherever hazards have to be mitigated as a result of asset specificity, process regulation occurs.

Intra-organizational asset specificity, managerial dilemmas, and corporate social responsibility

The "new" turn this study takes now is to apply asset specificity *intra*-organizationally, and to relate it to the emergence of corporate social responsibility standards. It is necessary to address certain assumptions about the nature of firms before the application of asset specificity to the *intra*-organizational setting. The following arguments for internal drivers of corporate social responsibility assume a context of imperfect vertical integration: central management is in control over the flow of organizational resources (see Demsetz 1991: 161–2) and therefore in a "take it or leave it" (Sappington 1991: 47) position vis-à-vis organizational subunits and individual subordinates. Analogous to markets, however, hierarchies are imperfect in that the information on the basis of which actors make decisions is incomplete (Hart 2010). "Hidden information" (Miller 1992: 138) and expert knowledge create information asymmetries. Consequently, decision-making in hierarchies is confronted with similar problems as in a market context. Opportunism, shirking, and "hidden action" (Miller 1992: 120) are pervasive. Hierarchy failure is a possible outcome as organizational steering is a constant challenge. Management deals with it via intra-organizational bargaining, negotiation, and coalition politics.[10]

So when management assigns a critical mass of organizational resources to an organizational subunit or to subordinates in order to support the fulfillment of a task, but subsequently fails to transfer this investment without a loss, the decision situation is transformed. Management becomes vulnerable and dependent on the subunit and loses its strong, authoritative "take it or leave it" position. Unforeseen events can no longer be dealt with through a reallocation of resources; they require a joint reaction. Opportunism and shirking become threats, while the disciplining effect of hierarchy is weakened. Central management thus finds itself in a situation in which it will have to bargain with the respective subunit over an intra-organizational governance order, sidelining asset-specific allocations of resources to safeguard its authority. This study treats situations in which the mode of intra-organizational social coordination is transformed from a hierarchy to one in which management becomes dependent on and vulnerable to the behavior of subordinates, as "managerial dilemmas" (Miller 1992).

Corporate social responsibility is key to resolving managerial dilemmas in two ways: first, it reduces information asymmetries. In situations of managerial dilemmas, corporate social responsibility is implemented to structure, document, and monitor work processes, identify areas of improvement, provide for performance measures, facilitate resource use efficiency, and define escalation procedures. Hence, a valuable side effect of the adoption of standards defining corporate social responsibility is that, in these situations, it enables management to collect information about *what* subordinates do and *how* processes can be improved.

Second, corporate social responsibility reduces uncertainty. Since the 1990s, environmental, social, health, and labor standards proliferate on the global level, addressing not only states but also firms. On the local level, however, and, by assumption, in a context of limited statehood,

---

[10] Such a "political" view of the firm's nature conceiving of organizations as bargaining arenas draws on the works of, among others, Alchian and Demsetz 1972; Dow 1985; Eccks 1985; Hart 2010; March 1962; Milgrom and Roberts 1988; Miller 1992; overview in Barney and Hesterly 2006. Also, Williamson himself refers to examples which imply this perspective on the *intra*-organizational setting (Williamson 1975: 59).

these standards are not enforced. This discrepancy between the global and the local is a source of uncertainty for companies. Firms that invest in an area of regulatory void in an asset-specific way worry about whether their investment decision will still be tenable in the future. They ask themselves, for instance, whether labor costs and energy prices will increase, or whether the firm will be forced to reintegrate negative externalities of production (caused, for example, by NGO campaigns or increasing prices due to resource shortages). Yet firms that from the very start adhere to the highest international standards in the asset-specific allocation of resources reduce this kind of vulnerability to changes in the environment: they have already prepared for such changes. Therefore, a management that has an asset-specific relationship with one or more subunits and so cannot close down a unit easily in response to a shift in its strategic environment will insist on implementing corporate social responsibility standards and policies.

It must be noted that these arguments, while they take into account the existence of external drivers for corporate social responsibility, are essentially about internal drivers. More precisely, the argument developed here is that two firms, exposed to the same external pressure factors and risk environment, will nonetheless show very different levels of corporate social responsibility in their behavior on account of the distinct internal managerial dilemmas they face.

Internal driver 1: *the human resources dilemma*

The first particular dilemma situation analyzed is the *human resources dilemma*. It refers to ongoing investments in skills of employees that are hard to attain on the labor market. Such investments create asset specificity in the employment relation in the sense that the required skills level can be achieved only subject to these investments.[11] In

---

[11] Human asset specificity can also be two-sided, if employees cannot redeploy their skills to another employment relation without great losses. Often, however, labor markets in transition countries suffer from a shortage of skilled labor. The mismatch between supply and demand often enables employees to transfer the investment in their skills to another labor relation, while employers, in turn, cannot redeploy the investment in the skills of employees to another labor contract. One-sided human asset specificity implies a stronger bargaining position for employees than two-sided human asset specificity. Hence, the outcome of bargaining processes marked by one-sided human asset specificity will be closer to the preferences of employees than the outcome of two-sided asset specificity.

comparison, ongoing investments in skills that are openly available on the labor market are not asset specific, or only less so. These investments could be easily reassigned to the task of headhunting for new employees on the labor market who can already boast of these required skills. Hence, in this case, management has strategy options for the procurement of the requisite skills level of production and thus remains in a "take it or leave it" position vis-à-vis employees.

The goal, asset-specific investments in skills – skills that are not attainable from the labor market or only with difficulty – pursues a higher productivity and/or specific production techniques for specialized niche-market products. Since management is in a "take it or leave it" position, employees can be forced to attend training courses that teach such skills. However, once employees have attained the required specific skills, the bargaining situation is transformed. For management, "turnover is costly, since a similarly qualified but inexperienced employee would have to acquire the requisite task-specific skills before he would reach a level of productivity equivalent to that of an incumbent" (Williamson 1975: 59). Hence, management cannot easily "hire and fire" employees anymore. The mode of social coordination has changed from a hierarchy to a situation in which management becomes dependent on employees, and vulnerable to their behavior. The dilemma situation emerges. More precisely, asset-specific investments in skills create expert knowledge and information asymmetries, in addition to related problems of opportunism, cheating, and shirking. Also, unforeseen events in the environment may affect the productivity of the investment, yet lie beyond the direct control of management and thus necessitate a joint response. Social conflict, disease, and drug abuse are examples of general societal developments with a potential negative impact on the productive value of the investment in skills. Hence, management has to find a way to cope with the uncertainty that persists with respect to the future productivity of the resource allocation and has to find a way to reduce emerging information asymmetries. This is how dilemma situations turn into a driver. They put management under pressure to act and find ways to deal with them.

This study argues that, in this specific situation, labor-related corporate social responsibility can resolve the dilemma and will, therefore, be the preferred strategy option of management. Labor-related corporate social responsibility can entail services which are so beneficial to employees as to discourage turnover, absenteeism, and low productivity. In addition, they also mitigate problems in the investment environment that could permeate the workforce and affect its productivity.[12] Corporate social responsibility may thus envisage premiums for workers upon satisfactory fulfillment of the tasks in question. Also, special pension schemes and insurances, extensive health care services, and services promoting physical wellbeing, regeneration, and a healthy lifestyle, can remedy potential threats in the environment that risk affecting the firm. In substance, the labor-related corporate social responsibility that emerges in situations of asset-specific allocation of resources depends largely on the features of the investment environment. More specifically, it depends on where public service provision and regulation are lacking, and needed. Thus, the question is: in which areas does management confront uncertainties and complexity as a consequence of limited statehood and thus engage in corporate social responsibility with the aim of reducing uncertainties and information asymmetries that may negatively affect the asset-specific investment?

In a context in which labor conditions are entirely unregulated or where the implementation of existing regulation is absent, the logically derived outcome, as argued here, is that firms will issue employees with steady and formal contracts, offer them insurance packages, and guarantee the payment of a minimum wage for limited working hours. If social problems, such as drug abuse, are widespread in the investment environment and impinge on the firm, the *human resources dilemma* will motivate management to set up and run anti-drug campaigns. The empirical assessment conducted further below analyzes businesses in South Africa in terms of their management's behavior regarding a major problem in the investment environment, HIV/AIDS, and the huge uncertainties and complexities this illness entails. Firms that confront the *human resources dilemma*, in this context, will set up HIV/AIDS workplace programs.

---

[12] An interesting aspect of this argument is that more commonly the relation between stakeholders and corporations is discussed the other way around: corporations are usually portrayed as violating stakeholder rights. The argument on the *human resources dilemma*, however, shows that stakeholders such as employees can harm corporations as well – which reflects current debates in stakeholder theory about corporate and stakeholder responsibility (Elms and Phillips 2009; Freeman *et al.* 2006; Goodstein and Wick 2007).

While it can be assumed that employees have a strong interest in such labor-related services, the mentioned governance provisions allow management to safeguard its power position during and after the allocation of organizational resources. However, in contrast to employees, such governance provisions are costly for management. Hence, it is in the management's interest to offer only the bare minimum in services necessary to maintain its authority, while employees will drive for a maximum in services. The extent of services resulting from the process of explicit (for example, in labor councils between representatives of management and of employees) and implicit (finding the best reply to the opponent's strategy) bargaining will therefore critically depend on the level of asset specificity created through the investment.[13] The more management becomes dependent on employees and vulnerable to their behavior, the greater will the uncertainty in the environment be perceived. The same is true for information asymmetries between management and employees. Hence, the broader and more sophisticated will be the labor-related corporate social responsibility services which management agrees to offer employees.

In summary, with respect to internal driver 1, I argue that *the human resources dilemma causes the engagement of firms in health, social, and other labor-related corporate social responsibility.*[14]

Internal driver 2: the *technological specialization dilemma*

The second internal driver for corporate social responsibility is the *technological specialization dilemma*. It elaborates in detail a factor that has already been considered in literature, though mainly as a control variable in econometric analyses of corporate social responsibility, which is the "level of technological advancement" of a firm (for example, Khanna *et al.* 2007). Technologically complex products often require a considerable amount of pre-commercial planning and allocation of resources. Once research and development (R&D) has a marketable product ready, central management allocates resources to start up production. It is in this phase that the *technological specialization*

---

[13] In addition, it is decisive whether human asset specificity is one-sided or two-sided, as argued in footnote 11.

[14] One-sided human asset specificity causes a stronger engagement than two-sided human asset specificity.

dilemma occurs on account of production-specific assets, i.e. *intra-*organizational asset-specific investments in the production unit and technology. Production-specific assets refer to the commitment that is made by management to support the task delegated to a subunit to start up and run production. The longer the period before envisioned return of investment and the more resources dedicated to the production unit, the greater is management's commitment. The production-specificity of the company's assets increases accordingly – in line with the ever growing managerial dilemma.

In comparison, if the period before envisioned return of investment is short, production-specific assets are absent.[15] In this case, if management is dissatisfied with the output of production, it can reallocate resources swiftly. The unit is closed or restructured. A new production site is opened or production is shifted to another site. Thus, management remains in a "take it or leave it" position vis-à-vis the subunit.

If a long period before return on investments is envisioned – that is, if production-specific assets are created – the situation changes and turns into a managerial dilemma. Management becomes dependent on and vulnerable to the behavior of the production unit. It will have to deal with unforeseen events that have an impact on production costs. In addition, the *technological specialization dilemma* implies the creation of expert knowledge about processes, specialized machinery, and production techniques within the production unit. Information asymmetries are a consequence and bear the risk of opportunism. Hence, management fears that the subunit will not fulfill the task as envisioned. Return of investment and the making of profits are at risk.

Standard economic instruments of organizational management, such as the creation of an internal price mechanism, according to which management incentivizes the subunit on a certain price per unit of the production output, does not provide for a way out of the dilemma. The *technological specialization dilemma* occurs in the period before production begins, the period during which the production site is being constructed. In this period, instruments of organizational steering that are related to the production output, such as a price per unit, are obviously not applicable.

---

[15] Likewise, if investments are absent or small, no commitment is made and production-specific assets do not exist.

On some occasions an incentivization on a price per unit is possible, but bears risks and may cause reverse effects. Where the technological specialization dilemma persists throughout long periods of production or over a whole production cycle – which is often the case in high technology production – price per unit incentives may even create a "moral hazard."[16] Management incentivizes the subunit on a low price per unit to inspire efficient production processes. However, price per unit is a rather short-term efficiency measure. Being fully aware that management will bail out the subunit in the event of a crisis in the future, this unit may take high risks and use up assets and resources to meet management's expectation of a low price per unit in the short run, but may thereby undermine its long-term efficiency and diminish the profitability over the whole production cycle. Insisting on the delivery of a certain price per unit in an early stage of the production cycle alone is therefore not a strategy by which management can overcome the *technological specialization dilemma.*[17] An additional governance order sidelining the asset-specific investment is instead necessary to reduce information asymmetries, uncertainties, and the risk of "moral hazard" in the relationship between management and the production unit.

Therefore, in order to reduce uncertainty and information asymmetries and to mitigate "moral hazard," a management that confronts the *technological specialization dilemma* will insist on strict production process standards. Such standards will structure, document, and monitor work processes, identify areas of improvement, provide for performance measures, facilitate resource use efficiency, and define escalation procedures. Hence, management will insist on the implementation of standards that facilitate information about *what* subordinates do and about *how* processes can be improved. Such standards, which will often take on the form of management systems, can be quality-oriented, such as in case of ISO 9001 quality management systems; not every process standard is thus an instance of corporate social responsibility.[18] However, in a context of regulatory void, and depending on the degree to which allocated resources are asset-specific, management will, in

---

[16] That is, where investments in the production will only generate returns after long periods of production.

[17] Price per unit may, however, be an effective incentive in combination with process standards.

[18] Quality management can but does not necessarily involve aspects of corporate social responsibility.

addition, insist on standards that extend to environmental aspects, as this guarantees resource-use efficiency and mitigates potential legal and reputational risks. Examples of such process-oriented environmental corporate social responsibility are ISO 14001 environmental management systems (Potoski and Prakash 2006), VDA 6.1, or TS 16949 integrated quality and environmental management standards in the automotive industry.

In the upcoming bargaining situation, it is common knowledge that management's authority vis-à-vis the subunit is diminished once resources have been allocated. Anticipating this transformation, the representatives of the unit will behave opportunistically and promise to fulfill the task of running production efficiently as envisioned by management, knowing that they can renegotiate the terms and conditions of the agreement from a better bargaining position after production-specific assets have been created – or simply pursue their own interests ignoring central management. Central management, however, anticipates this loss of authority as well. It will therefore insist on negotiations with the subunit that go beyond agreements based on "mere promise" (Williamson 2000: 601) and press for the installment of governance rules as a backup to the commitment through corporate social responsibility standards with strict information disclosure, monitoring, and sanctioning mechanisms. For the representatives of the subunit this is a suboptimal outcome, but since central management can still negotiate from a "take it or leave it" position it can impose corporate social responsibility unequivocally at this point.

This study therefore argues with respect to internal driver 2 that *the technological specialization dilemma causes production process-oriented (environmental) corporate social responsibility.*

Internal driver 3: the *foreign direct investment dilemma*

The third internal driver is the *foreign direct investment dilemma*. This is a specific instance of internal driver number 2, the *technological specialization dilemma*. More specifically, it involves central management, located in a highly regulating country, making a substantial investment with a long duration before returns are generated in a branch located in a foreign country with weak or limited regulatory capacities. The consequences of such investments are thus analogous to the ones that give rise to the *technological specialization dilemma*. The difference is, however, that the *foreign direct investment dilemma* also features a trans-border element in the relation between management and the subunit in which it invests, as well as diverging regulatory contexts, which make the dilemma appear more severe. These elements increase uncertainty and information asymmetries.

Managers who confront the *foreign direct investment dilemma* will consequently ask themselves whether the branch really organizes processes efficiently or whether it exploits the emergent information asymmetries and acts opportunistically. The question is whether the branch will make use of assets and resources, or of lax environmental, social, and health regulation in order to boost its short-term revenues and thereby risk undermining the long-term profitability and efficiency of its operations knowing that headquarters will come to the rescue in the event of a crisis ("moral hazard" problem). Analogous to the *technological specialization dilemma*, in situations characterized by the *foreign direct investment dilemma*, headquarters' management will insist on strict process standards to reduce information asymmetries and uncertainty with respect to changes in the environment of the branch and the mitigation of "moral hazard." In a context of limited statehood, just as in the case of the *technological specialization dilemma*, depending on the severity of the dilemma, management will insist on standards that extend from quality to environmental aspects as well, as this guarantees resource-use efficiency and mitigates potential legal and reputational risks.

However, unlike the *technological specialization dilemma*, management will, in its effort to hold the branch accountable to the highest attainable standards, insist on a transfer of standards from "home" to its operations "abroad" in the case of a strong *foreign direct investment dilemma*. Hence, the *foreign direct investment dilemma* is a driver of the diffusion of regulatory standards from highly regulating to weakly regulating countries. This is the main difference between the *foreign direct investment dilemma* and the *technological specialization dilemma* in terms of the impact they have on corporate social responsibility. As it features a cross-border element and a management located in a country with particularly strict and concise regulation, the *foreign direct investment dilemma* is a source of "race to the top" (Börzel and Thauer 2013; Vogel and Kagan 2004) dynamics, i.e. the convergence of international standards at the highest level. This is especially so when competitors confront similar *foreign direct investment dilemmas*. The efficiency and long-term profitability of the branches abroad then become a decisive competitive advantage.[19]

In this respect, the *foreign direct investment dilemma* links up with two arguments in literature, which both concern or derive from diffusion theory and research (DiMaggio and Powell 1991; Shipan and Volden 2008; Simmons *et al.* 2006). First, it specifies the "home country" hypothesis and closes a gap between quantitative and qualitative approaches. According to this hypothesis, firms originating from a highly regulating country will transfer the high standards from "home" to their operations in weakly regulating countries "abroad" (Greenhill *et al.* 2010; Prakash and Potoski 2007). While this claim finds confirmation in some econometric studies, qualitative analyses observe that subsidies of such firms often do not transfer any standards (Börzel *et al.* 2011; Héritier *et al.* 2009). This study specifies the hypothesis, thereby extending its validity to qualitative approaches. More specifically, it will be argued that while the hypothesis holds, it does so only under the condition that the operations abroad constitute an asset-specific investment for management at "home." It is therefore the *foreign direct investment dilemma*, and the degree to which it is present, that drives the transfer of standards from "home" to operations "abroad."

Second, it adds a "vertical" perspective to the analysis of diffusion dynamics, which so far have been analyzed from a strictly "horizontal" perspective. By a horizontal perspective, diffusion theorists understand a focus on interaction effects in large populations of cases: "what theorists of diffusion explicitly reject is the notion that processes of policy change can adequately be understood by conceiving of [actors] as making decisions independently of each other" (Simmons *et al.* 2006: 787). Accordingly, the phenomenon of diffusion refers to "any process where prior adoption of a trait or practice in a population alters the probability of adoption for remaining non-adopters" (Strang 1991: 325). The argument on the *foreign direct investment dilemma* contributes to the analysis of the diffusion of business standards as it defines (vertical) organizational characteristics as a precondition for (horizontal) diffusion effects. More precisely, it helps to define how and why an

---

[19] This argument implies that the likelihood of a policy transfer caused by the *foreign direct investment dilemma* increases over time, as previous policy transfers of competitors and the positive spin-offs thereof put firms that have not carried out a policy transfer under pressure to also manage their foreign assets more efficiently by adopting environmental standards.

individual firm may develop the idea to transfer "home" standards "abroad" in the first place, which is a necessary condition for diffusion dynamics to take place at a later stage. It may also contribute to the analysis of diffusion dynamics themselves as it helps us to identify which firms of an industry sector will be affected by diffusion dynamics, and when. The general argument, with respect to the former question, is that firms are affected by diffusion dynamics on account of the degree to which they confront the *foreign direct investment dilemma*. With respect to the latter, in the very moment a firm receives investments with long durations before returns are generated, it is affected by diffusion dynamics. Taken together, both arguments may help future research to identify which industry sectors are more and less prone to the diffusion of business standards. They may also contribute to a better understanding of the evolution and specific pathways of standard diffusion over time.

Note that while this argument relates to external drivers, it is essentially about internal drivers. The argument here is that two firms of an industry sector experiencing diffusion dynamics will show a different reaction to and participation in the diffusion process. This is due to the variant foreign direct investment dilemmas they are confronted with. Likewise, a single firm of an industry sector in an area of regulatory void may remain unaffected by diffusion dynamics up to the point it receives long-term investments.

To summarize, regarding the third internal driver of corporate social responsibility, this book argues that *the foreign direct investment dilemma leads to a transfer of high standards if the branch in the weak state "abroad" is a specific asset to management "at home" in the highly regulating country.*

Internal driver 4: the *brand reputation dilemma*

The fourth internal driver is the *brand reputation dilemma*. The argument with respect to this dilemma bears strong similarities to a hypothesis in literature which maintains that branded firms will engage in corporate social responsibility for reputational reasons (Börzel *et al.* 2013; Haufler 2001; Marx 2008; Mol 2001). The *brand reputation dilemma* emerges as a consequence of asset-specific investments in marketing to support alternative means of product differentiation to the price mechanism. Price-driven firms rely – in their interaction with consumers – on anonymous market forces.[20] Intra-organizationally, this strategy has no repercussions except that it implies decision-making by means of hierarchical steering and economic instruments such as an internal market, which gives subunits incentives to produce at a low price per unit. Short-term cost cutting is the strategy, production-specific assets are minimized and negative externalities are maximized while management remains in a "take it or leave it" position throughout the production process. However, once management decides to offer alternative means of product differentiation to consumers in order to support their decision to buy, intra-organizational repercussions will occur. Two investments in this respect can be differentiated.

First, resources can be allocated by management to support a differentiation of products according to their degree of sophistication, technical complexity and other quality-related features (Anton *et al.* 2004; Parker 2002). Such investments are made to target a high-end niche market in which consumers are willing to pay a premium for quality.[21] Management becomes thereby dependent and vulnerable in two ways: on the one hand, the allocation creates the *technological specialization dilemma* and therefore renders management dependent on the production unit; on the other hand, production-specific assets also imply one-sided asset specificity in relation to consumers.

More precisely, production-specific assets are investments made by management that lose their productive value when redeployed to another consumer segment, in which no premiums are paid (i.e. the mass segment). Hence, management becomes dependent on the high-end market segment. Asset specificity is one-sided in this relation, as consumers do not make any non-transferable investments when buying the products from a high-end market firm. Consumers do not commit themselves to purchasing a particular good from a specific brand or seller. They do not even commit to purchasing a certain type of product from the high-end market segment, since they can always choose the option to buy a cheaper product from a mass segment. Hence, should the firm not offer the expected price–quality ratio consumers will opt for another seller. These considerations reinforce the need for management to impose strict corporate social responsibility rules on the production unit as a means of

[20] "Faceless buyers and sellers ... meet ... for an instant to exchange standardized goods at equilibrium prices" (Ben-Porath 1980: 4).
[21] Ammenberg and Hjelm 2003; Anton *et al.* 2004; Bansal 2005; Parker 2002.

cost and quality control. The difference to the argument for the second internal driver, the *technological specialization dilemma,* is that this fourth driver goes beyond the explanation of intra-firm corporate social responsibility. It applies to the exchange between organizationally different buyers and suppliers as well. Consumers hold the brand, from which they purchase a product, responsible for its quality and the way it was produced. Even if much of the value added to a product was actually generated within a supply chain, they hold the brand responsible for what they have purchased nonetheless.

Second, management can allocate resources to the marketing unit for the creation of a brand name, which can be a powerful product differentiation mechanism.[22] Such an investment in the reputation of a firm is not necessarily competing, but rather complementary to a high-end market strategy. Strong branding can go hand in hand with a strong quality orientation. Indeed, branding can provide the end-consumer with information about the superior quality of a product. However, branding can also add value to products that have no material differences. To be more precise, investments in marketing can support the creation of a social status-value of the brand. As in the case of a high-end market orientation, an *intra*-organizational allocation of resources to support the creation of a brand name creates one-sided asset specificity. The resources lose their productive value if they are transferred to a mass or low-end consumer segment. *Intra*-organizationally, the asset "brand name" is also not redeployable, for example to support the creation of a more sophisticated production site, to upgrade R&D, or the level of skills of employees. High-end market consumers, however, are not dependent on the firm. They do not invest in their buying decision and are therefore free to choose between the full range of sellers and between different market segments. Just as investments in product quality, investments in a brand name have intra-organizational repercussions. Public outcry over bad business practices devalues the investments made to support a positive image. To safeguard its investment, management will therefore impose strict corporate social responsibility policies on the production unit and on its suppliers, for which firms are held responsible.[23]

---

[22] Auld *et al.* 2008; Deitelhoff and Wolf 2010; Flohr *et al.* 2010; Smith 2008; Spar and LaMure 2003.
[23] Similarly argue Hoffmann 2001; Schepers 2006; Trullen and Stevenson 2006.

In summary, *the fourth internal driver of corporate social responsibility is the brand reputation dilemma, which causes the engagement of firms in in-house and supply-chain corporate social responsibility.*

Scope conditions

The empirical analysis in the subsequent chapters will show that these arguments for internal drivers of corporate social responsibility are widely applicable and gain explanatory power in highly diverse contexts. However, three scope conditions apply. The first scope condition pertains to the institutional-political context. The arguments in this book apply to contexts of regulatory void, so-called areas of "limited statehood" (Krasner and Risse 2014; Risse 2011) – environments where the state is unwilling or incapable of setting high standards, providing essential services, or enforcing legal obligations. Everything else being equal, variation of internal drivers should, under these conditions, lead to variant levels of corporate social responsibility. In areas of consolidated statehood, by contrast, the theory of internal drivers does not apply in the same way. As the literature on the "varieties of capitalism" points out, consolidated statehood is explained historically, at least to a certain degree, by the emergence of regulation that mitigates the risks of predominant patterns of asset-specific investments in an economy (Busemeyer 2009; Hall and Soskice 2001; Iversen 2005). Interlocking webs of firmly established legal obligations and the provision of services by way of public institutions are therefore (usually) already present here. These webs reflect the specific needs of the prevailing type of capitalist order and its comparative advantages (Hancké 2010; Thelen 2004). In addition, social movements and organizations such as the environmental movement and NGOs or unions feed into this web of obligations and public services (Esping-Anderson 1990; Korpi 2006). In consequence firms often deem themselves to be over-regulated in contexts of consolidated statehood: they do not see the need for additional voluntary standards.[24] In Germany, for instance, there is a strong emphasis on skilled labor, a sophisticated web of obligations, and collective institutions that organize health care services including

---

[24] An indication for this is that self-regulation by business is here usually contingent on the "shadow of hierarchy" (Halfteck 2008; Héritier and Lehmkuhl 2008; Scharpf 1997), the regulatory threat by the state.

occupational health care for workers (Jackson and Deeg 2006; Streeck and Yamamura 2001). Firms usually do not exceed these levels, even if their workforce is highly skilled. There is simply no need for it: high levels of regulation and service provision are already in place. In areas of limited statehood, by contrast, interlocking systems of firm obligations and public institutions do not exist in the same way and the provision of services and governance is generally insufficient. Instead, the "shadow of anarchy" (Börzel and Risse 2010; Börzel and Thauer 2013; Scharpf 1997) looms over firms: the knowledge that the risks associated with asset-specific investments will remain unmitigated, if they do not adopt high standards voluntarily. Regulatory void – limited statehood – is thus a scope condition for internal drivers to be effective in the way predicted in this study.

Note, however, that areas of regulatory void (and, accordingly, the shadow of anarchy) are, according to the way the concept is understood here, *not* confined to failing, failed, or weak states – or to the "global south" (Draude *et al.* 2012: 11). "Area" here pertains to functionally, socially, historically, *or* territorially defined political spaces. Spaces of regulatory void can thus occupy parts of state territories or transcend state borders and be transnational or global in nature – or concern a specific policy field or historical period. In other words: there may be areas of regulatory void to be found in the midst of Germany, for example – known to be a rather "strong" state – or Denmark or the US.[25] The theory of internal drivers applies to all areas of limited statehood – within Europe or the US in the same way as in the emerging markets context of South Africa and China.[26]

The second scope condition pertains to the content of governance rules: more specifically to the common distinction in literature between standards in the area of "product regulation" and "process regulation" (Vogel 1995, 2005). Standards regulating products define the physical

---

[25] There are also areas of strong statehood in emerging markets such as South Africa and China.

[26] I chose the emerging markets contexts of South Africa and China to evaluate the theory of *internal* drivers – and not an area of limited statehood in, say, Germany – as the issue of limited statehood and firm behavior in relation to regulatory standards is much more relevant here. First, limited statehood is more typical in emerging markets compared to the EU or the US. Second, ever since the major trade liberalizations of the 1990s and 2000s, large proportions of global production take place in emerging markets – under conditions of regulatory void.

attributes of goods, such as quantity, size, and quality-related aspects (Vogel 1995: 18). Standards regulating the process of production formulate requirements in regard to the way a product is manufactured or otherwise made. Both follow different logics: product standards tend towards "race to the top" dynamics. The real issue, however, is process standards, which are particularly prone to "race to the bottom" dynamics (see above). The arguments presented in this study merely explain process standards, the more unlikely case of firm behavior in relation to regulatory standards. They do not explain product standards. The causal logic of the arguments set this scope condition: process standards reduce vulnerabilities, uncertainties, and information asymmetries in the period between an agreement among two exchanging parties and the execution of this agreement (that is, the delivery of a good in exchange for a price), which is the critical period in situations of asset specificity. Product standards, by contrast, are of no use here. They can be ascertained only with or after the execution of the agreement (i.e. upon delivery of goods in exchange for the agreed price). This is, from the perspective of the transacting parties, too late should the agreement involve asset-specific investments. In consequence, product standards do not help decision-makers in firms overcome the managerial dilemmas inherent in asset-specific investments, and are therefore not an outcome of the internal drivers theorized here.

Third, the argument for internal drivers applies to market, rather than politically driven firms. The rationale underlying internal drivers presupposes that the management of main assets and resources is a key variable for a firm's commercial success. That is to say that if assets are mismanaged, there is a good chance that the firm will endure a loss in efficiency and profitability and encounter debts or bankruptcy caused by a slump in competitiveness. It is these negative yet anticipated consequences of asset mismanagement that motivate managers to engage in the governance of asset-specific investments and to make use of corporate social responsibility standards, management systems, and policies. Politically driven firms, in comparison, find their key factor for success in public affairs management (Coen *et al.* 2010: 16–17). This is not to say that internal drivers are entirely irrelevant for firms that are more politically driven than market-driven. However, the game they play is a different one and it is more often than not the case that political pressure on firms regarding their behavior will trump the causal force of internal drivers. Examples of politically driven firms include most state-owned companies, such as Petrobras in Brazil, the energy provider Eskom in South Africa, or firms that rely disproportionally on public spending or subsidies such as the aviation industry or energy suppliers in general (Chick 2011). Likewise, firms whose business model relies on licensing by the state, as in large parts of the mining and military industries, are predominantly politically rather than market-driven (Baldwin and Cave 1999; Besley 2006). Moreover, many former communist countries, such as China or Russia, where considerable parts of industry sectors are still state-owned or partly state-owned, require foreign investors in strategic key industries to obtain licenses from the government to enter the market and/or do so in the form of joint ventures with local, often state-owned enterprises. Also in these cases – an example of which would be the automotive industry in China – firms are in all likelihood more politically driven than market-oriented.[27]

Within these limitations, the arguments addressed in this study can be applied to a whole range of cases. In fact they decisively contribute to a better understanding of corporate social responsibility for a significant part of global production. In cases where the state takes a distant stance towards industry regulation and does not own, license, or otherwise dominate the logic of an industry sector, the arguments of this book apply and may be tested with respect to their explanatory power. The empirical analysis will assess the arguments in the context of the South African and Chinese textile industry and its various subsectors and segments, as well as the South African automotive industry with its various subsectors and segments. The arguments developed here are applicable beyond that, though, as, for example, to textile and lower electronic production in South-East Asia, automotive production in Latin America, household items production in India, furniture manufacturing, high-tech electronics, and processor production in various countries around the world. Table 2.1 summarizes the main theoretical arguments for internal drivers and the scope conditions within which they apply.

---

[27] A similar argument can be made with respect to monopolists. If firms have no competition, negative consequences of a mismanagement of assets and resources are less severe. Hence, the effects of *internal* drivers will be much weaker in these cases than in cases of market-driven firms, so that the arguments for *internal* drivers do not apply.

Table 2.1 *Internal drivers of corporate social responsibility*

Internal driver	Managerial dilemma	Relation between managerial dilemma and CSR/type of CSR	Scope conditions
Driver 1	*Human resources dilemma*: emerges when investments are made in the skills of employees that are not available on the labor market or only with difficulty.	The more management invests in skills and the more these skills are unique to the task, the stronger will be the engagement in labor-related CSR.	
Driver 2	*Technological specialization dilemma*: defined by the amount of investment management makes in the production unit and the period before envisioned returns of investment.	The more management invests in the production unit with long durations before returns are expected, the stronger will be the engagement of the firm in production process-oriented (environmental) CSR.	
Driver 3	*Foreign direct investment dilemma*: created by central management, located in a highly regulating country, making a substantial investment with a long duration before returns are generated in a branch located in a foreign country with weak or limited regulatory capacities.	The more management invests in a branch abroad with long durations before returns are expected, the stronger will be the engagement for the firm in production process-oriented (environmental) CSR – and the more will high, "home" standards be transferred "abroad."	(1) Regulatory void; (2) process standards; (3) market-driven industry sector Arguments do not apply in the same way to areas of consolidated statehood, product standards, and politically driven industries.
Driver 4	*Brand reputation dilemma*: emerges as a consequence of asset-specific investments in marketing to support alternative means of product differentiation to the price mechanism.	The higher the investments in marketing, the stronger the CSR programs, in-house and in the supply chain.	

Before turning to an empirical evaluation of the theory, the next chapter will discuss in detail what corporate social responsibility is and how we can detect it. It will also lay out the organization and design of the inquiry, the case selection, and the institutional and policy context of the analysis.

3 | Corporate social responsibility: an inside-view approach and perspective

This book defined corporate social responsibility as *firms demonstrating a concern for the wellbeing of their workers, for the natural environment, and for society in general by adhering to international standards.* How is this understanding of corporate social responsibility relevant in the context of this study? Corporate social responsibility, in effect, owes its existence to a political idea (Carroll 1999; Frederick 2006; Vogel 2005: 6). It emerged by laying out what companies *should* do according to societal demands: treat workers well, respect the environment, and contribute to the wellbeing of society.[1] Rather than being concerned with these claims in themselves, however, this study attempts to explore what firms actually do in relation, and potentially, in reaction to them. Consequently, it has to conceptualize corporate social responsibility not in normative terms, but descriptively, as an empirically observable phenomenon. However, can we detect corporate social responsibility at all when we strip it of its moral judgment?

The challenge is to differentiate responsible from irresponsible behavior – or from behavior that is entirely unrelated to corporate social responsibility. Yet to make such distinctions is in itself a normative act. During apartheid, for instance, General Motors, Ford, and many other corporations in South Africa practiced racial segregation in the workplace (Black 1999; Williams 2004). Surely the intention of these companies was to thereby demonstrate to the ruling political regime that they assumed certain designated responsibilities showing that they were "good corporate citizens" – in the context of South African apartheid.

---

[1] In particular, in business ethics and management studies corporate social responsibility is often used in this normative way. Accordingly, the notion of corporate social responsibility is much wider, including profit-making, respect for the law, labor rights, innovation, environmental concerns, and sponsorship (for example, Carroll 1991; Carroll and Buchholz 2000; Freeman *et al.* 2006).

Obviously, in no way can we consider practicing racial segregation in the workplace as an instance of corporate social responsibility. Rather, we think of it as a clear case of corporate irresponsibility, of illegitimate support for a discredited political regime and exploitation of workers. But how can we make this distinction in an empirical study without becoming enmeshed in a normative debate?

The case of General Motors, Ford, and others in South Africa is insightful here. It is of defining importance for the emergence of corporate social responsibility as a political idea (Carroll 1999; Frederick 2006; Vogel 2005). The firms' loyalty to the oppressive racist regime backfired in the late 1970s, and badly so – from the perspective of the companies. Local activists in South Africa, in conjunction with transnational non-governmental organizations (NGOs), university students, and religious activists in the US formed one of the first "transnational advocacy networks" (Keck and Sikkink 1998) for corporate social responsibility in response to the firms' all-too-willing adoption of the regime's racist practices (Black 1999; Williams 2004). Apartheid South Africa was already delegitimized internationally at the time for having continuously infringed on basic international human rights norms (Black 1999). The activists reproached the firms publicly for supporting racism and demanded that these international human rights norms, which in origin and nature are state-based, be applied to firms as well. The consequent public debate resulted in the formulation and subsequent, widespread adoption of the "Sullivan principles" and the large-scale disinvestment of US firms from South Africa (Williams 2004).[2]

The way the activists asserted their claims accords to a core element of corporate social responsibility: compliance with international norms and standards (Levy and Kaplan 2008). Hence, the distinction between responsible and irresponsible firm behavior does not require the analysis here to render any normative judgment itself. Rather, it is international norms and standards (more precisely, the interpretation of firm behavior in relation to international norms and standards) that draw the line here. We can thus conceptualize corporate social responsibility

---

[2] Rev. Leon Sullivan, a priest, was a board member of General Motors. It was he who devised the principles to make basic international human rights norms applicable to firms in the context of apartheid South Africa. Rev. Sullivan died in 2002, but the principles he devised are still an important reference for corporate social responsibility, see: http://thesullivanfoundation.org/about/global-sullivan-principles (November 7, 2012).

descriptively by assessing the degree to which firm behavior conforms to international standards.

For instance, Crossley Carpets in Durban set up HIV/AIDS workplace programs according to the standards and recommendations of the World Health Organization (WHO) and the Global Health Initiative (GHI).[3] The sportswear and apparel firm Nike, producing in Zhejiang province in China, as another example showing corporate social responsibility, presses for the core labor standards of the International Labour Organization (ILO) among its suppliers (see Chapter 6). Other firms adopt the environmental management system ISO 14001 of the International Organization for Standardization in order to act in a socially responsible way (Prakash and Potoski 2006, 2007).

We can also identify firms that act irresponsibly this way, i.e. the negative value of the *dependent variable* "corporate social responsibility." When firms' practices infringe on international standards in the areas of labor and human rights, occupational and public health, and the environment, as in the cases of General Motors during apartheid times, they act irresponsibly. The luxury brand C is another example of such a firm. C has been presented as an example of a firm that exploits people and the environment. The behavior of C is indeed irresponsible. The firm violates basic labor and human rights norms as set by the ILO. Child labor, for example, is a common occurrence in the value chain of C and clearly in conflict with these norms (see Chapter 6).

This chapter sets out to indicate how this study will assess corporate social responsibility as well as the applicability, plausibility, and validity of internal drivers in the subsequent empirical case study analysis. It will thus define indicators for corporate social responsibility in line with the definition above, describe the logic and organization according to which internal drivers are evaluated, and render an account of the political-institutional and industry sector contexts of the cases.

Analyzing (drivers of) corporate social responsibility: an inside-view approach and perspective

How can we know corporate social responsibility when we wish to see it in empirical cases? Analyzing corporate social responsibility can be a

---

[3] Interview with the Director of Human Resources of Crossley Carpets, September 28, 2007, Durban.

challenge. What firms claim to be doing is not always what they are actually doing. Expressions such as "greenwashing" or "bluewashing" refer to such gaps between words and deeds (Cherry and Sneirson 2011; Marquis and Toffel 2012; Ramos and Montiel 2005). They imply that firms give themselves a "green," eco-friendly, or "blue" image in the context of the United Nations Global Compact to portray themselves as corporate citizens. They also suggest that firms do so in order to disguise their real, exploitative business practices. The luxury goods brand C may, again, serve as a case in point. An internationally recognized fashion brand, C has an all-encompassing corporate social responsibility policy (see Chapter 6 for details). The website of the group that owns C markets this policy prominently. The suppliers of C are according to this policy required to adhere to high international standards, such as the core labor standards of the ILO. In practice, however, C does not impress any such standards on suppliers, as its dealings with the leather firm CL demonstrate. Under pressure to meet C's demands – in particular the price C asks for – the leather firm races to the bottom as concerns labor, environmental, health and safety standards. C is aware of this, as it deploys "inspectors" (Héritier *et al.* 2009) to the leather firm to control the production process at any point in time. Hence, whereas the website of C communicates corporate social responsibility, the firm, in reality, has nothing but disdain for it.

From an analytical standpoint, the problem with cases such as C is that they may enter the data set as "false" positives: as cases of corporate social responsibility that are in reality cases of corporate irresponsibility. "False" positives would invalidate the analysis of drivers of corporate social responsibility and must therefore be avoided. However, "false" negatives are just as problematic. "False" negatives are cases in which the firm itself does not communicate much about corporate social responsibility activities. In particular smaller firms sometimes do not have formal corporate social responsibility policy documents or a communication strategy. Their policy is instead implied in their daily business practices.[4] An example of this is Crossley Carpets, which offers a sophisticated program to help their employees and their families affected by HIV/ AIDS, including comprehensive health care services (see Chapter 1). The firm has until recently not advertised or communicated any of this

---

[4] See also the debate about "implicit" end "explicit" corporate social responsibility: Hiß 2009; Jackson and Apostolakou 2010; Matten and Moon 2008.

to the general public. In light of the contested nature of HIV/AIDS in South Africa, the firm never found it opportune to publish its activities in this respect or to produce a policy document. Hence, when looking at Crossley Carpets from outside, the firm appears inactive in the area of HIV/AIDS and, thus, as a negative case of corporate social responsibility.

To ensure that cases are analyzed for what they really are, this study adopts an inside-view approach and perspective in the sense that it looks *inside* the firm and investigates the actual practices of employees and organizational subunits on the factory floor. It is here that we can find out about the level of environmental standards that is actually applied; it is here that we can come to assess the level of standards on which labor relations are really based; and it is on this level that we can verify whether a supply chain policy exists merely on paper or also as a practice. Hence, this study does not only look inside the firm in order to identify and analyze internal drivers of corporate social responsibility. It also adopts an inside-view perspective to detect corporate social responsibility in the practices of workers and subunits inside the firm. However, where precisely do we have to look in order to establish corporate social responsibility and irresponsibility?

Corporate social responsibility: policies, implementation, and practices

This study takes into consideration three dimensions of firm behavior: (1) policy; (2) compliance and implementation measures; and (3) policy practices. The first dimension concerns corporate social responsibility policies themselves and applies, of course, only to firms that have an explicit policy formulated. Policies can be found in policy documents or corporate social responsibility reports, websites, and other published material. They can vary in terms of the strictness of the standards they aim to achieve, the precision of the goals they formulate, and how demanding these goals are in comparative perspective.[5] The second

---

[5] These indicators refer to the "grammar of institutions" (Crawford and Ostrom 1995), which consists of *attributes, deontic, aim,* and *conditions. Attributes* are the actors the policy addresses. *Deontic* is the normative dimension of a policy: actors can, must, or must not do certain things according to the policy. A policy *aim* is the status of the world the policy envisions. *Conditions* delineate who is designated to do what, when, and how. Policy formulation is measured according to the degree of obligation and precision as well as depth and scope of stipulated provisions.

dimension, compliance and implementation measures, is more important than the first one. It considers how seriously firms actually take their policies (if they have any explicitly formulated), and what measures they take to implement them. Implementation pertains to the resources allocated in support of corporate social responsibility standards (financial and material, personnel, executive support etc.), and the degree to which this support is institutionalized (that is, through organizational subunits; compliance mechanisms). The third dimension, policy practices, is arguably the most important one. It is about the actual business practices. Is a firm's behavior in line with international social, labor, health and environmental standards? How demanding, encompassing and inclusive are the measures taken by a firm to protect the environment, labor standards, or the health of employees? Table 3.1 summarizes the three dimensions and lays out indicators according to which the empirical analysis assesses corporate social responsibility in the practices and behavior of firms.

The focus of the analysis will be on the practices of firms (dimension 3), as this study is concerned with the actual behavior of employers and employees, and subunits within firms on the factory floor. However, exceptions apply where this is, technically or practically, impossible or unreasonable. For example, in the context of environmental policies, the actual practices of firms are often impossible to directly observe or assess. Effluent levels, for instance, are hard to verify for a social science researcher and the same counts for emissions standards. In such instances, the other two dimensions will be used as proxies with a special emphasis on dimension 2, as this dimension entails a strong focus on behavioral sincerity. Special consideration will then be given to the degree to which independent external third-party experts verify that firms adhere to certain standards, and in how far such third-party monitoring is a constitutive part of the actual compliance measures firms apply.[6]

While this approach for detecting corporate social responsibility is capable of seeing through greenwashing and bluewashing, it requires extensive fieldwork and in-depth analysis. This is, however, also helpful. The establishment of internal drivers necessitates a similar inside-view approach and perspective and data on a similar level and of a similar

---

[6] On the importance of third-party monitoring and delegation see the literature on legalization/institutionalization (Abbot *et al.* 2000; Crawford and Ostrom 1995) and voluntary standards (Prakash and Potoski 2006, 2007).

Table 3.1 *Assessing corporate social responsibility – an inside-view perspective*

	The dependent variable: corporate social responsibility – a behavioral approach	
Dimension	Features/key questions	Measurement/assessment
(1) Policy	• How obligatory are policy goals? • How concise? • How demanding? • How encompassing?	• **Indicator 1a:** degree of obligation • **Indicator 1b:** degree of precision • **Indicator 1c:** depth (degree to which policies are demanding in terms of the strictness of standards) • **Indicator 1d:** scope (degree to which policies cover important areas comprehensively)	Weak
(2) Implementation measures	• Organizational resources and support • Institutionalization of compliance mechanisms	• **Indicator 2a:** personnel • **Indicator 2b:** material resources • **Indicator 2c:** financial resources • **Indicator 2d:** executive support • **Indicator 2e:** compliance mechanisms (sanctions, positive incentives, learning and support)	
(3) Practices	• To which degree do measures cover relevant areas? • To which degree are practices demanding? • To which degree are practices pursued in designated situations?	• **Indicator 3a:** scope (degree to which policy practices cover relevant areas) • **Indicator 3b:** depth (degree to which practices are demanding) • **Indicator 3c:** scale (extent to which practices are pursued systematically in designated situations)	Strong

quality. In consequence, each of the thirty-seven firm cases presented in this study are based on first-hand data collected specifically for it.[7] Thereby, the analysis draws on more than 200 personal interviews and factory visits.[8] Interviews were held with managers and employees on different hierarchical levels of firms, associations, NGOs, activists, unions, government agencies, international organizations, foreign development agencies (both public and private), journalists, experts, and academics. To triangulate the data (Denzin 2006), the book compared information provided by employees with information collected from other sources. For example, when a firm stated that it was the first to implement a full HIV/AIDS workplace program in a region, this information was crosschecked with competitors, NGOs, union representatives, government officials, associations, and experts.

If, for instance, a firm claimed to have a strict corporate social responsibility supply chain policy, a number of the suppliers of this firm were asked questions such as: who of the buyer firms of yours require you to adhere to social or environmental standards or fulfill certain requirements in this respect? What are these requirements? And in comparative perspective, which of the firms that source from you have strict and which ones rather lax standards? In which areas do the standards of different buyers differ, and by how far and in what respect? And what are the consequences if you do not meet these standards? Furthermore, in conducting interviews, factory floor visits were requested in order to compare what was said in the interviews with direct observations. In addition, the cases were established by also taking into consideration external data sources, such as financial

---

[7] The analysis draws on more than sixty firm cases in total. As this study conducts controlled pair-wise comparisons, many of them will not be presented here or mentioned explicitly as they do not fit in with this rather strict methodological design. However, all data and cases have been analyzed prior to writing this book. Wherever there is an individual case or piece of evidence that seemed to contradict any conclusion or inference drawn from the controlled pair-wise comparisons in this book, it is reported. For example, in Chapter 6 I invalidate my own argument on the *brand reputation dilemma* by reporting on what I found for the case of C in China – a luxury goods brand that infringes on social and environmental standards.

[8] The interviews were conducted in the period between February 2007 and May 2009; the duration of the interviews varied between 30 minutes and 4 hours; the average interview was approximately 1h30m and consisted of an interview part and a factory tour. The interviews were analyzed and coded according to the indicators developed for the dependent (see above) and independent variables (see below in the empirical chapters).

reports of firms and their websites, government reports, NGO websites and reports, journalist articles, and academic analyses.

Such triangulation is helpful in establishing valid "facts." But how does the analysis draw conclusions from these facts in order to assess the explanatory power of the theory of internal drivers of corporate social responsibility?

Organization of the study: logic(s) of causal inference and case selection

The main logic of causal inference in this book selects cases according to their variation of internal drivers (that is, on the *independent variable*) in order to assess them in controlled pair-wise comparisons (Ganghof 2005; King *et al.* 1994).[9] The unit of analysis is the firm. Highly similar firm cases are compared that, however, differ with respect to the degree to which they represent the internal driver under scrutiny. The inquiry then asks whether the internal driver really leads to corporate social

---

[9] While collecting the data I was aware of (the potential problem of) common method bias. Whenever possible, I asked for data for the independent (internal drivers) and dependent variables (corporate social responsibility) in separate interviews and with different managers. Where this was not possible, I collected data for the independent variables in a way that would not reveal my research interest in *internal* drivers. For example, in an introductory, preliminary part of the interviews I would discuss with interviewees all kinds of background information: the general situation of the firm, who are the competitors, products, market structure, its history, ownership structure, number of employees, turnover, and organizational particulars. In the context of this introductory part I would also inquire about the general conditions for business in South Africa or China, respectively, how long it takes the respective firm to find new employees, how that compares to competitors and other industry sectors, and whether the firm runs training programs, what these consist of etc. – thereby measuring, without the interview partner's recognition, asset-specific investments in skills of employees (see Chapter 4). After this introductory part I would begin asking questions in relation to rather obvious driving factors of corporate social responsibility: did the firm ever interact with NGOs in the past? Does it experience consumer demands for high standards? This second part was usually followed by a third part in which I inquired about the practices of firms with respect to corporate social responsibility, and a fourth, open-ended part that usually consisted of a general discussion about issues that came up during the interview. On account of the extensive triangulation of data described above and this approach to dealing with the potential problems of common methods bias, I trust that the data I collected with respect to internal drivers and their effects is valid. To account for remaining uncertainties, I decided to report only those cases I believe have a solid data basis.

responsibility in the way theoretically anticipated. Similarity of cases is established on the basis of company features, and by controlling for numerous potential external driver-based explanations.

"NGO pressure" is an example of such a potential external driver-based explanation, which will be controlled. According to this explanation, firms that are under the scrutiny of transnational NGOs adopt corporate social responsibility policies to prevent being publicly "named and shamed" by the NGOs for corporate misconduct. The analysis will neutralize this (potential) explanation in pair-wise comparative analyses by choosing only firms that are similarly affected by such NGO pressure – or not affected at all. Another example of a feature that will be held constant across comparative cases is firm size: the analysis will only compare firms of a similar size. Other control variables are the market orientation of a firm, membership in business associations, participation in public–private partnerships, the country of origin of a firm, and export/import orientation, to name a few. Table 3.2 summarizes this approach to comparative case study analysis.

In addition to this correlation-based logic of causal inference of controlled pair-wise comparisons, the analysis will also contain elements of process-tracing and thus apply a causal mechanism-based logic of inference (Brady and Collier 2010; George and Bennett 2005). In the context of correlation-based inferences variation of the dependent variable either reflects the corresponding variation of the independent variable or not – in which case the causal argument is rejected. Whatever happens in between cause and effect, however, remains empirically obscure. Tracing causal mechanisms sheds light on precisely these dynamics and processes in between cause and effect. Causal mechanisms are important for the validation or rejection of causal arguments, as they allow for a test of the logic of the argument itself (George and Bennett 2005; Tilly 1997). Process-tracing furthermore enables the analysis to test for potential alternative explanatory factors that correlate with the independent variable (and thus resolves problems of multicollinearity) or that are otherwise closely related to it.

To illustrate, one argument in this book is that asset-specific investments in production sites motivate firms to adopt high environmental standards (see Chapters 2 and 5). One may argue, alternatively, that it is not asset specificity that causes the emergence of environmental standards, but technological advancement. According to this alternative explanation, investments in production sites lead to new technology. New technology,

Table 3.2 *Controlled, pair-wise comparisons (correlation-based logic of inference)*

Type of comparison: cross-sectional or longitudinal (n ≥ 2)		Controlled pair-wise comparisons		
		Criteria for case selection		Causal inference: correlation-based
		(1) Control variables	(2) Variation of internal driver	
Organizationally distinct entities (cross sectional) or different periods of time (longitudinal)	Firm case 1	Highly similar firms as concerns basic firm features and potential external pressure factors for CSR: country/ region of operation; industry sector; production output (product type); policy field; firm size; high-end or low-end target market; NGO pressure; membership in associations or public–private partnerships; country of origin; problem pressure	High levels of asset specificity	High levels of CSR: confirming evidence; low levels of CSR: disconfirming evidence
	Firm case 2		Low levels of asset specificity	Low levels of CSR: confirming evidence; high levels of CSR: disconfirming evidence
				Does the variation of the independent variable correlate with the variation of the dependent variable?

in turn, raises the level of standards automatically as it is usually more resource use efficient. On the basis of controlled pair-wise comparisons we could not decide whether it is asset specificity or new technology that causes high environmental standards. Asset-specific investments almost always correlate with technological advancement; they may actually cause it. As a consequence, both potential explanations are inseparable in the context of pair-wise comparisons.

Process tracing is a method according to which these two explanations can be disentangled (George and Bennett 2005: 205–10): the causal path, sequence of events, and intermediary outcomes that can be reasonably deduced for the factor "technological advancement" are clearly different from the ones that can be ascertained for asset specificity (see Chapter 5 for details). They can therefore be empirically evaluated in comparative perspective within one and the same case. Table 3.3 summarizes the understanding in this study of process-tracing.

Table 3.3 *Process tracing (mechanism-based logic of inference)*

Process tracing		
Type of comparison	Case features/criteria for case selection	Causal inference: mechanism-based
Within-case (n = 1)	(1) Level of internal driver correlates with level of CSR (2) At least one other potential alternative or highly related explanatory factor or causal mechanism correlates with the internal driver (3) The case is representative for cases that are characterized by the internal driver in general, and is a likely case for the alternative explanation/ driver (i.e. a "hard" test for the internal driver mechanism)	Deduction of distinct and, possibly, mutually exclusive observable implications for the competing explanations/ mechanisms Do the observable implications confirm the theorized internal driver-mechanism or the alternative explanation? Do any of the observable implications allow us to rule out one of the explanations?

Apart from controlled, pair-wise comparisons and process tracing, the analysis will also make use of "backwards-looking" (Scharpf 1997: 18) logics of inference, which are empirical puzzle-oriented and thus select cases on the dependent variable in order to ask from there on what explains the asserted variation. More precisely, the empirical chapters will begin presenting puzzles of corporate social responsibility, showing that the established explanations in the literature, which mainly focus on external drivers, fail to explain them. The chapter will then continue to show that by applying "forwards-looking" (Scharpf 1997: 18) methods, which select cases on the independent variable (controlled, pair-wise comparisons and process tracing), the respective internal driver the chapter deals with can resolve the puzzle. An exception in this respect is Chapter 6. This chapter opens up with an empirical puzzle which effectively disconfirms internal driver 4, the *brand reputation dilemma*. Accordingly, the analysis will continue to proceed in a "backwards-looking" way from this point onwards in order to inquire about the whereabouts of this disconfirming evidence.

Another organizing principle of this study and the case selection is that the empirical analysis aims at hard cases-tests so as to demonstrate the general applicability, importance, and explanatory power of its arguments. To this end, this study will assess the validity of internal drivers in highly diverse contexts: cases will be chosen from within the South African automotive and textile industries, and from within the Chinese textile industry.

South Africa and China have in common that they are, in the policy areas the analysis features, areas of regulatory void (Risse 2011; Risse and Krasner 2014; see also Chapter 2). Apart from that, however, both countries are highly different: whereas post-apartheid South Africa is a liberal democracy with a strong civil rights constitution and, in principle, the rule of law, China is a socialist dictatorship. The policy fields in this study are, too, highly dissimilar. The analysis will assess the effects of internal drivers on companies' health programs, labor standards, and environmental policies. Whereas some of the corporate social responsibilities concern negative externalities of production (mostly so in the field of environment), others create benefits for workers and society and are thus related to the provision of common goods (as, for example, health programs). The industry sectors from within which the cases are chosen also differ significantly. The textile industry is labor-intensive and low-tech, does not involve high amounts of fixed capital or expert

knowledge and is, accordingly, a sector with limited potential for productivity gains. All in all, the industry exemplifies variation of asset
specificity on a relatively low level. Contrary to this, the automotive
industry is technology and capital intensive and offers highly productive
workplaces to skilled employees. Compared with the textile industry,
the auto sector illustrates variation of asset specificity on a high investment level. The idea behind choosing these highly different contexts is
this: should internal drivers turn out to explain corporate social responsibility in these contexts, we can conclude that they have general
explanatory power – that is, that they are valid irrespective of context
characteristics.

The remainder of this chapter describes the diverse empirical institutional and policy contexts as well as the industry and market contexts to
which the analysis will subject the arguments for internal drivers.

Institutional and policy context: corporate social responsibility in South Africa and China

The first internal driver, the *human resources dilemma*, will be assessed
in the context of South Africa and with respect to its predicted effects
on labor-related corporate social responsibility. More specifically, the
analysis will evaluate the explanatory power of this internal driver with
respect to South African-based firms' actions concerning HIV/AIDS
among their workforces.

South Africa is one of the countries most heavily affected by HIV/
AIDS. The first cases were diagnosed in the early 1980s (Dickinson and
Stevens 2005; Nattrass 2007; von Soest and Weinel 2006). In the 1990s,
the spread of the disease grew exponentially and, in 2004, prevalence
was believed to have well surpassed 10 percent of the total population.
Estimations are that between 15–20 percent of the population in the
sexually active age group have contracted the virus.[10] The policies of the
South African government in response to this have been sluggish at best
(Whiteside and Sunter 2000). After the democratic elections in 1994,
HIV/AIDS was declared a "Presidential lead project" (see Rosenbrock
1998). However, it turned out that this project fell prey to a lack of

---

[10] According to the United Nations Children's Fund (UNICEF), the estimated adult
prevalence rate (aged 15–49) in 2007 is 18.1 percent (www.unicef.org/
infobycountry/southafrica_statistics.html, January 5, 2011).

financial resources as well as human resources on the local level. To make it worse, the scarce financial resources that were made available were not used appropriately. By the end of the 1990s, the South African government revised its approach to HIV/AIDS in the "HIV/AIDS/STD strategic plan for South Africa 2000–5" (Department of Health 2000). This plan focused on prevention, but lacked any explicit commitment to anti-retroviral therapy and other medical treatment (Hickey *et al.* 2003) as well as a budget for implementation. In conclusion, it did not resolve any of the problems caused by the insufficient response to the disease, most importantly, the particularly limited involvement and capacity of local government (Hickey 2002; Müller-Debus *et al.* 2009a, 2009b).

By 2003, however, the government came under international and domestic pressure for its lack of action in this respect. The "Operational plan for comprehensive HIV and AIDS care, management and treatment for South Africa" (Department of Health 2003) is a direct response to this pressure. The plan envisioned universal, equitable, and free access to medication. According to it, it was the provinces that would provide the necessary medical services for this. However, again, lack of resources – medication, skilled personnel, and clinics – and for a long time also the lack of clear commitment on the part of government to the plan specifically, as well as to fighting the disease in general, undermined effective implementation.[11] Most patients who receive public health care have to wait long periods before they gain access to medication. The medication itself is insufficient by international medical standards. Also in view of industry regulation, government has so far not developed clear regulations on how to monitor and manage the disease in the workplace (see Dickinson and Stevens 2005).

Why does South Africa – as an emerging market with considerable resources, world-class universities, and medical know-how – show such a striking inability to cope with a problem as large and severe as the HIV/AIDS pandemic? One reason is certainly the fact that the country has had to deal simultaneously with an array of problems after transition from apartheid to democracy. The new African National Congress (ANC) regime was under great pressure to organize access to housing, fresh water, electricity, the job market, and education for the "black" impoverished masses. These problems of access and more

---

[11] See interview with automotive expert Dr Justin Barnes, October 1, 2007, Durban, and Müller-Debus *et al.* 2009a, 2009b.

equal distribution of the country's wealth have yet to be resolved. The government was insufficiently equipped from the very beginning to confront these problems, and so could not draw attention and resources on specific areas such as HIV/AIDS.

In addition, however, serious mismanagement and a vivid display of ignorance dominated on the highest political levels in relation to HIV/AIDS. The Thabo Mbeki governments – Thabo Mbeki was President of South Africa in the crucial years between 1999 and 2008 – rejected the so-called "international scientific consensus" concerning HIV/AIDS. This consensus refers to the fact that HIV causes AIDS and that medical treatment prolongs the time span before persons who have contracted HIV fall sick with AIDS. The government, however, publicly denied the relation between HIV and AIDS – in particular before 2003 – and was openly hostile towards any medical approach towards the disease.[12] In consequence, it abstained from making anti-retroviral medication available to persons who had contracted HIV and undermined any effort by international organizations to do so.[13] A key figure in the government's "denialism" of the international scientific consensus on HIV/AIDS was Mbeki's health minister, Ms Manto Tshabalala-Msimang, who proposed garlic, lemon juice, and beetroot as AIDS remedies.[14] A Harvard Study in 2008 thus accused the Mbeki government of being responsible for at least 365,000 premature deaths on account of suppressing the distribution of medication which would help prevent pregnant women from infecting their babies.[15] According to a *New York Times* report, President Mbeki even personally attacked anyone in South Africa who questioned his "denialist" position in relation to the

---

[12] Dugger, Celia W. (November 25, 2008) "Study Cites Toll of AIDS Policy in South Africa," *New York Times* (www.nytimes.com/2008/11/26/world/africa/26aids.html?_r=1&hp, December 5, 2012).

[13] Hickey 2002; Hickey *et al.* 2003; Nattrass 2007; Thauer 2013a; Whiteside and Sunter 2000.

[14] Dugger, Celia W. (November 25, 2008) "Study Cites Toll of AIDS Policy in South Africa," *New York Times* (www.nytimes.com/2008/11/26/world/africa/26aids.html?_r=1&hp, December 5, 2012); Robbie, John (September 14, 2000) "Don't call me Manto," BBC News (http://news.bbc.co.uk/2/hi/africa/924889.stm, December 5, 2012).

[15] Roeder, Amy (Spring 2009) "Wasted Lives," Harvard Public Policy Review (www.hsph.harvard.edu/news/magazine/files/hphrSPR09southafrica.pdf, December 5, 2012).

scientific consensus.[16] For example, he supposedly wrote a letter to Professor Malegapuru Makgoba, a leading South African immunologist, who publicly demanded the distribution of anti-retroviral medication, accusing him of defending "Western" science – which he deemed to be racist.

By 2003/04 the government's stance towards the disease changed, however, at least to a certain degree. President Mbeki had come under international and domestic pressure for his display of ignorance towards the disease and failure to fight it effectively (Dickinson 2004; Nattrass 2007; von Soest and Weinel 2006). In particular, the civil society pressure group Treatment Action Campaign (TAC) organized broad public resistance among South Africans against the government's policy. The TAC in conjunction with increasing international isolation forced President Mbeki into an agreement imposed on him by his own party according to which he had to abstain from any public debate on HIV/AIDS. The TAC also pressured the cabinet to draft a new governmental program which resulted in the mentioned "Operational plan for comprehensive HIV and AIDS care, management and treatment for South Africa" of 2003 (Department of Health 2003; Hickey *et al.* 2003). According to a *New York Times* report, it was in this situation that the former US president, Bill Clinton, met with President Mbeki at a dinner on the occasion of Nelson Mandela's eighty-fifth birthday and talked to him about AIDS. Clinton, according to the newspaper report, told President Mbeki how anti-retroviral treatment had reduced the AIDS mortality rate in the US whilst reminding him that "I'm your friend and I haven't joined in the public condemnation."[17] When Clinton offered to dispatch a team of experts to assist in devising a national treatment plan, President Mbeki agreed and thus in 2004 this team convened to implement the operational plan.

In practice, however, only little progress was made in the wake of these developments. The Mbeki government abstained from publicly denying the scientific consensus and ceased intimidating civil society organizations and individuals fighting the disease on the basis of

[16] Dugger, Celia W. (November 25, 2008) "Study Cites Toll of AIDS Policy in South Africa," *New York Times* (www.nytimes.com/2008/11/26/world/africa/26aids. html?_r=1&hp, December 5, 2012).
[17] *Ibid.*

scientific evidence. But South Africa remained an area of limited state-hood with respect to HIV/AIDS. The aforementioned health minister who had denied any relation between HIV and AIDS was able to remain in office until 2008. Most South Africans have hardly any access to health care services, in particular those living in the townships; these are the areas most affected by the disease. Drug coverage for persons sick with AIDS is an estimated 20 percent nationwide and it is much lower in the townships (Dickinson and Stevens 2005; Nattrass 2007; von Soest and Weinel 2006). As one prominent representative of the South African Business Coalition on HIV/AIDS (SABCOHA) – a business-based pressure group – summarizes the situation: "In South Africa, the government is hugely constrained in its ability to deliver for a whole host of reasons: corruption, incompetence, poor leadership, incapacity, legacy of apartheid, you can carry on."[18]

The second and third internal drivers, the *technological specialization dilemma* and the *foreign direct investment dilemma*, will be subject to evaluation as well in the context of South Africa, yet in terms of their predicted effects on environmental standards. South Africa is also an area of limited statehood in this policy field. However, whereas it is the failure of the government to provide for essential health services in the field of HIV/AIDS, it is the lack of effective industry regulation that defines the country as an area of regulatory void in the field of the environment.

Firms can, by and large, do as they wish in South Africa in terms of environmental pollution. While the country's legislation has adopted the main international environmental standards and norms, implementation on the local level is not taking place. The South African government started to introduce environmental legislation from the mid-1990s onwards in an attempt to reintegrate the country into the international community after decades of apartheid isolation (DEAT 2000; Groenewald 2005; Lund-Thomsen 2005). The most important legal provision in this respect is the Bill of Rights (No. 108/1996), which relates environmental to human rights by, for example, stipulating a fair and sustainable management of South Africa's natural resources. Section 24 of the Bill of Rights guarantees environmental rights to the South African people. These basic principles have been specified by additional environmental legislation on the national level, of which

---

[18] Interview with a representative of the South African Business Coalition on HIV/AIDS (SABCOHA), March 19, 2007, Johannesburg.

the National Environmental Management Act (NEMA) is the central document.[19] NEMA formulates principles for environmental decision-making and details the scope of action of state agencies as well as compliance and enforcement mechanisms and environmental information disclosure.[20] Other acts specify the law regarding air quality, water management, or biodiversity.

Thus, the policy arena in the field of environment is fully established on the national level in South Africa. However, implementation, when delegated to the local and provincial levels, does not take place. There is a lack of specification of abstract framework legislation into local standards, guidelines, by-laws, and limits. Enforcement and monitoring is not pursued (Hönke *et al.* 2008; Lund-Thomsen 2005).[21] Some provinces, such as the Western Cape, have stronger regulatory capacities than, for example, the Eastern Cape – a particularly poor province where socio-economic development is lagging behind. However, even the relatively well-off and progressive Western Cape government employs only a handful of staff for local implementation of environmental laws and standard setting, which is insufficient for effective regulation.[22] To increase the effectiveness of environmental regulation, the government has invented an environmental task force policing group, the "green scorpions."[23] While this group has indeed given recent cause to minor improvements vis-à-vis the enforcement of existing regulation, the resources and personnel of the "green scorpions" are still too few to make a substantial difference. In addition, this group can only enforce existing legislation and thus does not tackle the problem of lax or entirely lacking environmental regulations on the local level. Hence, whenever companies adopt environmental standards, the analysis considers this an instance of corporate social responsibility, since through such measures the firm reintegrates negative externalities of production on a voluntary basis.

[19] Act 107/1998 amended by Act 56/2002, Act 46/2003, Act 8/2004.
[20] Specified for firms in the legislation on environmental impact assessments (EIA).
[21] On the national level, the Department of Environmental Affairs and Tourism (DEAT) lacks personnel and expertise. On the local level the budget for environmental agencies is in addition to that problem insufficient.
[22] Interview with the Assistant Director of the Department of Environmental Affairs and Development Planning of the Western Cape, September 15, 2008, Cape Town.
[23] See http://emi.deat.gov.za (30 December 2012).

The fourth dilemma situation brings about corporate social responsibility policies across the board in-house and in the supply chain on account of asset-specific investments in the brand reputation of a firm. The analysis will subject this internal driver to the different contexts of South Africa and China as this driver turns out to be invalid and in need of further specification. In South Africa, corporate social responsibility across the board is mainly concerned with environmental policies. Labor-related corporate social responsibility, as defined by the core ILO-labor standards and demanded by the Global Compact, is in this context of minor relevance only. The country has a rather strict labor law in place. With respect to HIV/AIDS workplace programs the reputational risks seem rather limited. While such programs certainly fall into the realm of corporate social responsibility, they are not part of what international institutions, such as the Global Compact, consider minimum standards defining corporate social responsibility in the eye of the public. Accordingly, firms do not face accusation or criticism for not running a HIV/AIDS workplace program.

With respect to China, the analysis is concerned with labor relations and environmental policies. Not unlike South Africa, framework legislation exists in China, too, but is rarely implemented.[24] The first Chinese environmental law dates back to 1979 and was subsequently developed into an environmental policy arena by complementary area specific legislation (see Sternfeld 2006: 36). Today, laws prohibit the pollution of water, sea, and air, and set guidelines for deforestation, protection of resources, and environmental heritages. Examples of legislation include the Cleaner Production Bill (2002) as well as a bill on waste management and recycling (2005). As some commentators conclude, "China has made some substantive progress" (Chan *et al.* 2008: 291) regarding environmental policies in recent years. However, while abstract laws exist and increase in depth and scope, implementation is lagging behind. China "seems to lack the will or capability" (Chan *et al.* 2008: 291) on the local level to support compliance with the laws.

The central actor in the field of environment in China is the State Environmental Protection Administration (SEPA), which was founded in 1984 and gained ministerial status in 1998. SEPA suffers from

---

[24] See Chan *et al.* 2008; Chatham House 2007; OECD 2007; Sternfeld 2006; Task Force on Environmental Governance 2006.

shortcomings in expertise, personnel, and financial resources to effectively supervise and manage the transfer of abstract national legislation into local regulation. In addition, SEPA often fails to display the necessary political will for this task (see Task Force on Environmental Governance 2006). Many legislations and regulations are not publicly accessible. Monitoring and sanctioning of firms that infringe on the law happens on rare occasions only. On the local level, government agencies in the field of environment are particularly weak or entirely absent. Environmental policy in China is therefore only "responding to pollution problems once they occur, rather than being proactive and preventive" (Task Force on Environmental Governance 2006: 5).

It should be mentioned, though, that the economically developed provinces at the coast have started to adopt stricter regulations over the last few years. In the province of Zhejiang, in which the Chinese case studies are located, the German Gesellschaft für Internationale Zusammenarbeit (GIZ), for example, has assisted the government in setting up regulatory capacities. Since implementation had not taken place at all before, this development, according to the GIZ assistance program, will take many years before effects are visible on the level of company behavior.[25]

With respect to labor relations, the situation is analogous. National framework legislation exists and has increased in depth and scope recently.[26] In 1995, the Meeting of the Standing Committee of the Eighth National People's Congress issued the Labor Law of the People's Republic of China. This piece of legislation is oriented towards international standards and contains provisions about the most important areas usually covered by labor law: regulated are individual and collective contracts, working hours, minimum wages, health and safety at the workplace, dispute resolution, and obligatory insurances. However, implementation of the law has not taken place, as the director of the human rights program at Reebok in China pointed out in 2002: "Who enforces Chinese labor law? Nobody. If it was enforced, China

---

[25] Interview with a program manager and a technical advisor of SEPA and the environmental ministry of Zhejiang, April 11, 2008, Hangzhou.

[26] See Chan 2003 and 2005; *New York Times* (January 1, 2008) "New Labor Laws Introduced in China"; *Newsweek* (February 24, 2008) "Chinese Union. New labor Regulations designed to protect China's workers are already having an impact, according to American-based watchdog."

would be a better place for millions of people. But it is ignored more than in any other country."[27]

Despite profound structural alterations of the legal framework governing labor relations, the situation has not significantly changed in respect to prevailing implementation deficits since 2002. A new labor law was issued in December 2007. The law stipulates severe penalties for employers who hire persons without contracts to prevent undercutting the minimum wage, imposing excessive over-time on workers, or refusing to insure them.[28] It also demands one month's pay per year of employment for workers who have been let go and open-ended terms of employment for those who have completed two fixed terms.

However, the law is structurally new as it is contract law. This implies that the workers themselves are supposed to enforce implementation vis-à-vis employers by means of litigation or complaints submitted to the Department of Labor. On the one hand, this structural-legal alteration may strengthen the position of workers in the future and therefore is a potential improvement. On the other hand, however, it has not yet resulted in any significant changes.[29] The courts in China are not independent and few workers would dare to file a lawsuit without securing the consent of political authorities beforehand. In addition, even if access to courts was equitable, contract law causes "bottleneck" problems – a few, understaffed courts would have to administer millions of potential lawsuits from workers whose rights have been violated. Hence, implementation is still sluggish at best.

The industry and market context: automotive and textile

The cases analyzed in the subsequent chapters feature firms in the automotive and textile industry sectors. The two industries are very

---

[27] Director of the human resources program of Reebok in China, May 29, 2002, Hong Kong, quoted in Chan 2003: 45.

[28] However, hiring persons without contract is more often the rule than the exception in some industries such as textiles.

[29] Interviews with the China Program Manager of the World Watch Institute (WWI), China Watch, March 11, 2008, Washington, DC; the China Workplace Program Manager of Social Accountability International (SAI), April 2008, Beijing; the Senior Program Officer of The Asia Foundation, April 15, 2008, Beijing.

different. The automotive industry illustrates high degrees of fixed capital and high barriers to market entry, high-tech production, high productivity, skilled labor, and a technically complex production output. The textile industry, by contrast, stands out for its relatively low capital investment, low market entry barriers, low productivity, high labor intensity, and relatively simple products. Most importantly, however, the analysis concentrates on cases from these two industry sectors because they are strikingly different with respect to the degree to which managerial dilemmas characterize them.

While the automotive industry is marked by substantial, asset-specific allocation of organizational resources in human resources and production technologies, the textile industry serves as an opposite example, i.e. it exhibits low levels of such resource allocation. Hence, if the arguments for internal drivers were to hold for comparative cases in both industries despite their distinctiveness, this would indicate their validity and explanatory power on different levels of intensity of managerial dilemmas and independent of the different sector contexts.

In addition, the two industry sectors have been chosen because they are particularly relevant for the economic development in transition countries. Hosting a textile industry is generally regarded as a "first step" to industrialization and modernization (Gereffi and Memedovic 2003). The industry is inclusive and its entry barriers are low (Jai-Ok *et al.* 2006; Nordas 2004). Even with limited access to credits and a shortage of industrial expertise, it is possible to become a textile entrepreneur. The industry is labor intensive and offers jobs even to unskilled workers. They usually constitute the majority of the population in newly industrializing countries.

In contrast to the textile industry, entry barriers are high in the automotive industry. The sector is considered a catalyst for modernization, innovation, and technological upgrading and therefore the "next step" to industrialization.[30] Automotive companies often invest substantially if they decide to enter industrializing markets as producers. They transfer technology and high standards of production. Spillover effects upgrade the economy with respect to the technologies used and efficiency. Besides, the industry is regarded as important from a modernization perspective. It creates a demand for skilled labor and pays

---

[30] See Lorentzen 2006; Lorentzen and Barnes 2004: 473; Lorentzen *et al.* 2004; Meyn 2004: 14.

relatively well – and is therefore crucial for the emergence of an edu-
cated middle class.

In South Africa, the analyses will include cases from both industry
sectors. The configuration in the two industry sectors today is a direct
outcome of the political liberalization process pursued by the government in the 1990s after the end of apartheid. Before liberalization, the
South African market and its industries were isolated and highly inefficient by international standards. After the political transition phase
from apartheid to democracy between 1989–94, the goal of the first
democratically elected government under the new liberal constitution in
1994 was to integrate the country into the global market in order to
rationalize, modernize, and develop the economy, generate economic
growth, attract foreign direct investment, and create a competitive job
market (see Meyn 2004: 10). For the automotive industry the Motor
Industry Development Programme (MIDP) was implemented in 1995
to liberalize the auto market and incorporate the South African industry
into the World Trade Organization/General Agreement on Tariffs
and Trade (WTO/GATT) free trade system. Key features of the MIDP
were:

- the immediate reduction of import tariffs from 115 percent to
  65 percent and a phase-down of tariffs which is faster than required
  by WTO obligations;
- the gradual abolition of all local content requirements;
- general duty-free allowances;
- the invention of an import/export complementation scheme by which
  rebate credits can be earned on exports of vehicles and components;
  rebate credits can be used for duty-free imports of vehicles and
  components.[31]

The program is generally considered a success. Exports grew from *circa*
9,000 cars in 1995 to 58,000 in 2000; 114,000 cars were exported in
2005, increasing to 170,000 in 2007 and 280,000 in 2011.[32] Today, the

---

[31] See Barnes and Black 2003; Black 2001; Black and Mitchell 2002; Lorentzen and
Barnes 2004; Meyn 2004. Several revision rounds of the MIDP have adapted the
detailed provisions to the current market situation in South Africa.

[32] See NAAMSA 2006; Statistics South Africa (www.southafrica.info/business/
economy/sectors/automotive-overview.htm, June 19, 2009); see also US
Department of Commerce 2005: 1 and NAAMSA media release: Comment of the

automotive industry is the third largest economic sector after mining and agriculture and the largest of all manufacturing sectors in South Africa, accounting for approximately 30 percent of the country's manufacturing output. Car production contributes about 7.7 percent to the gross domestic product (GDP) and circa 15 percent to the total exports. Hence, the automotive industry in South Africa is particularly well established, still growing and increasing production depth.

Like the automotive industry, the textile industry of South Africa underwent a process of liberalization from the mid-1990s onwards. Accession to the World Trade Organization in 1994 and a quick phase-out of protection levels exposed the industry to global competition (see Müller-Debus *et al.* 2009a: 15–18). Throughout the late 1990s, the textile industry profited immensely from liberalization and the new access to the global market. In particular when the South African Rand depreciated in the late 1990s, exports grew and remained competitive against imports (Vlok 2006). This trend was considerably strengthened by the US and the EU providing South Africa with preferential access to their markets.[33]

However, substantial appreciation of the Rand in 2002 reversed this trend. Exports were annihilated and an import surge was initiated which resulted in the textile and clothing industry experiencing considerable difficulties.[34] In fact, the industry has become import-driven with the majority of imports coming from China. This, in turn, was clearly to the disadvantage of the manufacturers in South Africa. South African retailers, however, take great advantage of cheap Chinese imports. An interesting aspect regarding the retail market in South Africa is that it is still largely in the hands of genuinely South African firms such as Edgars, Foschini, the South African Woolworths, Massmart, and Mr. Price, just to name a few.

In China, the empirical investigation comprises cases from the Chinese textile industry. Before 2005, the country faced export restrictions

---

October 2011 new vehicle sales statistics (www.naamsa.co.za/flash/press.htm, November 5, 2011).

[33] Granted to South Africa by the African Growth and Opportunities Act (AGOA) and a South Africa–EU trade agreement. Since 2005, the textiles and apparel sector has been subject to the GATT.

[34] Today, Statistics South Africa estimates that the textiles, clothing, leather, and footwear industries contribute approximately 4.6 percent to the total value of manufacturing sales.

for almost three decades.[35] The world's largest markets of the EU and the US restricted Chinese imports under a system of international export quotas established by the Multi-Fibre Arrangement (MFA) and its successor, the Agreement on Textiles and Clothing (ATC). Nonetheless, Chinese exports increased at twice the rate world exports increased in the 1990s and at that time that China was already on its way to become the textile factory of the world (Mahtaney 2007: 10–12).[36] At the beginning of 2005, the MFA/ATC-inflicted restrictions on exports were lifted and the clothing and textile trade became part of the general WTO provisions. Exports grew immediately and continue to do so to this very day with the result that "China is the most important exporter of textiles and clothing in the world" (Eberhardt and Thoburn 2007: 177).

These developments have caused a diversification of the industry into firms that target the domestic market and those that export. Generally, the export-driven firms operate on higher profit margins and standards of production than those parts of the industry that sell to the domestic market. The latter are often still operating with quality and efficiency standards from the early 1990s. This study, however, will exclusively concentrate on those firms in the Chinese textile industry that export exclusively. This is a sector which has recently come under strong economic pressure. The appreciation of the currency, the Renminbi, has made Chinese imports less competitive in Europe and the US. The government has reduced hidden subsidies for the industry. The new labor laws, irrespective of prevalent implementation problems, have poisoned the general investment climate. Some textile firms have therefore relocated to India and Vietnam. These developments notwithstanding, China is still the most important textile producer worldwide.

With respect to sector structures, the automotive industry is in general – that is, worldwide – composed of four distinct subsectors: raw material

---

[35] Interviews with the China Program Manager of the World Watch Institute (WWI), China Watch, March 11, 2008, Washington, DC; the China Workplace Program Manager of Social Accountability International (SAI), April 2008, Beijing; the Senior Program Officer of The Asia Foundation, April 15, 2008, Beijing.

[36] Quota regimes are generally problematic instruments for a regulation of trade flows in the textile industry. Textile production is highly fragmented. Even a relatively simple jacket may be produced by the collaborative effort of dozens of factories and it is often very difficult for customs to trace the places of production.

production (for example, steel, glass, fibers), component manufacturing (tools, electronics, braking systems, windows), original equipment manufacturing (finishing, assembly), and after sales services (garages, insurance). However, this study only concentrates on manufacturing, that is, on original equipment manufacturers (OEM) and component manufacturers. OEM account for 30–40 percent of the total value added in the industry; they are multinational corporations that dominate the world market for cars and have the buying power in automotive production chains. Component manufacturers are either first, second, or third tier suppliers to the OEM. First tier suppliers are often huge multinationals, as for example Robert Bosch AG or Schaeffler; they deliver high-tech products, such as brake systems, directly to the OEM. Second tier suppliers are usually medium-sized, although there are some multinationals among them as well. Second tier suppliers do not deliver directly to the OEM, but to first tier suppliers. Third tier suppliers are often small and medium-sized firms. Their products are only car-specific to a certain degree as they usually sell to other sectors as well. Generally, the industry is a high-tech, high-skills, and high investment industry. However, the further down a firm is in the supply chain, usually the smaller its operations and the less it relies on skills, technology, and other investments (see Figure 3.1).

The cases selected for this study from the South African automotive industry include major OEM with plants in the country, such as BMW, Ford, General Motors, Mercedes Benz of South Africa, Nissan-Renault, and Volkswagen. The sector structure of component manufacturing is

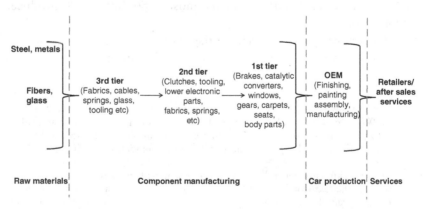

Figure 3.1 The structure of production in the automotive industry

more fragmented than in the OEM sector. While there are only a few OEMs operating in South Africa and worldwide, there are many more firms in the business of manufacturing of components. Hence, comprehensive coverage could not be achieved in the case selection. However, the nine cases featured are highly representative for the component manufacturers of South Africa. The cases feature the firms August Laepple, Capewell Springs, Shatterprufe, Schaeffler Group (with the brands LUK, INA, FAG), Firstpro Engineering, Feltex Automotive, Vacuform, Robert Bosch AG, Beier Albany, and SANS Fibre.

The textile industry is – in comparison to the automotive industry – generally much more fragmented. The value added chain consists of five distinct sectors: raw materials (for example, oil, cotton, silk), textile production (petrochemicals, yarn, weaving, knitting), clothing (cut, make and trim, sewing), trading agencies that import and export finished textiles, and marketing/retailing. The retailers and their purchasing power dominate the sector. However, trade agencies are becoming more and more important. They organize the production for retailers, search for the best prices, control quality, and assume all associated risks. Most Western brands, but also the retailers in South Africa, purchase large proportions of their textile products via this "middle man"-sector (see Figure 3.2).

The textile cases of this study include firms from all textile subsectors, except for raw materials. Many firms are active in more than one

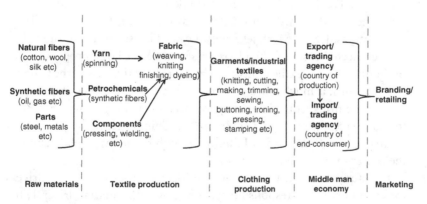

Figure 3.2 The structure of production in the textile industry

subsector and will thus be listed under different categories. In South Africa, brands/retailers that are analyzed include: Adidas; Jordan and Co. (with the brands Asics, Tiger Brands, Jordan Footwear, Olympic, Bronx); Woolworths; Billabong; Foschini; DB Apparel (with the brands Playtex and Wonderbra); Massmart; Nike; Edcon (with the brands Boardman's, CAN, Edgars, Prato, Red Square, Temptations, Jet, Jet Mart, Jet Shoes, Legit); Levi's; Gap; Mr. Price; and Falke. Clothing firms featured in this study are: Jordan and Co.; Monviso; International Trimmings and Labels; Capewell Springs; DB Apparel; Levi's; Edgars; Foschini; Falke; and Billabong. Textile firms are: Feltex; Frame; International Trimmings and Labels; Migra Textiles; Capewell Springs; Beier Albany; SANS Fibre; Crossley Carpets; Paltex; and Team Puma. In China, the following clothing factories were the subject of investigation: NTS Ltd.; Ningbo Silk Trend Garment Co., Ltd. (factory of Polymax Group Company Ltd.); LP apparel, Inc.; Hangzhou Dadi Garments Co., Ltd.; Futan – Hangzhou Futan Knitting Co., Ltd.; Cosieleather Garments (Hua Tong Group); and Dhawoo Co., Ltd. Trade agencies operating in China included are: Wonderful Earth (Far East) Ltd.; NTS Ltd.; Polymax Group Company Ltd.; MDC International (HK) Ltd.; and Dragon Up Holdings Limited. Retailers incorporated in this study that source from China are: Steilmann (C&A, Peek and Cloppenburg); LP apparel Group; Lloyd Textile Trading Limited; Accurate Limited; H&M; and Gap. In addition, the following already mentioned South African retailers and brands source extensively from China: Jordan and Co. (with the brands Tiger Brands, Jordan Footwear, Asics, Olympic, Bronx); Woolworths; Billabong; Foschini; Playtex and Wondebra; Massmart; Nike; Edcon (with the brands Boardman's, CAN, Edgars, Prato, Red Square, C&A, Temptations, Jet, Jet Mart, Jet Shoes, Legit); Levi's; Mr. Price; and Falke.

The selected cases are highly representative for large proportions of the South African textile industry. The representativeness of the Chinese cases, in turn, is much more limited. The sample includes only clothing and textile firms from Zhejiang province. Zhejiang province accounts for 22 percent (see Wick 2007: 36) of Chinese textile exports; it is located in the "backyard" of Shanghai with the town of Hangzhou as the center of trade and production.

The study will now turn to the empirical analysis of internal drivers for corporate social responsibility. It begins with internal driver 1, the *human resources dilemma* and focuses on textile and automotive companies in South Africa. HIV/AIDS is heavily affecting the productivity of firms in the country. Most people with HIV/AIDS do not have access to health care. Does the *human resources dilemma* motivate firms in this context to take on the fight against the disease among their workers and to this end develop HIV/AIDS workplace programs?

4 | *Internal driver 1: the* human resources dilemma

Many firms do business in emerging market contexts as they offer cheap, unskilled labor with subsequently larger profit margins (Blanton and Blanton 2009; Cohen 2007). It is precisely these firms to which arguments about an alleged regulatory "race to the bottom" refer. Regulatory standards and corporate social responsibility are cost factors for these firms, which they will obviously seek to avoid. They thereby force states competing for foreign direct investment into a regulatory "freeze" (Madsen 2009: 1298) or compel them to downsize regulation (Bohle 2008; Chan and Ross 2003; Gill 1995). However, emerging markets also attract businesses that rely on more complex input factors than cheap labor alone.[1]

A case in point is the South African hotel carpet manufacturer Crossley Carpets. Hotel carpets are the output of a sophisticated production process – unlike the manufacturing of rugs, for example, which is more simple. Accordingly, whereas rug making relies mostly on cheap, unskilled labor (Siedmann 2007), hotel carpet manufacturing is "highly specialized," as a manager of Crossley Carpets reports, relying on "unique skills: we cannot just hire people from the labor market."[2] Newcomers to the firm have to undergo extensive training before they become employable to the firm. In addition, workers are constantly trained on the job in special training courses so that incumbents can be recruited for higher-level technical and management positions. Crossley Carpets is thus a firm that illustrates internal drivers, more specifically, the *human resources dilemma*, which emerges on account

---

[1] See Blanton and Blanton 2009. For individual country studies in this respect – in particular in the BRIC countries (Brazil, Russia, India, China) – see Dossani 2012; Farrell *et al.* 2007; Simon and Cao 2008; Wang 2011.
[2] Interview with the Director of Human Resources of Crossley Carpets, September 28, 2007, Durban.

of investments in employee skills that are difficult to come by on the labor market (see Chapter 2).

The example is not overly exceptional. Just as Crossley Carpets, many firms with complex processes produce in emerging market contexts such as South Africa. As they are often confronted with skills shortages, they seek to alleviate such conditions by running sophisticated training programs within their factories.[3] Some firms in the car industry in South Africa, China, Brazil, Mexico, or Russia, for example, spend more than 10 percent of their labor costs on such programs.[4] However, how do such in-house training programs have a bearing on corporate social responsibility? Do firms that make asset-specific investments in skills behave differently in relation to labor standards when compared to firms that rely on cheap, unskilled labor?

This chapter answers this question in the affirmative. Crossley Carpets is illustrative in this respect. When the HIV/AIDS pandemic hit South Africa with full force in the mid/late 1990s, the firm was "losing some very good, experienced workers who had received training and so attained the unique skills we need here."[5] Similarly to many other firms, Crossley Carpets was unsure of how to react to this crisis at first. The government did not provide any guidelines. It also appeared unwilling and incapable of resolving it. Public health care provision was – and is still – not adequately equipped to effectuate any significant measures in this respect. The government, clinging to its ideological stance regarding the disease, was not doing much to contain its further spread (see Chapter 3). Facing these circumstances, management at Crossley Carpets came to learn that workplace programs can effectively mitigate most of the negative economic

[3] In South Africa, this lack of skills is according to many observers, including the government, a main obstacle to more economic growth in the country (Lorentzen and Barnes 2004; Rodrik 2008). Other emerging market countries confront similar shortages, see Dossani 2012; Farrell *et al.* 2007; Simon and Cao 2008; Wang 2011.

The Vice President of Manufacturing of Mercedes Benz South Africa says that car firms do so to create a "skills pipeline to cater for the ongoing increase in technical complexity". See www.mercedes-benzsa.co.za/media-room/news/15032387403/mbsa-east-london-training-initiative (January 1, 2013).

[4] A case in point is BMW, but the same applies to other large car producers. See www.bmw.co.za/products/automobiles/bmw_insights/key.asp (January 3, 2013). Lorentzen 2006; Lorentzen and Barnes 2004; Lorentzen *et al.* 2004; Meyn 2004; US Department of Commerce 2005.

[5] Interview with the Director of Human Resources of Crossley Carpets, September 28, 2007, Durban.

effects of HIV/AIDS from a study that had been released by the energy provider ESKOM.[6]

Thus faced with a "human resources crisis," the firm decided to implement a workplace program as "a way of trying to retain the unique skills we [had] built among our employees."[7] This statement exemplifies empirically the nexus between internal drivers and labor-related corporate social responsibility, as theorized earlier in Chapter 2: investments in rare skills make firms run benefits programs for employees to assure that they remain healthy and productive.

The literature supports the general conclusion which derives from this: the relationship between firms and labor standards in international trade is far more complex – and in particular less deterministic – than presumed by the "race to the bottom" argument. Analyses abound in which firms voluntarily adhere to high social and labor standards in areas where the state is weak.[8] Macro-quantitative econometric studies even argue that labor and human rights policies spread with international trade (Blanton and Blanton 2007; Cottier 2002; Hafner-Burton 2005; Richards *et al.* 2001). This argument has been specified: exporting to countries with high labor standards leads to a surge for such standards in weakly regulating production countries (Cao *et al.* 2013; Greenhill Mosley and Prakash 2009).

However, while these studies have improved our understanding of the relationship between international trade and labor standards significantly, they mostly focus on external pressure factors and do not consider internal drivers for corporate social responsibility and the spread of global standards.[9] The explanatory model suggested in support of the transfer of standards from highly regulating countries to weakly regulating ones assumes a non-governmental organization (NGO) and consumer pressure-induced international "California effect" (Cao *et al.* 2013; Greenhill Mosley and Prakash 2009; Vogel 1995). NGOs and consumers in countries with strict regulation and a strong emphasis on

---

[6] See for this study UNAIDS 2005: 35.

[7] Interview with the Director of Human Resources of Crossley Carpets, September 28, 2007, Durban.

[8] Börzel and Thauer 2013; Deitelhoff and Wolf 2010; Flohr *et al.* 2010; Kell and Ruggie 1999; Vogel and Kagan 2004.

[9] Notable exceptions are Blanton and Blanton (2009), who conceptualize skills as a factor for labor standard diffusion; this chapter elaborates this factor further for the firm level.

labor and human rights (i.e. the "Western" world) put pressure on firms to have their entire business practices – including those in offshore production locations and supply chains – comply with basic human rights and labor standards. Such pressure from NGOs and consumers has made importing firms in Western countries source from exporting, offshore production locations and from firms in these locations with a good human rights and labor standards record. This preference of importing firms, in turn, makes exporting firms in emerging markets contexts adopt high labor standards and lobby their governments to improve human and labor rights (Cao *et al.* 2013; Greenhill Mosley and Prakash 2009).

Analyzing nine cases of small to large manufacturing firms in South Africa, this chapter argues first that important empirical puzzles remain in relation to the emergence and spread of labor-related corporate social responsibility, which external driver-oriented analyses cannot resolve. Second, it explains these puzzles by showing that *intra*-organizational, asset-specific investments in employee skills motivate firms to engage in labor-related corporate social responsibility. Third, the chapter traces the *intra*-organizational processes unleashed by this internal driver and so shows how and why skills specificity leads to labor standards.

The nine firms consist of four large (Sä, Sh, Fe, and AL) and three small to medium-sized (FE, V, and CS) suppliers in the automotive industry – and of two medium to large textile firms (CC and DBA). The firms are deeply embedded in global production networks. These networks are oriented towards Western markets – the EU and the US – where labor rights, and the concern for these rights, are strong. The automotive firms supply intermediate products for car production directly or indirectly to one or more of the seven large multinational car firms in the country: BMW, Ford, General Motors, Mercedes Benz, Nissan, Toyota, and VW. These so-called original equipment manufacturers (OEMs) pursue a dual strategy in terms of sales: they target the South African growth market, but are also highly export-oriented at the same time.[10] About 60 percent of their production output is

[10] Figure 4.1 also indicates in grey where these OEMs would be in this mapping. While the empirical fieldwork for this chapter included the OEMs, I decided against presenting them as cases here. The level of asset-specific investments in skills and the resulting HIV/AIDS workplace programs are more or less the same across all OEMs in South Africa. Hence, the cases do not illustrate variation and are thus of no value for the analysis (though some variation has recently emerged

exported to the US and Europe.[11] In fact, one major incentive for the automotive industry to produce in the country is the privileged terms of trade with the US that have been granted to South Africa by the African Growth and Opportunity Act (AGOA) and to the EU under similar preferential trade agreements (Meyn 2004).[12] The textile firms consist of the aforementioned hotel carpet manufacturer Crossley Carpets, which sells to firms such as the Hilton Group and Marriot, as well as to casinos and cruise ships in the US and Europe. The second textile firm is DBA, a firm which produces the Wonderbra and Playtex products in South Africa. Hence, in terms of structural preconditions, the nine firms are most likely candidates for trade-based diffusion of labor standards in that they are integrated in supply chains that end up in highly regulating markets. Figure 4.1 maps the cases according to the level of involvement on which the nine firms run HIV/AIDS workplace programs.

The nine firms are representative for other small to large goods-producing firms in South Africa. The mapping thus indicates the emergence and spread of HIV/AIDS programs among small to large manufacturers in general. Figure 4.1 can be interpreted as in line with arguments about trade-based diffusion of standards from highly regulating home countries to weakly regulating ones on account of California effects (Cao *et al.* 2013; Greenhill Mosley and Prakash 2009). However, Figure 4.1 also indicates that the external pressure

as a result of the financial bankruptcy of General Motors and the financial crisis of Ford from 2007 onwards: the two firms had to drastically cut costs and so downgraded their HIV/AIDS programs. However, in the context of this study this is not a finding of great interest). In addition, OEM cases cannot be taken as comparative cases for large supplier firms, for instance. OEMs and suppliers differ in too many respects: OEMs are huge corporations – much larger than the supplier firms. OEMs are in addition very different from supplier firms in that they have a brand name and sell to end consumers.

[11] See Chapter 3 and NAAMSA 2006; Statistics South Africa (www.southafrica. info/business/economy/sectors/automotive-overview.htm, June 19, 2009); see also US Department of Commerce 2005: 1 and NAAMSA media release: Comment of the October 2011 new vehicle sales statistics (www.naamsa.co.za/ flash/press.htm, November 25, 2011). Around 65–70 percent of the exports go to Europe, the US and some minor parts to Australia, New Zealand, and Japan – that is, markets in which labor standards are strict. For information about where the exports go see the website of the Automotive Industry Export Council (AIEC) under: www.aiec.co.za/TopExportsContinents.aspx (January 5, 2013).

[12] Information about AGOA available at: www.agoa.info/index.php? view=country_info&country=za. (January 23, 2011), see also Meyn 2004.

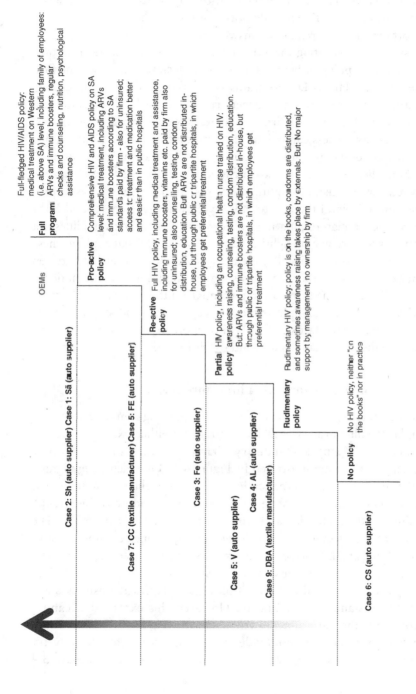

Figure 4.1 HIV/AIDS programs of suppliers in the automotive and textile industries in South Africa

factor-oriented perspective on the relationship between firms and labor standards in international trade does not give us the complete picture. Important questions remain unanswered.

Aside from indicating the emergence and spread of workplace programs, the mapping in Figure 4.1 also demonstrates that the nine firm cases operate HIV/AIDS programs on strikingly different levels. As mentioned before, Crossley Carpets runs a workplace program on a relatively high level. The firm organizes sexual education programs, HIV/AIDS awareness campaigns and anti-discrimination training, distributes condoms and information material concerning the disease, offers medical services to treat so-called "secondary diseases" such as tuberculosis, hands out immune boosters, and, in selected cases, provides anti-retroviral therapy to employees who have contracted HIV/AIDS. The German-originating car company CS, by contrast, does not show any involvement in fighting the disease at all. What explains these differences? More specifically, with respect to the relationship between firm behavior and labor standards under conditions of international trade, why are some firms driving standard diffusion, while others do not? Which firms in an industry sector, country or production network through which standards diffuse will be more or less affected? In sum, what are the preconditions of standard diffusion?

In search of an explanation: a literature review

The literature suggests a number of drivers pushing firms to adopt high standards voluntarily, which concentrate on either external pressure factors or company and industry characteristics. Can any of these explain the variation illustrated in Figure 4.1? One factor highlighted in the literature on governance in areas of consolidated statehood is the regulatory threat by state agencies – the "shadow of hierarchy" (Halfteck 2008; Héritier and Lehmkuhl 2008; Scharpf 1997). The argument alleges that when given the option, businesses choose not to be regulated at all. When circumstances are such that this option is not available, businesses prefer voluntary self-regulation to state regulation. Thus, when confronted with a credible regulatory threat, businesses will adopt high standards voluntarily. However, this explanation cannot account for the variation illustrated above (Figure 4.1). The South African government has not made any attempt to regulate the industry in regard to HIV/AIDS (see Chapter 3). By contrast, before 2003/4 instances occurred where the government undermined attempts by businesses to take up a fight against HIV/AIDS. For example, in 2003 businesses, local government, civil society organizations, and the Global Fund joined to set up a project for the purpose of making available HIV/AIDS medical services in communities in Durban. At the last minute, the national government under President Thabo Mbeki intervened and managed to stop the project (Börzel *et al.* 2012; Hönke and Thauer 2014). Thus, the shadow of hierarchy is not what drives the firms' workplace programs.[13]

Another potential explanation concerns the size of firms, given that the firms in Figure 4.1 differ to some extent in this respect (Börzel and Thauer 2013; Udayasakar 2008; UNIDO 2002). Size determines the relative costs per employee for HIV/AIDS-related health care programs. Such programs require investments in infrastructure, such as a clinic and medical personnel. Larger firms can use this infrastructure more efficiently. Therefore relative costs decrease with increasing firm size.[14] However, a closer look at the nine cases reveals that firm size cannot account for the overall variation. For example, AL is a relatively large auto supplier, whereas V is a much smaller car firm.[15] According to the factor firm size, AL should have the more demanding HIV/AIDS program. However, V's HIV/AIDS program is more sophisticated and comprehensive than AL's. Another example demonstrating that firm size does not explain the variation in Figure 4.1 is the textile firm Crossley Carpets. The firm is smaller in comparison with the auto firms Fe and AL.[16] Nonetheless, Crossley Carpets operates a workplace program on a higher lever than Fe and AL. Firm size can also not explain why firms of similar size nevertheless engage on very different

---

[13] Even if the government was to make a credible regulatory threat, the "shadow of hierarchy" would not explain the asserted variation. All firms would be exposed to this threat so this would not explain the variation of HIV/AIDS programs either.

[14] This feature is a suppressor/enhancing variable rather than a full driver (Börzel *et al.* 2013). However, firm size could explain the different levels of HIV/AIDS programs among the firms under the assumption that there are additional incentives (for example, reputational concerns or NGO pressure) for the firms to adopt such programs in the first place.

[15] Whereas AL has about 1,000 employees in South Africa, V has 60–70 employees (see detailed analysis below).

[16] Fe employs 2,200 persons in South Africa, Crossley Carpets has 500 employees (see detailed analysis below).

levels in the fight against HIV/AIDS: for example, CS is roughly as large as FE and V and all three are car suppliers.[17] However, while FE has a strong program, CS does not have any program at all – and V is somewhere in between both cases in this respect.

While firm size can be excluded as an explanation for the puzzle, another potential factor concerns supply chain governance. The nine firms are part of production networks of international brands, which may impose strict standards as well as monitoring and control mechanisms (Guthrie 2006; Héritier *et al.* 2009). However, this factor cannot explain the firms' differences with respect to their HIV/AIDS programs either. The nine firms state that buyer firms regulate them in many respects. For example, they set strict targets concerning product quality, price, environmental standards, and also labor standards as far as this concerns the ILO core labor standards (see detailed analysis below). However, this strict supply chain governance does not extend to the issue of HIV/AIDS. The firms unequivocally report that they have never had any interaction with their buyers in relation to the disease. Hence, we can also exclude this factor as a potential explanation. Besides, a number of the firms featured in Figure 4.1 supply to the same group of buyers. Sä, Sh, AL, Fe, FE, and V directly supply to the large OEMs of their industry sector, among them BMW, Mercedes, VW, Ford, General Motors, Toyota, and Nissan. However, they fight HIV/AIDS to very different degrees. Supply chain governance can therefore not account for the variation illustrated in Figure 4.1.

Another well-established explanation in the literature for voluntary business standards concerns the "home country" of the featured firms. Multinational corporations often bring their "best practices" from their home markets to their emerging markets operations and so transfer high standards from highly regulating countries to weakly regulating ones (Garcia-Johnson 2000; Moran *et al.* 2005; Sethi and Elango 1999). While some of the nine firms – Sh, V, FE, Fe, DBA, and Crossley Carpets – are South African-owned, the auto suppliers Sh, CS, and AL originate from Germany. Since Germany is generally considered to be a highly regulating country while South Africa is deemed to be a country with weak regulatory capacities (Börzel and Thauer 2013), this difference may account for the variation illustrated in Figure 4.1. However, in Germany there is no industry regulation

---

[17] They have between 50 and 100 employees.

concerned with HIV/AIDS.[18] Neither do Sä, AL, or CS address the issue of HIV/AIDS in their factories and organization in Germany. Consequently, there are no standards in the first place that could be transferred to South Africa. Hence, the home country argument does not explain the asserted variation. Besides, the three German-originating firms Sä, AL, and CS operate HIV/AIDS programs on strikingly different levels, despite sharing the same home country. CS is even the "negative" case in the sample of cases presented in Figure 4.1 – the firm is not involved in the fight against the disease at all.

While the home country argument can thus be excluded as a factor to explain the variation illustrated in Figure 4.1, sector differences could be a potential explanation. The auto industry is often presumed to be a driver of standard diffusion (Lorentzen 2006; Lorentzen *et al.* 2004; Thauer 2013a). In contrast to that, the textile industry is usually associated with rather low standards and as an industry driving a regulatory "race to the bottom" (Börzel *et al.* 2013; Chan 2003; Chan and Ross 2003). And indeed, the textile manufacturer DBA confirms this presumption. The firm's HIV/AIDS program is rather weak. Crossley Carpets, however, shows that textile firms can also engage in the fight against HIV/AIDS, and, on a higher level than many of the car firms featured in the analysis. In addition, it is the automotive supplier CS, and not a textile firm, which is the negative case in the context of Figure 4.1. The firm shows absolutely no activities in the area of HIV/AIDS. Sector characteristics, therefore, cannot explain the variation among the nine firms either.

Local communities or local civil society organizations pressuring firms to treat workers well and fight the HIV/AIDS pandemic may be counted as additional push factors for labor standards (Bray and Thauer 2014; Kirton and Trebilcock 2004). However, none of the nine firms have ever had any interaction with local organizations concerning the disease. While thus not a factor explaining the puzzle of HIV/AIDS policies among the nine firms, another potential explanation points to self-regulation in the context of business associations as a factor for corporate social responsibility (Ronit and Schneider 2000). However, this potential driver, too, does not explain the asserted variation: the automotive firms in Figure 4.1 are members of the

---

[18] Prevalence rates in Germany are comparably low and public health care provides comprehensive medical treatment. Hence, there is no demand for industry regulation.

National Association of Automotive Component and Allied Manufacturers (NAACAM) of South Africa. NAACAM has recently started a program in its local action groups (LAG) to assist suppliers in developing HIV/AIDS policies.[19] Hence, organizational support that reduces the costs of setting up HIV/AIDS programs is theoretically available to these firms. Moreover, the South African Business Coalition on HIV/AIDS (SABCOHA) has indeed approached some of the firms, among them DBA and Crossley Carpets. SABCOHA is a cross-sector industry association composed of large automotive firms, retailers such as the South African Woolworths, and the Electricity Supply Commission (ESKOM). The association was originally founded as the industry's lobby in the field of HIV/AIDS (Müller-Debus *et al.* 2009).[20] Over the years, the association has taken on the additional task of offering support and services to small and medium-sized businesses. SABCOHA provides firms with industry-specific tool-kits for the development of HIV/AIDS workplace programs. Thus, just as the car suppliers in the context of the LAGs of NAACAM, Crossley Carpets and DBA had access to assistance in setting up a workplace program as well. The factor "associations" is therefore equally available to all of the nine cases featured in Figure 4.1; it also cannot explain the striking variation they display with respect to HIV/AIDS workplace programs. Inasmuch as they are equally available to the featured firms, none of them actually made use of the assistance the associations offered them; hence, we can exclude the factor "associations" altogether for the nine cases.

A final factor potentially accounting for the firms' HIV/AIDS programs concerns the "problem pressure" they experience (Börzel and Thauer 2013). On account of different prevalence rates of HIV/AIDS in their factories, the firms may not be similarly inclined to see the need to fight the disease. FE, CS, and V confront prevalence rates of about 15–20 percent among their workers, Crossley Carpets and DBA of more than 20 percent, and Sä, Sh, Fe, and AL of an estimated 10 percent (see analysis below). However, the variance with respect to HIV/AIDS programs within these three groups of affectedness turns out to be almost as stark as between firms that differ with respect to

---

[19] Interview with the Managing Director of NAACAM, September 29, 2008, Johannesburg.
[20] Interview with the CEO of SABCOHA, March 19, 2007, Johannesburg.

"problem pressure." FE, for example, runs a relatively strong work-place program, whereas CS – which is similarly affected by the disease – does not have a program at all. Similarly, Crossley Carpets is a firm that demonstrates a strong approach in response to the disease. Contrary to that, DBA is a negative case in this respect, despite a similarly high prevalence rate. Hence, it is not prevalence rates *per se* which explain why and under which conditions firms fight HIV/AIDS. While a minimum problem pressure is certainly a precondition for HIV/AIDS programs to emerge, it cannot explain the variation among such programs illustrated in Figure 4.1.

What, then, is the explanation? This study will now turn to the theory of internal drivers to resolve the puzzle of the differential levels of HIV/AIDS programs represented in Figure 4.1. This allows us to return to – and systematically investigate – the initial question raised at the beginning of this chapter: do firms that make asset-specific investments in skills behave differently in relation to labor standards when compared to firms that rely on cheap, unskilled labor?

Asset specificity: driving HIV/AIDS programs?

The theory of internal drivers of corporate social responsibility argues that asset-specific investments in employee skills give rise to managerial dilemmas, which in turn motivate management to take on the fight against HIV/AIDS in the workplace. The case of Crossley Carpets illustrates this argument empirically. However, does the theory hold when applied to cases in a comparative perspective? Everything else being equal, do different levels of asset specificity cause different levels of labor-related corporate social responsibility?

To address these questions, this study changes the logic of the inquiry here. The nine firms in Figure 4.1 will be divided into three groups. This allows the analysis to conduct a systematic assessment of this internal driver in a way consistent with the *ceteris paribus* clause: comparisons that neutralize potential other explanations (such as firm size or sector characteristics, see above) so as to assess the isolated effects of investments in employee skills.[21] The first group consists of the medium- to large-sized automotive suppliers Sä, Sh, Fe,

---

[21] While the discussion of the empirical puzzle illustrated in Figure 4.1 followed a "backwards-looking" (Scharpf 1997: 18) approach, the analysis now changes

and AL. The second set of firms features three small- to medium-sized automotive component manufacturers: V, FE, and CS. The two large textile manufacturers Crossley Carpets and DBA constitute the third group.

Apart from allowing the analysis to conduct controlled, pair-wise comparisons, this separation into three groups has several advantages. It subjects the argument for internal driver 1 to diverse industry sector contexts and considers its effects on different levels of intensity of the driver. The textile industry is usually associated with low entry barriers: it is a low investment, low-tech, low skills, cheap labor industry – and, consequently, one that is usually presumed to drive "race to the bottom" dynamics. The car industry, by contrast, is known for its high entry levels. It is a high investment, high-tech, high skills industry, which is often regarded as a driver of innovation and positive spillover effects (see Chapter 3). If the argument for internal driver 1 were to hold for all three controlled comparisons, irrespective of these differences, this would indicate their general validity.

The cases also illustrate variance of asset-specific investments in rare employee skills on different levels of intensity. Generally, the skills level – and skills specificity – in the automotive industry is much higher than in the textile industry. Automotive firms in South Africa, for example, spend on average 3–7 percent of their labor costs on training, with some firms spending more than 10 percent; textile firms, in turn, spend less than 1 percent.[22] Similar differences persist within the sectors. Smaller firms usually invest less in training than larger firms. If it could explain HIV/AIDS programs across the three comparisons irrespective of the level of intensity of the driver, this would indicate a strong causal force of internal driver 1.

The analysis will also allow us to resolve the puzzle in Figure 4.1. The variance of HIV/AIDS programs within the three groups of cases is much larger than the variance between them. So should internal driver 1 fully explain the variation within the three groups, this means that it would automatically explain most of the variation in Figure 4.1.

---

into a "forward-looking" one, which selects cases on the independent variable (internal driver 1) in order to assess the isolated effects thereof. After this "forward-looking" analysis, however, the chapter will relate its results back to the puzzle and thereby resolve it.

[22] Interview with the Human Resources Manager of Monviso, September 16, 2008, Cape Town.

Measuring internal driver 1: the human resources dilemma

How can we know asset specificity when we want to see it? Asset-specific investments have two dimensions. In case of the *human resources dilemma* – that is, internal driver 1 – the *asset* dimension refers to the quantity of resources spent on training and skills development. The *specificity* dimension refers to the uniqueness of skills created through resource allocation. Together, the two dimensions are a measure for the dependence of management vis-à-vis employees. With respect to the measurement of the *asset* dimension, I rely on a proxy indicator: the proportion of the workforce that receives training, and the frequency and duration of training, as well as the personnel allocated for training.[23] The greater the proportion of the workforce that receives training, the more frequent and longer it is, and the more personnel dedicated to the task of organizing training the greater the resource allocation, leading to higher scores in this dimension, and vice versa.

With respect to the second dimension, *specificity*, this study suggests that skills uniqueness is indicated by the extent to which skills are available on the labor market. The analysis therefore measures skills uniqueness by considering the number of personnel mobilized to find new employees and the time spent doing so, and/or the availability of the skills level the production processes require from employees (in terms of qualifications) hired from the labor market. The higher the number of personnel dedicated to headhunting and the more time invested in sourcing new employees, and/or the greater the scarcity of the skills required, the higher the scores in this dimension, and vice versa.

The absence of any of the two dimensions indicates the absence of asset specificity. If the first dimension is absent, this means that no resources are allocated to support the training of employees. Consequently, management is not dependent on employees and so

---

[23] Many firms do not systematically collect data indicating their costs for training and skills development, which would be the more direct and intuitively plausible indicator. When they do collect this data, it turns out that the methods firms apply to define costs for training differ significantly between firms, with the effect that the data cannot be compared without risking severe measurement bias. Hence, I decided against measuring the costs firms spend on training and skills development according to their self-assessment.

Table 4.1 *Indicators for the* human resources dilemma

Internal driver 1: the *human resources dilemma*		
Concept: asset specificity	Indicators	Assessment
Dimension 1: asset creation *Extent of training*	**Indicator 1a:** proportion of the workforce that receives training; frequency and duration of training	**High vs. low** **High**
	Indicator 1b: number of personnel conducting training	**High vs. low**
Dimension 2: specificity *Uniqueness of skills created through training and headhunting*	**Indicator 2a:** personnel dedicated to the task of finding new employees and the time spent on headhunting for newcomers	**High vs. low**
	Indicator 2b: availability of the trained skills on the labor market	**High vs. low** **Low**

no managerial dilemma will emerge (see Chapter 2). Wherever the second dimension is insignificant, it implies that the skills level a firm's production processes rely on could also be attained from the labor market. In this case, management could reallocate the resources it invests in training and skills development any time to hiring new, more skilled, staff. Therefore, resource allocation would in this case not be asset-specific and not create significant dependence of management on employees. Asset-specific allocation of resources in training thus requires positive values in both dimensions. The more resources allocated to support the training of employees and the greater the uniqueness of skills that are thereby created, the higher the degree of asset specificity, and the more severe the managerial dilemma the case illustrates, and vice versa (see Table 4.1).

This study now turns to an analysis of internal driver 1 in the first group of cases, which consists of medium to large supplier firms in the car industry. Which are these firms and how do they differ with respect to asset-specific investments in employee skills?

Medium to large automotive component manufacturers

The analysis begins with a consideration of Sä, which is part of a large industry group with headquarters in Herzogenaurach, Gemany. The group comprises eighty-six companies, has 69,000 employees and had a worldwide turnover of €8.9 billion in 2007. In South Africa, Sä employs 500–700 people and generates a turnover of ZAR400 million.[24] Sä South Africa produces clutches and clutch systems. AL is also a German-originating global player in the automotive component industry, albeit smaller. The Heilbronn-based group has fourteen operations worldwide, employs 4,000 people and had an annual turnover of €622 million in 2007.[25] In South Africa, operations consist of two plants and 1,000 employees manufacturing automotive body parts and body systems. The South African-based Fe Group owns eighteen factories in the country, had an annual turnover of ZAR1.2 billion and employed 2,200 people in 2007.[26] Fe automotive – the part of the group featured in the analysis – manufactures covers of gearboxes, components for catalytic converters, and car carpets. Sh is part of the PG Group and specialized in the manufacturing of car glass and windows.[27] In 2007, Sh had four production sites in the country that generated a turnover of ZAR800 million and employed 1,500 people.

Domestic sales of the four companies go mainly to the large multinational car firms in the country – BMW, Ford, General Motors, and Mercedes – and account for more than 50 percent of the four firms' sales

---

[24] Depending on the season and customer demand employment varies. The factory has existed for more than forty years, but it has been part of the Sä Group only since 2003/2004. Interview with the Human Resources Manager, the Manager of Integrated Systems, and the Key Accounts and Export Manager of Sä, September 22, 2008, Port Elizabeth.

[25] The factory was established in 1972. During apartheid times the German firm held minority shares only. After political liberalization in 1994, the Group gained full ownership of the branch. Interviews with the Environmental and Safety Manager and the Human Resources Manager of AL, September 13, 2007, Rosslyn; websites of AL Germany and South Africa (January 12, 2009).

[26] Interviews with the Safety, Health and Environment (SHE) Manager and the Procurement Manager of Fe, September 25, 2008, Durban; website of Fe (January 13, 2009).

[27] The PG group was founded in 1897 and is an internationally operating, South African firm by origin with an annual turnover of ZAR2 billion and sales offices in various African countries. The group specializes in glass making. Sh is the division that manufactures car windows. Interview with the Product Engineering and Corporate Quality Assurance Manager of Sh, September 22, 2008, Port Elizabeth; websites of the PG Group and of Sh (January, 11 2009).

volume. The firms sell components to these large multinational car firms for the production of their cars. However, these large domestic customers of the four firms export more than 60 percent of their production output, which means that the bulk of the 50 percent of domestic sales of Sä, Sh, Fe, and AL is *indirectly* exported by firms such as Ford, Toyota, Nissan, or VW – mainly to the US and Europe. The rest of the four firms' sales volume is directly exported, mostly to Europe and the US. The four cases have been chosen in the context of this analysis as they illustrate different degrees of presence and gravity of the *human resources dilemma*. The *human resources dilemma* is strong in the cases of the manufacturer of clutches and clutch systems Sä and the producer of car windows Sh; it is significantly less apparent in the case of the manufacturer of car carpets Fe and almost completely non-existent at the producer of automotive body parts AL. This study will now substantiate these assertions by providing a detailed analysis of the four firm cases, thereby establishing both dimensions of asset specificity: the *asset* dimension and the *specificity* dimension.

Extent of training: is skills development an asset?
With respect to the *asset*-dimension of the *human resources dilemma*, the proportion of the workforce participating in training programs is nearly 100 percent in all four companies. This finding illustrates the relatively high level on which variation of the *human resources dilemma* takes place across the four cases – for example when compared to the one of the small to medium-sized automotive firms featured in the second comparison. At the car glass firm Sh and the manufacturer of clutches Sä, employees on the lowest level of employment participate in training courses for at least three hours per week.[28] For higher-level workers training is more frequent and individualized and consists of different course modules on the one hand, and of continuous on-the-job training on the other hand. Hence, for both firms in-house training is a significant asset.

The manufacturer of auto body parts AL, by contrast, offers training courses to the entire workforce for one hour, once per week.[29] Aside

---

[28] The analysis refers here to *Indicator 1a*. Interviews with the Manager of Integrated Systems of Sä, September 22, 2008, Port Elizabeth and the Product Engineering and Corporate Quality Assurance Manager of Sh, September 22, 2008, Port Elizabeth.

[29] Interview with the Environmental and Safety Manager and the Human Resources Manager of AL, September 13, 2007, Rosslyn.

from that, learning has not been integrated into daily operations. Fe, the car carpet manufacturer, resembles AL in this respect: the duration and frequency of training courses is on a similarly low level when compared to Sh and Sä.[30] However, one difference is that, unlike AL, Fe has also implemented the idea of on-the-job training. Continuous learning is organized whenever the need for additional skills arises. In summary, as concerns the frequency and duration of training, the clutch maker Sä and the car glass maker Sh invest heavily in skills, while the auto body manufacturer AL does not show much commitment in this respect; for the car carpet firm Fe, training is more important in terms of duration and frequency than for AL on account of continuous on-the-job training, but clearly much less so than for Sh and Sa.

The personnel structure reflects these findings.[31] Sä employs one human resources manager exclusively for the task of organizing and conducting training and training plans for the 500 employees. In addition, Sä has hired an external provider for the lower-level skills training. At the car glass manufacturer Sh, the training program is also managed and organized by one human resources manager per 500 employees. The auto body firm AL and the car carpet manufacturer Fe, by contrast, do not employ anyone specifically for the task of organizing training.[32] Hence, in terms of personnel, Sä shows the highest commitment to skills development, closely followed by Sh. For AL and Fe skills development is much less relevant in this respect.

Quality of trained skills: readily substitutable or unique to the task?
Assessing the *specificity* dimension of the *human resources dilemma* in comparative perspective, the analysis reveals similar differences between the firms as in the *asset* dimension.[33] In terms of the time it takes the firms to fill an open position, the skills which Sä and Sh rely on are highly specific. It takes the two firms three to six months to fill an

---

[30] Interview with the Safety, Health and Environment (SHE) Manager of Fe, September 25, 2008, Durban.

[31] I turn now to the measurement of *Indicator 1b*.

[32] Interview with the Safety, Health and Environment (SHE) Manager of Fe, September 25, 2008, Durban.

[33] The analysis turns now to the evaluation of *Indicator 2a*. Data concerning the number of personnel dedicated to headhunting is not systematically available for the four cases; the assessment will therefore concentrate on the time spent on headhunting.

open position. The car carpet firm Fe manages to find new employees within three months on average. The auto body firm AL, by contrast, says that it has no problems at all finding new employees; the time spent on searching for new employees is negligible according to the firm.

To fully establish the degree to which the skills the four firms depend on are unique or, conversely, readily substitutable from the labor market, let us also consider the availability of qualifications the firms search for on the labor market.[34] It becomes apparent that the manufacturer of clutches Sä demands high skills qualifications that are rather hard to find on the labor market. On the lowest level of employment, the minimum requirement for new employees at Sä is the Matric – the successful graduation after twelve years of schooling and a demonstration of practical skills. However, only a small proportion of the workforce of Sä consists of lower level employees such as floor operators.[35] Instead of employing workers on this level in a formal capacity, the company prefers to lease them from a labor broker. Besides, the business model of Sä in South Africa is to make small volumes of highly sophisticated products. As a consequence, production is "not very automated when compared with a mass-production plant in Germany because changeovers would take too long." Instead, manufacturing at Sä "relies on manual labor."[36] This manual labor, however, uses complex production techniques for which high and specific skills are required. Accordingly, the skills required for most jobs at Sä (more than 60 percent) are rare: Sä predominantly fills high-level positions that require a degree in engineering. Such a degree implies at least three years of university education. These skills are, according to the assessment of a manager of Sä – which is also confirmed by managers of other firms, experts and observers interviewed for this study – very hard to obtain on the South African labor market. In addition, the in-house training that

---

[34] I thus turn now to an assessment of *Indicator 2b*, the availability of the skills level the production processes require from employees on the labor market.

[35] Sä has adopted the model of the "breathing factory" once created by Peter Hartz at VW in the mid 1990s and now widely applied in the German automotive industry. This model aims at giving firms greater flexibility in times of crisis – through the creation of flexi-time and the hiring of lower-level employees from labor brokers, which can be released circumventing the normal labor law provisions. Interview with the Manager of Integrated Systems of Sä, September 22, 2008, Port Elizabeth.

[36] Interview with the Manager of Integrated Systems of Sä, September 22, 2008, Port Elizabeth.

introduces employees to the processes of making clutches at Sä are highly specific. Sä has no direct competitor in the country, which makes this training unique to the task in the South African context.[37]

In comparison, the skills AL depends on are much less specific. "We require minimum skills, but that is all," pointed out the human resources manager of the auto body maker.[38] "Minimum skills" refer to "employability" – i.e. basic literacy and numeracy. At the car carpet manufacturer Fe, the requirements are similarly low: "You must be able to understand English. You must be able to read and write. So it's basic employability."[39] While employability is a big issue in the context of South Africa – and the lack of it one reason for the country's mass unemployment – it is a much lower and therefore more available minimum requirement than the various degrees that Sä demands. In addition, the in-house training AL and Fe provide is not unique to the task of production at all. The program at AL has the goal to maintain employability.[40] The firm has recently invested in new computerized machinery for the making of auto body parts. Operating these machines presupposes operators to be literate and numerate. AL, however, has a number of long-term employees who lack these basic skills. To ensure that the older staff – who are not easily let go on account of South African labor laws – can continue to work efficiently, the mentioned courses have been created recently to upgrade skills to this minimum level.[41] At Fe, the asserted training courses are also directed at these rather basic skills to maintain the level of employability on the factory floor to allow for changing technology and production techniques. In other words: the skills Fe and AL seek on the labor market and create

---

[37] Interviews with the Manager of Integrated Systems of Sä and the Product Engineering and Corporate Quality Assurance Manager of Sh, September 22, 2008, Port Elizabeth. The employees who have obtained the specific skills, however, could easily find a new, similarly ranked and paid job as at Sä and Sh, given the shortage of engineering skills and work experience in the country. Hence, asset specificity is in this case more one-sided than two-sided.

[38] Interview with the Human Resources Manager of AL, September 13, 2007, Rosslyn.

[39] Interview with the Safety, Health and Environment (SHE) Manager of Fe, September 25, 2008, Durban.

[40] Interview with the Human Resources Manager of AL, September 13, 2007, Rosslyn.

[41] This implies that the firm was able to operate on a particular low-skills level before and only now begins to invest in employees.

in the context of their training programs are non-specific and relatively easy to substitute.

The car glass producer Sh, by contrast, searches for job applicants with relatively high skills, which are not readily available on the labor market. The firm requires the Matric as a minimum. For higher positions, a degree in engineering is the condition for employment. The proportion of employees with higher-level jobs is, however, smaller than at the manufacturer of clutches Sä, because the car glass firm Sh does not collaborate with labor brokers. This has an effect on the recruitment policy, which, in the case of the clutch maker Sä, predominantly targets the high-skills level, while the car glass manufacturer Sh aims at the lower skills level as well. The in-house training of Sh is, however, as highly specific as in the case of the manufacturer of clutches Sä. This training is unique to the task in the South African context since Sh does not have a competitor in the country.[42] A representative of Sh explains: "you could take an employee out of General Motors and put him into Volkswagen. He would transfer his skills. We in the glass industry are different. We are unique in South Africa as we do not have any competition."[43] With respect to the specificity dimension the results are thus as follows: Sä is highly dependent on unique skills, followed by Sh; Fe and AL are last.

Small to medium automotive component manufacturers
The second comparison includes vacuforming and blow-molding firm V, the precision engineering firm FE, and the spring manufacturer CS, which are all small to medium-sized component manufacturers in the automotive industry. V makes plastic, carpet, and thin metal sheet components, as for example, overflow bottles and surface components. The company is South

[42] Interviews with the Manager of Integrated Systems of Sä and the Product Engineering and Corporate Quality Assurance Manager of Sh, September 22, 2008, Port Elizabeth. The employees who have obtained the specific skills, however, could easily find a new, similarly ranked and paid job as at Sä and Sh given the shortage of engineering skills and work experience in the country. Hence, asset specificity is in this case more one-sided than two-sided.

[43] Interview with the Product Engineering and Corporate Quality Assurance Manager of Sh, September 22, 2008, Port Elizabeth. The interviewee further illustrates the specific task uniqueness at Sh with an example: "We have some CNC equipment. Now you could have had some experience with some CNC equipment elsewhere and you could adapt some of that to our industry. But the heart of our business is the furnace, and the tools in our furnace are adjustable, they have to be fine-tuned during a production run, and that only comes with the specific, even unique skills, training, and experience of the glass industry."

African-owned, has sixty to seventy employees, and an annual turnover of ZAR18 million.[44] Customers of V are the South African branches of large multinational corporations such as Nissan, Ford, and BMW, and a couple of small South African-originating OEMs as, for instance, the manufacturer of caravans, Jurgens. FE is also South African-owned and employs sixty to seventy-five people.[45] The precision engineering firm makes connecting rods, parts of water pumps, and manifolds. Most of their business is with VW. CS employs eighty-five to one hundred people, generating a yearly turnover of ZAR24 million. Since 1999 the manufacturer of springs is owned by a large German-based group specializing in the making of springs and clips of all kinds.[46] Their main customers are the South African branches of large multinational first-tier suppliers, such as Federal Mogul, Autoliv, TRW, Bosch, and Takata which use the products of CS for the making of braking systems and car seat belts. The analysis finds that the spring manufacturer CS does not confront any noteworthy human resources dilemma. Management of the precision engineering firm FE, by contrast, has to deal with a rather strong dilemma situation. The vacuforming company V takes a middle position.

Extent of training: is skills development an asset?
More specifically with respect to the *asset* dimension of the *human resources dilemma*, the proportion of the workforce receiving training as well as the frequency and duration of training is almost 100 percent at the precision engineering firm FE.[47] The workforce attends training courses on an ongoing basis.[48] The vacuforming firm V also offers most of its workforce training courses on a regular basis.[49] In contrast to that, the spring maker CS does not see a need for training and therefore does not offer any courses.

---

[44] Interview with the Director of V, October 1, 2008, Rosslyn; website of the firm.

[45] Interviews with the CEO, the Quality Manager, and the Human Resources Manager of FE, September 23, 2008, East London. Figure for turnover is classified information.

[46] Interview with the Production Manager of CS, September 18, 2008, Cape Town.

[47] The analysis thus begins by measuring *Indicator 1a*.

[48] Interviews with the CEO, the Quality Manager, and the Human Resources Manager of FE, September 23, 2008, East London.

[49] "We have done training for all of the staff," interview with the Director of V, October 1, 2008, Rosslyn.

If we consider the number of personnel conducting training in order to get a full picture of the asset dimension, the results are analogous.[50] Whereas one person in the human resources department spends about half of her time on organizing training courses at the precision engineering firm FE, the human resources manager at the vacuforming company V spends on average one working day per week on organizing training. The spring manufacturer CS does not employ any personnel conducting or organizing training courses. Thus, with respect to the *asset* dimension, the precision engineering firm FE invests most in training in terms of frequency and durations of training and personnel dedicated to organizing skills development, followed by the vacuforming firm V; the spring maker CS does not invest in training in a significant manner.

Quality of trained skills: readily substitutable or unique to the task?
Turning to the evaluation of the *specificity* dimension of the *human resources dilemma*, how much time do the three firms spend on average to fill a vacant position?[51] For FE it is three months of headhunting for a new employee.[52] For the other two firms it is "not difficult at all" to employ newcomers according to the respective human resources managers: "we take anyone off the streets, and there are many … so it does not take time."[53] Hence, hiring costs are negligible for V and CS, but high for FE. Very similar are the findings if we consider the skills level – and its availability on the South African labor market – which the firms look for when hiring new employees.[54] CS requires only "common sense, not more."[55] In addition, the company does not train any task-specific skills. Similar conclusions follow from what a

---

[50] I turn now to an evaluation of *Indicator 1b.*

[51] The analysis begins by assessing the specificity dimension with *Indicator 2a.* As in the previous analysis, data on the personnel dedicated to finding new employees is not available. The analysis will therefore concentrate on the time it takes to hire a new employee.

[52] Interviews with the CEO, the Quality Manager, and the Human Resources Manager of FE, September 23, 2008, East London.

[53] Quote from interview with the Production Manager of CS, September 18, 2008, Cape Town; similarly the Director of V, October 1, 2008, Rosslyn.

[54] The analysis thus turns now to the measurement of *Indicator 2b.*

[55] Interview with the Production Manager of CS, September 18, 2008, Cape Town. The information concerns the average job postings only. Aside from this, the company employs a handful of skilled toolmakers and production engineers as well. In addition to these upper-level blue-collar workers, CS has a management and a small administration. If positions in these departments are renewed, higher

manager of the vacuforming firm V says: the firm "targets the unskilled segment" of the labor market.[56] Hence, the skills V seeks are available. The in-house program of V aims at basic employability,[57] and "to bring about literacy, computer literacy and numeracy as far as we can."[58] Given the shortage of even the most basic skills in the country such a training program establishes some degree of specificity, albeit on a rather low level.[59]

The entry level at the precision engineering firm FE, by contrast, is relatively high. The company's core business and pride is the tool room apparently being "one of the best in East London."[60] Accordingly, the workforce predominantly consists of skilled toolmakers and trained machinists. In fact, the firm hires hardly anyone without seeing a future toolmaker in that person. The condition of employment at FE is the Matric – the South African high school diploma – and a degree in mechanical engineering, which implies "three years college or university education."[61] In addition, the in-house training programs at FE are oriented towards hand-made tooling and precision engineering. FE is one of the last factories in the country to offer this craft. For example, to benchmark its processes FE compares itself to Indian precision engineering firms. Competitors in South Africa are non-existent. Hence the skills required at FE, for which the training programs aim, are unique in the country.[62] Therefore, the precision engineering firm FE has the highest level of skills dependency, also in view of the *specificity* dimension, followed distantly by the vacuforming firm V. The spring maker CS scores lowest. In summary, the management of the precision engineering

---

skills requirements apply. However, about 80–85 percent of the company's employees are floor operators to whom no particular skills requirements apply.

[56] Interview with the Director of V, October 1, 2008, Rosslyn.

[57] Employability refers to the ability to communicate in English; it also refers to literacy and numeracy and basic social skills (punctuality, reliability, rule abidance, and the absence of negative attributes such as obvious drug abuse and the use of sexually discriminating language).

[58] Interview with the Director of V, October 1, 2008, Rosslyn.

[59] Employees can transfer these basic skills to another employment relation without a loss. Hence, "human asset specificity" is in this case one-sided.

[60] Interviews with the CEO, the Quality Manager, and the Human Resources Manager of FE, September 23, 2008, East London.

[61] Ibid.

[62] Ibid. While toolmakers are difficult to substitute for FE, they could easily find a new, similarly ranked and paid job as at FE, given the shortage of engineering skills in the country. Hence, asset specificity is in this case more one-sided than two-sided, even though the skills the training at FE aims at are quite unique to the task.

firm FE confronts a severe managerial dilemma, while the dilemma of the management of the vacuforming firm V is rather moderate; the spring maker CS does not confront a managerial dilemma at all.

Textile manufacturers

The third comparison considers firms from the textile manufacturing industry sector. The carpet manufacturer Crossley Carpets employs 500 people in its main factory and another 130 in the sister company Sy.[63] Crossley Carpets produces Axminster and Wilton carpets that are of a much higher quality and value ($200 to $500 per square meter) than rugs. Most of the products are exported; customers include the Hilton Group and Marriott. A striking characteristic of Crossley Carpets is that the firm has vertically integrated almost the entire production process, which is exceptional for a textile firm. Only some of the basic raw materials like raw wool are delivered to Crossley Carpets directly "off the sheeps' backs."[64] DBA has about 1,200 employees and was owned by Sara Lee until 2006, when Sun Capital bought DBA.[65] The business model of DBA has become extremely rare in the textile industry. The company markets brands and manufactures garments. More precisely, DBA makes and sells pants, bras, and t-shirts under license for international brands that sell to a high-end consumer market in South Africa. The production process at DBA is, as the one of Crossley Carpets, to a high degree vertically integrated. The analysis shows that Crossley Carpets has to deal with a much more intense *human resources dilemma* than DBA.

Extent of training: is skills development an asset?

Concerning the *asset* dimension, 100 percent of the employees of both firms are offered training courses.[66] However, participation in training

---

[63] Crossley Carpets was established in the 1960s under the name of Romatex Group, which was subsequently bought by the Irish firm Ulster Carpets. When Ulster went bankrupt, a former manager bought the South African factory. Interviews with the Director of Human Resources, the Assistant to the Managing Director, the Chief Engineer, and the Environmental Manager of Crossley Carpets, September 28, 2007, Durban.

[64] Interview with the Chief Engineer and Environmental Manager of Crossley Carpets, September 28, 2007, Durban.

[65] Sara Lee is a large American textile group. Interviews with the Director of Manufacturing, the Manager of Human Resources, and the Supply Chain Manager, September 25, 2008, Durban; website of DBA (January 26, 2009).

[66] The analysis thus assesses here *Indicator 1a.*

courses is voluntary at the underwear maker DBA and the attendance rate is low, as the human resources manager explains: "The employees are very embarrassed about the fact that they cannot read or write; and they tease each other for it."[67] Hence, they stay away from training to avoid social stigmatization. At Crossley Carpets, by contrast, "the employees have to fulfill various requirements in terms of training, such as electrical or mechanical engineering or textile-related courses. The training department oversees all of these training activities."[68] In addition, there is a mentorship program that governs the training plans at an individual level. As a consequence, the attendance rate is high. The underwear firm DBA offers training for the duration of one hour per week during work time.[69] At Crossley Carpets, the training is carried out on the factory floor via a mentorship program and takes place continuously, but at least twice per week for the duration of two hours.[70]

The differences between the two firms in terms of their investment in training programs becomes even more apparent if we consider the personnel structure.[71] The underwear firm DBA designates a half-time position per 600 employees to the organization of training.[72] While this is already remarkable for a textile manufacturer, Crossley Carpets involves more dedicated personnel. The firm tasks two full-time staff with the organization and steering of training for its 600 employees. Hence, with respect to the *asset* dimension constituting the human resources dilemma, Crossley Carpets has a much greater stake in the training programs it runs than DBA.

[67] Interviews with the Director of Manufacturing, the Manager of Human Resources, and the Supply Chain Manager of DBA, September 25, 2008, Durban.

[68] Interviews with the Director of Human Resources, the Assistant of the Managing Director, the Chief Engineer, and the Environmental Manager of Crossley Carpets, September 28, 2007, Durban.

[69] Interviews with the Director of Manufacturing, the Manager of Human Resources, and the Supply Chain Manager of DBA, September 25, 2008, Durban; email questionnaire answered by the Director of Manufacturing of DBA, January 12, 2009.

[70] Interviews with the Director of Human Resources, the Assistant of the Managing Director, the Chief Engineer, and the Environmental Manager of Crossley Carpets, September 28, 2007, Durban.

[71] The analysis thus turns now to the measurement of *Indicator 1b*.

[72] Interviews with the Director of Manufacturing, the Manager of Human Resources, and the Supply Chain Manager of DBA, September 25, 2008, Durban; email questionnaire answered by the Director of Manufacturing of DBA, January 12, 2009.

Quality of trained skills: readily substitutable or unique to the task?
However, the most important difference between the two firms concerns
the *specificity* dimension. In terms of personnel dedicated to the task of
finding new employees, the skills Crossley Carpets needs are much more
specific than those of DBA, which designates half the personnel that the
manufacturer of hotel carpets earmarks for the task of finding new
employees.[73] More precisely, Crossley Carpets designates one full-time
position for this task, whereas DBA one half-time position.[74]

Regarding the availability of the required skills on the labor market,
more differences between the two firms become apparent.[75] The skills
requirement at the underwear firm DBA for basic work such as carry-
ing, packaging, or cleaning is literacy in English.[76] For higher-level
workers such as machinists that operate the sewing machines, DBA
"takes qualified people: they have to function socially and be able to
count, read, write, and sew."[77] Accordingly, the condition of employment is employability and some form of sewing experience, which
means that the skills DBA seeks need to be searched for, but are not
too difficult to find on the labor market in South Africa. In comparison,
the hotel carpet maker Crossley Carpets has stricter skills requirements.
The condition of employment is, even on the lowest entry level, the
Matric.[78] Higher-level operators such as machinists are expected to at
least hold an additional degree in engineering, that is, a three-year
university education. Clearly, these skills are more difficult to find in
comparison to those required by the underwear firm DBA.

Considering the in-house training of Crossley Carpets and DBA, the
degree to which learned skills are unique to the task has to be analyzed
separately for the different levels of employment. On the lowest level,

---

[73] The analysis thus begins with an assessment of *Indicator 2a*. Data on the time
  spent on headhunting for newcomers was not revealed. Hence, "skills
  requirements" are used as a proxy indicator for "hiring costs."
[74] Email questionnaire answered by the Director of Manufacturing of DBA,
  January 12, 2009 and interview with the Manager of Human Resources of DBA,
  September 25, 2008, Durban. Interview with the Director of Human Resources of
  Crossley Carpets, September 28, 2007, Durban.
[75] I am analyzing here *Indicator 2b*.
[76] Interview with the Manager of Human Resources of DBA, September 25,
  2008, Durban.
[77] Ibid.
[78] Interview with the Director of Human Resources of Crossley Carpets,
  September 28, 2007, Durban.

the differences between Crossley Carpets and DBA are marginal only. The courses in both cases aim at basic literacy, numeracy, and computer literacy and thus consist of skills that are available in the South African context. On a higher level, however, the extent to which training is specific is greater at Crossley Carpets than at DBA. Both firms' training programs are focused on production techniques. For DBA, this involves manual sewing and the operation of sewing, gluing and molding machines. While these tasks are more delicate than, for example, in the making of t-shirts, they are not unique. DBA has a number of competitors in South Africa, among them Triumph or Falke. Hence, the respective sewing and operational skills are available on the labor market. By contrast, training for higher-level workers at Crossley Carpets involves electrical and mechanical engineering skills specific to the production process of the carpet maker: "most of the skills we require here cannot be found anywhere in the country because we use specialized machines."[79]

The *human resources dilemma*: summary of findings

The nine firms illustrate different degrees of presence and gravity with regard to the *human resources dilemma*. For the four medium- to large-sized automotive supplier firms, the analysis finds high presence of the dilemma in the cases of the manufacturer of clutches and clutch systems Sä and the producer of car windows Sh, a significantly weaker managerial dilemma at the manufacturer of car carpets Fe, and no or hardly any human resources dependency of management at the producer of automotive body parts AL. As concerns the three small- to medium-sized automotive firms of the second comparison, the inquiry asserts no *human resources dilemma* for the spring manufacturer CS yet a relatively high degree in the precision engineering firm FE. The vacuforming company V takes a middle position. As regards the textile firms analyzed in the context of the third comparison, the hotel carpet manufacturer Crossley Carpets exemplifies high dependency of management on employees on account of extensive training and the unique skills the firm makes use of in production processes. The bra, underwear, and other garments producer DBA, by contrast, illustrates a situation in which management does not confront a severe dilemma. Table 4.2 provides a summary of these findings.

[79] Ibid.

Table 4.2 Empirical cases illustrating (variance of) the human resources dilemma

The *human resources dilemma*: empirical cases

Indicators	Comparison 1: automotive industry — Medium to large first tier component manufacturers								Comparison 2: automotive industry — Small to medium component manufacturers						Comparison 3: textile industry — Large manufacturers			
	Case 1 (manufacturer of clutches) Sä		Case 2 (manufacturer of car windows) Sh		Case 3 (manufacturer of car carpets) Fe		Case 4 (manufacturer of body parts) AL		Case 5 (precision engineering) FE		Case 6 (blow-molding and vacuforming) V		Case 7 (manufacturer of springs) CS		Case 8 (manufacturer of hotel carpets) CC		Case 9 (manufacturer of garments) DBA	
	Results	Assessment	Results	Assessment	Results	Assessment	Results	Assessment	Results	Assessment	Results	Assessment	Results	Assessment	Results	Assessment	Results	Assessment
Indicator 1a training	100% of workforce receives training every second day for 1–2 hours		100% of workforce receive training twice per week for 1 hour		Majority of employees participate in training once per week for 1 hour		40–50% of the workforce participates in training once per week for 1 hour, rest: no training		100% of the workforce participates in training regularly		70–80% of the workforce participates in training regularly		No training		100% of workforce receives training every second day for 1–2 hours		Attendance in training courses is low; training course 1 hour per week	
Indicator 1b personnel conducting trainings	1 person full time for 500 employees		1 person full time for 500 employees		No personnel dedicated to the task of training		No personnel dedicated to the task of training		0.5 person dedicated to the task of training		0.2 person dedicated to the task of training		No personnel dedicated to the task of training		2 persons full time for 600 employees		0.5 person full time for 600 employees	
Indicator 2a personnel dedicated to finding new employees, time spent headhunting newcomers	3–6 months headhunting for new employees	High scores	3–6 months headhunting for new employees	High scores	3 months headhunting per new employees	Medium to low scores	Time spent on headhunting negligible	Low scores	3 months headhunting for new employees	High scores	Time spent on headhunting negligible	Medium scores	Time spent on headhunting negligible	Low scores	1 person full time for 600 employees	High scores	0.5 person full time for 600 employees	Low scores
Indicator 2b availability of the skills level on the labor market	Hard to find (university degree in engineering, highly specific practical experience)		Skills required available, but not common (high school diploma, highly specific practical experience)		Common skills (basic literacy, some practical experience)		Common skills (basic literacy, demonstrated employability)		Hard to find (university degree in engineering, highly specific practical experience)		Common skills (basic literacy, demonstrated employability)		Common skills (basic literacy, demonstrated employability)		Rare skills, (high school diploma plus highly specific practical experience)		Common skills (basic literacy, demonstrated employability)	

Firm characteristics and control variables

Controlled comparisons imply a selection of highly similar cases. Case selection for the evaluation of the effects of the *human resources dilemma* must therefore take into account a number of control variables (CVs). These are

- CV 1: firm size – indicator: number of employees of the firm;
- CV 2: level of technology/the *technological specialization dilemma*;
- CV 3: collaboration with associations and/or corporate social responsibility initiatives – indicator: active participation in meetings, exchange of minutes and notes, and presentation of progress to the association (public–private partnership, multistakeholder forum or else) on HIV/AIDS;
- CV 4: NGO pressure – indicator: campaigns of NGOs targeting a specific firm;
- CV 5: problem pressure – indicator: prevalence of HIV/AIDS among the workforce;
- CV 6: supply chain regulation – indicator: the extent to which a firm is controlled and regulated by buyer firms;
- CV 7: brand name/target market – indicator: marketing expenses of a firm or the end-consumer target market (high-end vs. low-end);
- CV 8: level of industry regulation in home country – indicator: strictness of regulation in the issue area of the dependent variable in the country of headquarters.

Table 4.3 establishes the nine cases with respect to these control variables (for the causal arguments underlying these control variables see "In search of an explanation: a literature review" above).

Labor-related corporate social responsibility: HIV/AIDS workplace programs

In South Africa, where HIV/AIDS is heavily affecting the productivity of firms, internal driver 1 – the *human resources dilemma* – should result in workplace programs that mitigate the risks that the disease poses to firms (see Chapters 2 and 3). To evaluate this claim, the analysis will concentrate on the practices of firms in this respect. More specifically,

Table 4.3 *Empirical cases, analyzed with respect to the control variables*

Control variables: analysis of the *human resources dilemma*

Control Variables	Comparison 1: automotive industry Medium to large first tier component manufacturers				Comparison 2: automotive industry Small to medium component manufacturers			Comparison 3: textile industry large manufacturers	
	Case 1 Sä (clutches)	Case 2 Sh (car glass)	Case 3 Fe (car carpets)	Case 4 AL (body parts)	Case 5 FE (precision engineering)	Case 6 V (blow-molding and vacuforming)	Case 7 CS (manufacturer of springs)	Case 8 CC (hotel carpets)	Case 9 DBA (garments)
CV 1 Firm size	Medium to large firm size (500–1,000 employees)	Medium to large firm size (500–1,000 employees)	Medium to large firm size (500–1,000 employees)	Medium to large firm size (500–1,000 employees)	Small to medium (60–75 employees)	Small to medium (60–70 employees)	Small to medium (85–100 employees)	Large (600–1,000 employees)	Large (600–1,000 employees)
CV 2 The technological specialization dilemma/ complexity of production	High-tech production	High-tech production	High-tech production	High-tech production	Low-tech production (most technology and machinery 20–30 years old)	Low-tech production (most technology and machinery 20–30 years old)	Low-tech production (most technology and machinery 20–30 years old)	Medium to high for a textile firm	Medium to high for a textile firm
CV 3 NGO pressure	No	No	No	No	No	No	No	No	No
CV 4 Association/ PPP initiative	Associated, but not with respect to HIV/AIDS	Associated, but not with respect to HIV/AIDS	Associated, but not with respect to HIV/AIDS	Associated, but not with respect to HIV/AIDS	No. However, received SABCOHA tool kit for suppliers	No. However, received SABCOHA tool kit for suppliers	No. However, received SABCOHA tool kit for suppliers	No	No

CV 5 Problem pressure	Estimated prevalence rate of HIV among workers: 10%	Estimated prevalence rate of HIV among workers: 10%	Estimated prevalence rate of HIV among workers: 8–12%	Estimated prevalence rate of HIV among workers: 8–12%	High (15–20% HIV prevalence rate)	High (15–20% HIV prevalence rate)	High (ca. 17% HIV prevalence rate)	High (15–20% HIV prevalence rate)	High (15–20% HIV prevalence rate)
CV 6 Supply chain regulation	Not with respect to HIV/AIDS	Not with respect to HIV/AIDS	Not with respect to HIV/AIDS	Not with respect to HIV/AIDS	Not with respect to HIV/AIDS	Not with respect to HIV/AIDS	Not with respect to HIV/AIDS	Not with respect to HIV/AIDS	Not with respect to HIV/AIDS
CV 7 Brand name/target market	B2B	B2B	B2B	B2B	B2B	B2B	B2B	B2B	Mostly B2B, otherwise high-end market
CV 8 Home country regulation	Not with respect to HIV/AIDS	Not with respect to HIV/AIDS	Not with respect to HIV/AIDS	Not with respect to HIV/AIDS	Not with respect to HIV/AIDS	Not with respect to HIV/AIDS	Not with respect to HIV/AIDS	No regulation	No regulation

this chapter considers the scope and depth of policy practices as well as the degree to which practices are pursued in designated situations (scale).[80] In substance, these practices can have two dimensions.

The first dimension entails disease prevention measures: free condom distribution, safer sex campaigns, training that aims to prevent the spread of the disease or disease-related stigmatization, and voluntary counseling and testing campaigns (VCT), as well as a peer educator program. In the context of VCT, employees are told their status anonymously and subsequently offered medical and psychological services. Peer educators are chosen from especially outspoken and respected members among the workforce. They promote safer sex and try to breach the social stigma associated with the disease. Peer educators also provide information to HIV positive employees about available medical assistance.

The second dimension refers to the assistance and support that employees are granted should they have already contracted HIV. Such assistance can include disease management as, for instance, the making of appointments with doctors or the harmonization of treatment with work plans, free treatment of "secondary diseases," the provision of immune boosters, and anti-retroviral (ARV) therapy on the level that usually only privately insured patients avail of.[81]

The practices can vary in scope in the sense that they can cover these relevant areas to different degrees. Some companies may, for example, provide immune boosters but not anti-retroviral therapy, while others offer both to employees. The more aspects are covered, the wider in scope are the practices. Depth refers to the degree to which the practices are demanding. For example, medical treatment can cover anti-retroviral therapy on different levels. It can be on the level of private health care institutions and thus on the most advanced level available, or on the level of South African public health institutions and thus on a much lower level. Scale concerns the inclusiveness of policy practices – i.e. the proportion of the workforce that can benefit from it – and the degree to which the practices are applied in designated situations. The higher the proportion of the workforce

---

[80] Scope refers to *Indicator 3a* in the context of the approach to corporate social responsibility and its measurement as laid out in Chapter 3. Depth concerns *Indicator 3b*. The degree to which policy practices are applied in designated situation measures *Indicator 3c*.

[81] The weakening of the immune system through the virus causes additional illnesses such as tuberculosis, which are so-called "secondary" or "opportunistic" diseases.

benefitting from the programs, and the more successful implementation is in this respect, the higher the values for scale. The indicators for measuring scope, depth, and scale of policy practices are listed in Table 4.4. The greater the prevention measures and the more services offered to employees who contract the virus, the stronger the program, and vice versa.

Medium to large automotive component manufacturers

The analysis begins with a consideration of the scope of policies, and the four medium- to large-sized automotive first-tier suppliers Sä, Sh, Fe, and AL.[82] The four firms cover the areas of condom distribution and information provision in relation to HIV/AIDS, and include peer educators as a minimum.[83] Differences among the four firms persist with respect to medical treatment, disease management, and voluntary counseling and testing (VCT), which are policy practices at the clutch maker Sä, the car glass firm Sh, and the car carpet firm Fe, but not at the automotive body producer AL.[84] However, counseling and testing is not organized by management but by the Southern African Clothing and Textile Workers' Union (SACTWU) in the case of car carpet manufacturer Fe. SACTWU is very active in the field of HIV/AIDS. Differently from SACTWU, the National Union of Metalworkers of South Africa (NUMSA) – the organization of the other three firms' employees – shows no engagement in the fight against HIV/AIDS at the workplace.[85]

---

[82] The analysis thus begins with the assessment of *Indicator 3a*. I shall mention that of the four firms, only Sä and Sh have a formal policy. The policies are weakly formulated, lack precision and strictness, and are shallow with respect to the goals that are delineated. They are also outdated since they do not detail and prescribe the full range of policy practices of the two firms. Hence, the firms' policies lag behind policy practices and are therefore not of essential relevance for the analysis. The policy documents of Sä and Sh were sent to me on January 10, 2009 by email.

[83] Hence, a first finding is that in comparison with the small to medium component manufacturers analyzed in the next section, the HIV/AIDS programs are more comprehensive.

[84] Interview with the Human Resources Manager of AL, September 13, 2007, Rosslyn.

[85] In the textile industry, margins and productivity are low and most firms cannot afford an HIV/AIDS program. Hence, SACTWU decided to support textile firms in the fight against the disease. The automotive chapter of NUMSA, by contrast, is dominated by the interests of the workers of resource-rich OEM such as VW, BMW, General Motors, or Toyota. These firms are forerunners with respect to HIV/AIDS workplace programs. Hence, there was no need for NUMSA to engage in additional activities, which are costly (and financed through wage deductions).

Table 4.4 *HIV/AIDS workplace programs – practices*

Corporate social responsibility: HIV/AIDS workplace programs Analyzed as outcome of the *human resources dilemma*		
Dimensions	Policy practices	Assessment/measurement
Dimension 1 *Prevention measures and conflict resolution*	• Free distribution of condoms and information material • HIV/AIDS training courses or other campaigns (such as safer sex programs and anti-discrimination campaigns) • VCT • Peer educator program	Weak
Dimension 2 *Medical support and treatment*	• Disease management support (coordination and organization of work and treatment plans offered to employees by firm) • Secondary disease treatment in on-site clinic • Firm takes over immune booster provision (either in on-site clinic or at a private doctor; either on the level of South African public health care or on private health care) • ARV therapy (either in on-site clinic or at a private doctor; either on the level of South African public health care or on private health care)	• **Indicator 3a:** scope (degree to which policy practices cover relevant areas) • **Indicator 3b:** depth (degree to which practices are demanding) • **Indicator 3c:** scale (extent to which practices are pursued systematically in designated situations) Strong

Hence, with respect to VCT the case of Fe exemplifies the effect of the factor "union" rather than that of "human asset specificity." As a consequence, the aspect VCT will be exempted from the analysis of Sä, Sh, Fe, and AL. In summary, the practices of Sä and Sh are widest in scope, followed by Fe. The program of the manufacturer of auto body parts AL is in comparative perspective rather basic.

Turning to the assessment of the depth of policy practices, the program parts the firms have in common – condom distribution, information provision, and peer education – are established by demanding practices.[86] For example, the activities of the firms go far beyond the distribution of pamphlets and the teaching of "facts" in the area of information provision. AIDS activists and NGOs are invited to the factories to discuss safer-sex practices with employees, the relation between HIV and AIDS, and the problem of social stigmatization associated with the disease. Moreover, industrial theater groups perform in the factories and facilitate the opportunity for reflection on social aspects that contribute to the spread of HIV as, for example, the role of men and women in society, sexual violence, drug abuse, and promiscuity. Differences in depth concern disease management and medical treatment.[87]

The negative case is, again, AL, the German-originating manufacturer of auto body parts. AL does not provide treatment. Positively tested employees may coordinate their treatment in the public health care system with work plans, which obviously makes for hardly any disease management practice at all. Public health clinics are usually under-equipped in South Africa. They lack personnel and resources. Waiting times are long and distances to the clinics can be considerable. In addition, medical treatment in public hospitals is poor and below international standards.[88]

---

[86] Depth concerns *Indicator 3b*.

[87] The number of designated personnel for the HIV/AIDS program reflects these differences as well. Sä and Sh employ two occupational health nurses full-time to organize VCT and disease management. Fe has hired one nurse for these tasks; AL does not employ a nurse with a specific HIV/AIDS training.

[88] In public clinics ARV treatment is initiated much later than in Europe, for instance. Patients are already rapidly deteriorating when they take up ARV therapy. Moreover, the treatment itself does not include an individualized drug cocktail that targets specific viruses. It consists of a general cocktail that is used on every HIV infection. This explains why life expectancy for patients on ARV medication in South Africa is much lower than in Europe. Another problem for patients on public health care is that it is often difficult for them to obtain the

The positive cases are the manufacturer of clutches Sä and the car glass producer Sh. Both firms have contracts with private health care clinics to which they refer HIV-positive employees. Unlike public health clinics, private clinics or company clinics are close to the factory or homes of employees and not overcrowded. The treatment in private clinics accords with international standards. In these clinics, employees receive immune boosters and vitamins prior to the outbreak of AIDS and anti-retroviral therapy should they reach a more critical stage. The level of medication conforms to the most advanced international standards and well beyond that of public health care. The incurring costs are covered by the firms. In addition, they take over the coordination of work and treatment plans, make appointments with doctors, and organize transportation. Hence, the two firms Sä and Sh practice their HIV/AIDS programs at a highly demanding level.

Fe takes a middle position between the negative case AL and the positive cases Sä and Sh. The producer of car carpets engages in disease management in a remarkable way, though it does not provide for medication. Fe has negotiated an agreement with a local public health care clinic that grants employees preferential access to treatment. Considering that this saves the patients bound to the public health care system incalculable waiting time, the disease management of Fe must be qualified as demanding. In addition, the human resources manager of Fe also arranges the appointments in this clinic personally to coordinate disease management with work plans and to assist infected employees. In sum, the German firm specialized in clutches Sä as well as the South African car glass maker Sh have deep policy practices, whereas those of AL are shallow; Fe takes a middle position.

Evaluating the scale of policy practices, i.e. the extent to which practices are pursued systematically in designated situations, the firms attain unitary high values in the program areas they have in common, which are condom distribution, information provision, and peer educators.[89] The respective factory visits confirmed that condoms are distributed for free in toilets, peer educators are identifiable and actively approach employees in all units of the factories, and 100 percent of the

immune boosters, nutrition supplements, and vitamins, that help to prevent infected persons from falling sick with AIDS.

[89] Measurement is undertaken according to *Indicator 3c.*

workforce regularly attends information and awareness raising events such as industrial theatre group plays. However, the peer educators often find it problematic to draw their colleagues into debates about the disease. HIV/AIDS is stigmatized in South Africa, rendering the implementation of any program tackling the disease a challenge.

Fear of stigmatization is also probably behind implementation problems regarding the disease management and treatment programs of Sä, Sh, and Fe.[90] At the manufacturer of car glass Sh and the clutch maker Sä private medical aid coverage for HIV/AIDS is 100 percent. However, the attendance rate in the medical treatment program is rather low. For example, in a recent anonymous VCT at the manufacturer of clutches Sä the attendance rate was 70 percent. Of these employees, 3 percent were tested positive. Out of this 3 percent only a small proportion signed up for the treatment program.[91] Sä furthermore reckons that the vast majority of HIV-positive employees abstained from the VCT.[92] However, without prior participation in a VCT, employees cannot access the treatment program. Hence, only a very small percentage of infected employees attend the medical aid program. This finding applies to Sä, Sh, and Fe in a similar fashion.[93]

In conclusion, the manufacturer of clutches Sä and the car glass firm Sh show the strongest response to HIV/AIDS in the workplace. The two firms have the most demanding and comprehensive policy practices in this respect as they offer full-scale private medical treatment to HIV-infected employees. The analysis ascribes the weakest policy to the manufacturer of body parts AL. The firm has a full program, but does not offer medical treatment and only little assistance for disease management. The car carpet maker Fe takes the middle position. The firm does not provide for medical treatment, but has a very ambitious disease management program, which accounts for relatively demanding policy practices.

---

[90] As revealed by the measurement of *Indicator 3b*, AL is lacking such programs.
[91] The company would not disclose exact data on this as the issue appears to be too sensitive. The exact number or percentage is not overly important here.
[92] Interviews with the Human Resources Manager, the Manager of Integrated Systems, and the Key Accounts and Export Manager of Sä, September 22, 2008, Port Elizabeth.
[93] For Fe, the assertion applies to the disease management program that grants employees preferential access to a local public health clinic, as Fe does not have an in-house medical aid program for infected employees.

Small to medium automotive component manufacturers
The analysis begins considering the activities of the manufacturer of springs CS in relation to HIV/AIDS workplace programs.[94] In 2004, the South African Business Coalition on HIV/AIDS (SABCOHA) sent a tool-kit for HIV/AIDS workplace programs to CS. This inspired the firm to draw up an in-house program. More precisely, the management of CS "planned" to install "boxes full of condoms in the toilets" and to put "signs up and posters."[95] In addition, the firm "theoretically" set up a peer educator program.[96] "Theoretically," the scope of policy practices at CS thus covers three basic areas: condom distribution, information provision, and peer educators: "That is as far as it goes."[97] However, in reality, the extent to which these practices are pursued is nil. In consequence, scope and depth of policy practices are nil, too.[98] At the time of the factory visit in September 2008, condoms were not distributed and information provision was not pursued. Also, the peer educator program was not in action.[99] Considering that management declared that it was not enforcing the program, these findings are not surprising.[100]

In contrast to the spring manufacturer CS, the vacuforming firm V is not fighting HIV/AIDS in the workplace in theory only, but also in practice. V offers free condoms to employees, actively informs about the virus and safer sex practices, and has a peer educator and disease management program in place.[101] Hence, the policy of the vacuforming firm V is

---

[94] CS, as V and FE, does not have a formalized, written policy on HIV/AIDS. Small firms are generally more informally organized than large firms. Therefore they often lack these features – even if they show substantial policy practices. Decisive is, however, the support of top-management (see operationalization in Chapter 3, *Indicator 2d*), which will therefore be described in addition to the findings for *Indicators 3a–c* as well.

[95] Interview with the Production Manager of CS, September 18, 2008, Cape Town.

[96] Ibid.   [97] Ibid.   [98] Thus, measuring *Indicator 3a–c* results in no scores.

[99] Usually peer educators can be spotted immediately as they are wearing t-shirts or stickers promoting HIV-related messages. In addition to that, they have an office for private consultation. At CS, no such signs for a peer educator program were there. When asked why there is an absence of such signs and, more generally, of signs that would indicate an active HIV/AIDS program on the factory floor, the representative of CS admitted that the policy has never been implemented.

[100] Interview with the Production Manager of CS, September 18, 2008, Cape Town. The program is "just something to say 'yes we do have it,' but apart from it, we do the least that we need to do." Interview with the Production Manager of CS, September 18, 2008, Cape Town.

[101] Interview with the Director of V, October 1, 2008, Rosslyn.

wider in scope compared with the actual policy of the manufacturer of springs CS (which is, as mentioned, nil) and also with the planned policy at CS, as it encompasses disease management as well.[102] More precisely, V assists infected and sick employees in the organization of their medical treatment. For example, the firm provides employees with information about clinics that are licensed for ARV treatment in the vicinity of the factory, offers transport to the clinics, and coordinates treatment plans with work plans. These practices are also demanding.[103] For example, to raise awareness V does not only distribute information brochures, but organizes regular HIV/AIDS training courses for the entire staff as well. Also, the practices that support disease management are ambitious. The firm actively influences its environment to improve the situation for infected employees. "One of the next steps in the LAG [the Local Action Group of NAACAM] for me will be to organize mobile clinics," says the Managing Director of V, indicating that he is involved in the planning of NAACAM-affiliated clinics that will offer public health care services in the vicinity of the factories exclusively for employees of automobile suppliers.[104] These clinics could reduce the waiting and travelling time for patients. However, concerning the degree to which these practices are pursued systematically in designated situations, the results for V are mixed.[105] Condom distribution and information provision are widely implemented.[106] The peer educator program is implemented throughout the factory as well.[107] However, the peer education itself often proves to be difficult on account of the stigma associated with the disease. Generally, employees do not want to talk about the issue; this is an important obstacle for a more effective implementation of the program.

For the same reason, participation in the disease management program is low. Upon anonymous testing, most positively tested employees "disappear."[108] They do not want to reveal their status, which, however, is a precondition for receiving benefits. Disease management is therefore

---

[102] These aspects refer to *Indicator 3a*.
[103] The analysis assesses here *Indicator 3b*.   [104] Ibid.
[105] The analysis assesses here the scale of policy practices, *Indicator 3c*.
[106] The factory tour revealed clear indications of an active implementation. For example, there is an on-site clinic at V dedicated to information provision and peer education.
[107] The peer educators are regularly trained and wear colorful t-shirts on which HIV/AIDS-related messages are posted.
[108] Interview with the Director of V, October 1, 2008, Rosslyn.

seldom put into practice, despite the fact that many employees could benefit from it given the high prevalence rate among the workforce. V has, nonetheless, implemented a medium-strong policy covering basic areas of HIV/AIDS abatement (which is relatively wide in scope) and is within these areas relatively demanding (i.e. the policy has some depth). This occurs even though some parts of the program are practiced on a limited or small scale only, for reasons closely connected to the social stigma associated with the disease in South Africa. Still, for a rather small firm, these findings are remarkable. Usually firms of the size of V lack the infrastructure and capacity for an active HIV/AIDS program. In case of V, however, the program seems to receive strong executive support.[109] The managing director is personally propelling the program and says that "categorically, wherever we from top-management can, we assist [employees with HIV/AIDS.]"[110]

While V shows – considering its size – a relatively strong engagement in the fight against the disease, the precision engineering firm FE's is even more profound. FE distributes free condoms, actively provides information and has organized a peer educator program. Furthermore, the company offers voluntary counseling and testing (VCT), whereby employees are told their status anonymously and subsequently offered medical and psychological services. FE offers disease management to positively tested employees and beyond that also facilitates and pays for medication: "if the need arises and an infected employee comes forward, we will facilitate the necessary treatment. We have done it and we will continue to do it in the future."[111] When asked what "facilitating" means in this context, the reply was that the firm organizes and fully covers medical treatment, ranging from immune boosters to anti-retroviral (ARV) therapy in a private clinic. With respect to the scope of policies the finding is therefore

---

[109] For example, the Managing Director of V who also co-owns the company wanted to personally answer the interview questions about the problem of HIV/AIDS at the workplace and the program. This indicates his personal ownership of the program.

[110] Interview with the Director of V, October 1, 2008, Rosslyn. This claim is credible, as the Director was able to give examples of assistance. Aside from this, indicative for his support is that he organizes, develops, and sets up large parts the HIV/AIDS workplace program personally by participating in the Local Action Group (LAG) of NAACAM on HIV/AIDS.

[111] Interviews with the CEO and the Quality and Human Resources Manager of FE, September 23, 2008, East London.

that FE's policy practices are highly comprehensive – clearly more comprehensive than V's.[112]

Also, the degree to which the policies are demanding is higher.[113] Whereas infected employees at V remain in the public health care system, FE organizes and pays for private health care, which is taken to a much higher level. Public health clinics are under-equipped, lack personnel, and lack resources. Waiting times and distances to the clinics are considerable.[114] More importantly, however, medical treatment in public hospitals is poor and below international standards.[115] Contrary to that, private clinics are close to the factory or homes of employees, and not over-crowded. The treatment in private clinics is on the level of international standards. While the HIV/AIDS program of FE is thus clearly wider in scope and more demanding than V's, the extent to which practices are followed systematically is similar.[116] Condom distribution and training courses are organized regularly and successfully, and the peer educator program is very active and visible.[117] However it is often not able to fully reach out to employees "because there is still prejudice amongst people."[118] The same is true for disease management and the medication program. 100 per cent of the employees of FE who are known to be HIV positive attend the medication and disease management programs and accordingly receive medical treatment from private clinics. However, the number of people that have actively taken advantage of the program is

---

[112] The analysis considers here *Indicator 3a*.
[113] Considering *Indicator 3b*. Regarding condom distribution and information provision FE and V show similar policy practices. As with V, FE organizes regular training courses and awareness-raising campaigns for the entire staff.
[114] However, the NAAMSA-affiliated mobile clinics may change this in the future for employees of V.
[115] In public clinics ARV treatment is initiated much later than in Europe for instance. Patients are already rapidly deteriorating when they take up ARV therapy. Moreover, the treatment itself does not include an individualized drug cocktail that targets specific viruses, but consists of a general cocktail that is used on every HIV infection. This explains why life expectancy for patients on ARV medication in South Africa is much lower than in Europe. Another problem for patients on public health care is that it is often difficult for them to obtain immune boosters, nutrition supplements, and vitamins keeping infected persons from falling sick with AIDS.
[116] Turning to an evaluation of *Indicator 3c*.
[117] There are areas on the factory floor specifically dedicated to HIV/AIDS information provision and peer education as a factory visit confirmed. The peer educators were identified as they wore red baseball caps.
[118] Interview with the Quality and Human Resources Manager of FE, September 23, 2008, East London.

only two. According to the estimation of FE, this means that only a very small percentage of the total workforce that is HIV positive participates in the benefits program. Hence, disease management and medication are deficiently implemented.

Summarizing the findings for FE, the precision engineering firm has a strong policy implemented, which is not only comprehensive but also demanding because it pays for private health care medication. As in the case of V, the finding is that there is strong support from the Managing Director of FE for the program.[119] However, the parts of the program specifically aimed at infected employees are not thoroughly implemented; the attendance rate among employees is low, mainly because of the fear of stigmatization.

Textile manufacturers

The practices that the hotel carpet manufacturer Crossley Carpets and the producer of underwear DBA have in common are free condom and information material distribution, awareness raising, and safer sex and other educational health-related campaigns including a peer educator program.[120] The latter program is organized by SACTWU. More precisely, SACTWU trains the shop stewards of Crossley Carpets and DBA on HIV/AIDS-related issues, and organizes and monitors their work as peer educators.[121] Furthermore, the two firms have in common that they operate on-site clinics with nurses that have received specific training on HIV/AIDS. Hence, the analysis finds for both Crossley Carpets and DBA that the scope of the respective HIV/AIDS programs covers the basic areas. Beyond that, however, stark differences persist, especially with

---

[119] The Human Resources Manager reports, for example, that an employee of FE had been recently diagnosed with a so-called "secondary disease" of HIV/AIDS. Following the diagnosis he did not go to the local hospital for his treatment. The Managing Director, however, personally investigated with the hospital if the employee complied with the treatment plan and was therefore – after he found out that the employee was not receiving treatment – able to put pressure on him to regularly see a doctor. This had the intended effects. The employee subsequently complied with the treatment plan and "today he appears as healthy as we do." The example reveals strong personal interest in the program. Interview with the Human Resources Manager of FE, September 23, 2008, East London.

[120] The analysis thus begins with the evaluation of *Indicator 3a.*

[121] Shop stewards are elected by workers to represent their interests in negotiations with management. In "closed" union firms such as Crossley Carpets and DBA elections are organized by the union.

respect to the range of services offered to infected employees. These are much wider in scope at Crossley Carpets than at DBA.

The clinic of DBA provides occupational health-related services only – the treatment of smaller work injuries or minor illnesses such as 'flu etc – and does not actively engage in the management or treatment of serious or chronic diseases such as HIV/AIDS. By contrast, the clinic of Crossley Carpets offers HIV positive employees various services. The clinic assists in managing the disease, as, for example, in the setting up of treatment plans and the integration of treatment plans into work plans. Moreover, the firm runs, unlike DBA, regular voluntary counseling and testing (VCT) campaigns to ensure that employees can know their status and are informed about the assistance and support Crossley Carpets offers.

In addition – and in contrast to DBA – Crossley Carpets treats the secondary diseases of HIV, which are a dominating factor in the lives of HIV-positive patients, in the on-site clinic, for free. The clinic also provides HIV-infected employees with immune boosters to prolong the period before the disease develops into AIDS. Finally, a major difference regarding medical services concerns the procedure that is initiated upon the deterioration of HIV-positive employees in need of ARV. While the HIV/AIDS program of DBA does not include any ARV treatment at all, that of Crossley Carpets does, albeit for only parts of the workforce. Hence, the workplace program of Crossley Carpets is much wider in scope than that of DBA.

Considering the depth of policy practices of the two textile firms, the mentioned common aspects of the two programs are constituted by demanding practices.[122] The medical treatment program and the VCT campaigns of Crossley Carpets are demanding as well. At Crossley Carpets, the goal is to provide for full medical care at least to the point at which patients develop AIDS – and in selected cases even afterwards. As asserted before, DBA has no such goals for its in-house clinics, but externalizes all aspects of medical care onto public or SACTWU-run clinics (which are also accessible to the workers of Crossley Carpets who are also SACTWU members). At SACTWU clinics, waiting time is shorter than at public clinics. For the rest, however, they offer the same services and

---

[122] Measuring *Indicator 3b*. As in the previous analyses this implies that information provision goes beyond the mere "facts." Crossley Carpets and DBA, for example, invite industrial theater groups and activists to tackle the social stigmatization associated with the disease or to highlight deeply embedded social structures that contribute to a spread of the virus.

medication as in public clinics, which are below the standard offered in the clinic of Crossley Carpets. Besides, SACTWU clinics are not an outcome of the firm policy of DBA. In fact, they are organizationally independent from DBA and are therefore not part of DBA's practices.[123] Concerning the depth of policy practices, the inquiry therefore asserts relatively high scores for Crossley Carpets, whereas DBA's score is lower as a consequence of medical and treatment aspects absent from the program.

A stronger engagement of Crossley Carpets in the fight against HIV/AIDS than DBA is also indicated by the extent to which practices are pursued systematically in designated situations.[124] For example, the attendance rates of awareness-raising, sex education, and other HIV/AIDS-related training courses "are very low" at DBA, while training is a pervasive practice for workers at Crossley Carpets.[125] These differences are effectuated by the differential implementation measures taken by DBA and Crossley Carpets respectively. Human resources management at Crossley Carpets monitors and enforces the participation of employees in at least one HIV/AIDS-related training course per year. In addition, positive incentives for more frequent participation are given, as the courses count as paid work time. Also, management organizes HIV-related training courses in a way that participation is convenient: the groups are not larger than twenty and "the audience is homogeneous to avoid embarrassment and communication problems."[126] At DBA, by contrast, mechanisms that would facilitate compliance with the HIV/AIDS training policy do not exist. Attendance is voluntary and neither monitored, enforced, nor encouraged. The courses are held after work or during lunch breaks and do not count as paid work time. In South Africa, where stigmatization and myths regarding HIV are

---

[123] A fact that reemphasizes the role the unions play in HIV/AIDS abatement, which has been pointed out already in the previous analysis. SACTWU clinics are also accessible to the workers of Crossley Carpets.

[124] That is, concerning *Indicator 3c*. Other programs are properly implemented in both cases. A factory visit revealed that HIV/AIDS as a topic is present on the factory floors, as inferred from condom distributors in the toilets and information sheets, campaign posters, and pamphlets in the factory. Also, the peer educators were clearly identifiable and have a room in the factory designated specifically for their task.

[125] Interview with the Manager of Human Resources of DBA, September 25, 2008, Durban.

[126] Interview with the Director of Human Resources of Crossley Carpets, September 28, 2007, Durban.

all pervasive, this absence of compliance mechanisms inevitably leads to low participation rates.

While these considerations clearly indicate that the extent to which policy practices are pursued systematically is greater at Crossley Carpets than at DBA, the scores for Crossley Carpets regarding the program parts that go beyond DBA's – participation of employees in the disease management and treatment program of the firm – are rather low. On the one hand, the fear of stigmatization discourages employees from taking advantage of the services the firm offers to the general workforce.[127] To tackle this problem Crossley Carpets organizes the VCT campaigns, through which it is hoped that employees will find their way into the firm's program. In spite of these measures, still relatively few of the employees profit from the treatment of secondary diseases, disease management, immune booster provision, and the general medical supervision offered.[128] On the other hand, with respect to the specific aspect of ARV treatment, a low attendance rate is a result of the firm policy itself. In contrast to the other described program parts – disease management, treatment of secondary diseases, immune booster provision – offered universally to the workforce, Crossley Carpets does not provide ARV therapy on a private health care level to everyone. Only "if it is somebody who is doing a job which is highly skilled, because this will affect the company negatively" will Crossley Carpets cover the private health care ARV therapy, "because the skills that we require here, most of them cannot be found or recruited from anywhere [else] because we use specialized machines."[129]

Hence, the same logic that was theorized to result in an engagement of firms in HIV/AIDS programs inclines Crossley Carpets also to limit

---

[127] Interestingly, the same problems persist for SACTWU-run clinics. According to the Human Resources manager of DBA, employees usually do not make use of the better treatment facilities in SACTWU clinics. Instead, they either opt to live in denial without treatment or consult a public hospital. The main reason for the low acceptance rate of the program is, again, the fear of stigmatization. "They do not want it to be highlighted" and decide to go to a clinic "at some place they are not known." Interview with the Manager of Human Resources of DBA, September 25, 2008, Durban.

[128] Data is a company secret. "Relatively few" refers to the assertion of the Human Resources management of Crossley Carpets that many more could be included in the program.

[129] Interview with the Director of Human Resources of Crossley Carpets, September 28, 2007, Durban.

ARV medication to those employees who are highly valuable to the firm. While these considerations strongly support the causal process theorized for the *human resources dilemma*, they also point at potential intra-firm segregation into different benefit groups based on different levels of asset-specific investments in employees within a firm. Table 4.5 summarizes the findings of the analysis of the automotive and textile cases with respect to HIV/AIDS programs.

Summary of the findings

What do the comparative analyses reveal with respect to the theoretically stipulated relation between the *human resources dilemma* and the firms' adopting of labor-related corporate social responsibility policies? The first comparison, which featured four automotive cases, corroborates the theoretical argument that the *human resources dilemma* causes management to engage in labor-related corporate social responsibility. The manufacturer of clutches Sä as well as the car glass maker Sh are cases that exemplify the *human resources dilemma*. The two firms invest in the training of skills that are otherwise difficult to find on the South African labor market. Consequently, they have full-fledged HIV/AIDS workplace programs implemented. These range from condom distribution and information campaigns to disease management, medication, and even anti-retroviral therapy on a level high above South African public health care. The producer of body parts AL, by contrast, does not go far beyond condom distribution in its HIV/AIDS-related activities on account of low and non-specific resource allocation in the realm of human resources. The car carpet manufacturer Fe takes a middle position – between AL on the one hand and Sä and Sh on the other hand – with respect to the extent management confronts the *human resources dilemma* the HIV/AIDS workplace program.

The analysis of the four large first-tier suppliers demonstrates the validity of the theoretical argument for internal drivers for firms operating on a relatively high level of asset-specific investments in skills of employees. Yet the second comparative analysis shows that the argument holds even when variation of the *human resources dilemma* takes place on a relatively low level of intensity of the dilemma. The precision engineering firm FE, the firm that confronts the dilemma most seriously, shows the deepest engagement in HIV/AIDS abatement. Apart from condom distribution, a peer education program, and awareness-raising, the precision engineering firm covers the costs for medical treatment in private hospitals for infected employees. In this respect, FE goes beyond the efforts of the vacuforming firm V that too is actively tackling the problem of HIV/AIDS in the workplace, but – as a consequence of medium investments in specific skills – does not pay for private health care. The spring manufacturer CS does not confront a managerial dilemma in the realm of human resources and accordingly does not engage in the fight against HIV/AIDS. In particular as the firms of this second analysis are rather small in size, these findings are noteworthy, as they imply that the argument for the *human resources dilemma* holds when subjected to a hard test. The three firms of this comparative analysis lack the resources and infrastructure to run full-fledged workplace programs. Hence, when firms such as FE and to a lesser extent V decide to actively engage in the fight against HIV/AIDS, they have to build up a whole infrastructure specifically for this task and dedicate to this end a disproportionate amount of resources compared to larger firms.

The findings for the two textile firms Crossley Carpets and DBA are additional confirming evidence. The management of the hotel carpet maker Crossley Carpets confronts a much stronger *human resources dilemma* than the garment manufacturer DBA's. Accordingly, the HIV/AIDS program of Crossley Carpets is much more comprehensive and demanding than that of DBA and includes medical assistance and anti-retroviral therapy – services not offered by DBA.

Taken together, the nine cases display – more or less – a linear relationship between asset-specific investments in employee skills and HIV/AIDS workplace programs, as Figure 4.2 shows.[130] The slight deviation of the cases from an ideal linear relationship can be traced back to the differences in firm size among the firms. While firm size cannot explain much of the overall variation in Figure 4.1 – and is by itself also not a factor motivating firms to practice corporate social responsibility (Börzel *et al.* 2013) – it enhances or diminishes the effects of internal driver 1: the larger the firm, the stronger the effect of the driver.[131] Hence, the puzzle of differential levels of HIV/AIDS workplace programs among South

---

[130] A disclaimer applies: the measurement of both asset specificity and HIV/AIDS programs was undertaken in relation to the firms' comparative cases in the context of the respective controlled comparison – and is thus neither absolute nor exact.

[131] Figure 4.2 shows in this respect that the relationship between asset specificity and workplace programs is almost ideal linear within the groups of cases that were formed in order to conduct controlled pair-wise comparisons.

Table 4.5 Empirical cases, analyzed with respect to labor-related corporate social responsibility (HIV/AIDS workplace programs)

Labor-related CSR
HIV/AIDS workplace programs

	Comparison 1: automotive industry — Medium to large first tier component manufacturers								Comparison 2: automotive industry — Small to medium component manufacturers						Comparison 3: textile industry — Large manufacturers			
	Case 1 — Sä (manufacturer of clutches)		Case 2 — Sh (manufacturer of car windows)		Case 3 — Fe (manufacturer of car carpets)		Case 4 — Al (manufacturer of body parts)		Case 5 — FE (precision engineering)		Case 6 — V (blow-molding and vacuforming)		Case 7 — CS (manufacturer of springs)		Case 8 — CC (manufacturer of hotel carpets)		Case 9 — DBA (manufacturer of garments)	
Stage matrix	Assessment	Degree of implemen-tation	Assessment	Degree of implemen-tation	Assessment	Degree of implemen-tation	Assessment	Degree of implemen-tation	Assessment	Degree of implemen-tation	Assessment	Degree of implemen-tation	Assessment	Degree of implemen-tation	Assessment	Degree of implemen-tation	Assessment	Degree of implemen-tation
Stage 1 — Free condoms, information distributed, raising awareness measures	Yes		Yes		Yes		Yes		Yes		Yes		No		Yes		Yes	
Stage 2 — HIV/AIDS training	Yes (demanding training, high attendance)		Yes (demanding training, high attendance)		High		Yes (demanding training, low attendance)		Yes (demanding training, high attendance)		Yes (demanding training, medium attendance)		No		Yes (demanding training, high attendance)		Yes (demanding training, low attendance)	
Stage 3 — VCT (voluntary counseling and testing)	Not part of the assessment	High	Not part of the assessment	High	Not part of the assessment	Medium	Not part of the assessment	Low	Yes (low attendance)	Medium to high	No	Medium	No	None	Yes (low attendance)	Medium to high	No	Low
Stage 4 — Disease management	Yes (comprehensive services offered; there are a number of employees benefiting from these services)		Yes (comprehensive services offered; there are a number of employees benefiting from these services)		Coordination services offered, but low participation		No disease management		Yes (comprehensive services offered; attendance low)		Yes (comprehensive services offered; attendance low)		No		Yes (comprehensive services offered; attendance low)		No disease management	
Stage 5 — Secondary disease treatment in on-site clinic	Yes (default practice; there are a number of employees benefiting from these services)		Yes (default practice; there are a number of employees benefiting from these services)		Yes, but low participation rate		No, only work related injuries are treated in on-site clinic		Yes (comprehensive services offered; attendance low)		No, but employees can get preferential access to cooperating public clinic		No		Yes, but low participation rate		No, only work related injuries are treated in on-site clinic	

Table 4.5 (cont.)

Stage 6 Immune booster provision	Yes (default practice; there are a number of employees on this medical scheme)	Yes (default practice; there are a number of employees on this medical scheme	No, but employees can get preferential access to cooperating public clinic	No	Yes (comprehensive services offered; attendance low)	No, but employees can get preferential access to cooperating public clinic	No	Yes (default practice; but attendance low)	No
Stage 7 ARV therapy	Yes, on the level of private health care (there are a number of employees benefiting from ARV therapy)	Yes, on the level of private health care (there are a number of employees benefiting from ARV therapy)	No, but employees can get preferential access to cooperating public clinic	No	Yes, on the level of private health care (attendance: low)	No, but employees can get preferential access to cooperating public clinic	No	Yes, on the level of private health care, but only for those employees that have long work experience	No

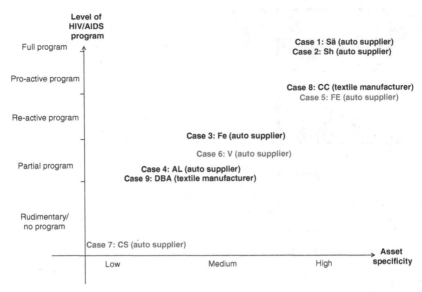

Figure 4.2 HIV/AIDS programs in relation to asset specificity (internal driver 1)

African manufacturing firms is solved: it is predominantly explained by internal driver 1 – asset-specific investments in employee skills (with some marginal contribution of the factor firm size).

Tracing the process: managerial decisions versus employee power

The analysis in the previous sections showed that asset-specific invest-ments in rare skills correlate with HIV/AIDS workplace programs, *ceteris paribus.* However, the inside-view approach and perspective in this book (see Chapter 3) can do more than demonstrate correlations. It can also trace the causal process (Brady and Collier 2010; George and Bennett 2005: 205–10; Tilly 1997). Process tracing allows the analysis to assess whether the causal mechanisms leading from asset specificity to HIV/AIDS workplace programs are really the ones explaining the cases as theorized in Chapter 2 – or if other mechanisms are at work. The analysis will thereby consider an important, potentially alternative explanation for the relation between asset specificity and HIV/AIDS programs: employee interests and their bargaining power vis-à-vis management. What is this alternative explanation about, and how far could, potentially, asset specificity bring about HIV/AIDS programs by influencing employee interests and their bargaining power?

Albeit on a different level of analysis, a recent debate in comparative political economy makes some suggestions in this respect. In "varieties of capitalism," Hall and Soskice (2001) propose, based on the idea of asset specificity, an "employer-centered" (Korpi 2006) explanation of welfare state policies. A main competitive advantage of firms in coordinated market economies (CMEs) vis-à-vis firms in liberal market economies (LMEs) is that they can make complex products (Busemeyer and Trampusch 2011; Hall and Soskice 2001; Mares 2001). This advantage, however, crucially depends on the willingness of employees to invest in skills specialization. In CMEs, social policies provide for strong incentives for such asset-specific investments. They protect employees with specific skills from having to accept job offers that do not correspond to their qualification. In consequence, firms that depend on specialized skills, as in the dominant industries in CMEs, emerge as main supporters of strong social welfare state policies.

While theoretically plausible, this "employer-centered" account has provoked criticism. In particular, authors who study welfare state development historically – as Esping-Anderson in *The Three Worlds of Welfare Capitalism* (1990) – argue that welfare state policies have rarely been created by capitalists (Korpi 1978, 2006). They are instead the result of class conflict in which strong working class organizations in coalition with left wing parties succeeded in pressing for social reforms *against* capitalist interests. As a consequence of this criticism, the comparative capitalism approach abandoned the idea of an "employer-centered" mechanism in relation to asset specificity and adopted the idea of an "employee-centered" one (Iversen 2005; Iversen and Soskice 2001, 2009): "individuals who have made risky investments in skills will demand insurance against the possible future loss of income from those investments" and therefore "have strong incentives to support social policies" (Iversen and Soskice 2001: 875) – whereas employees who have not made such investments have no such incentives.

Asset specificity can thus, potentially, lead to social policies on account of two distinct mechanisms. The "employer-centered" mechanism intends that employers – or managers – assume the responsibility for the wellbeing of employees; it is therefore they who will seek to create social policies. The "employee-centered" mechanism assumes that employees will take matters into their own hands and demand social policies themselves. This idea of potentially two distinct mechanisms relating asset specificity to social policies also applies to the analysis of corporate social responsibility in this book: unlike unskilled workers, employees with specialized skills have bargaining power vis-à-vis their employers (see Chapter 2). If we assume that workers in general have an interest in HIV/AIDS workplace programs, this difference in bargaining power may account for the firms' different levels of policies in relation to asset specificity.[132] This alternative, "employee-centered" explanation contrasts with the one suggested in this book which suggests an "employer-centered" – more specifically, management-centered – mechanism: managers first invest in specific skills of employees, then confront risks on account of this investment (such as that employees contract HIV/AIDS and so devalue the investment), which they in turn mitigate through social policies (i.e. HIV/AIDS workplace programs). Which mechanism prevails? Or do both occur equally and at the same time?

Process tracing is a method that allows us to disentangle alternative causal mechanisms and decide which one prevails empirically. It involves making inferences on the basis of observable implications that logically follow from alternative causal mechanisms (George and Bennett 2005: 205–10). This study suggests three sets of observable implications for the "employer" and "employee-centered" explanation, respectively.

The first set (1) concerns the sequence of events leading from asset specificity to HIV/AIDS programs. According to the "employer-centered" approach here, this sequence begins with management taking the initiative to set up and run an HIV/AIDS program (or new program parts when a program exists already). This decision is followed by attempts to make employees enroll in the new program so as to make

---

[132] While the comparative capitalism approach assumes that workers define their interests in relation to social policies differently on account of the asset-specific investments in skills specialization they have made and, accordingly, the different market risks they are exposed to, the same does not apply here. HIV/AIDS affects skilled and unskilled workers in the same way (i.e. independent of asset specificity). We can therefore not assume that skilled workers have a specific preference for HIV/AIDS programs when compared to unskilled workers. However, as I have argued in Chapter 2, asset specificity gives workers a strong bargaining position vis-à-vis employers, which may allow them to push their preference for social policies through.

it effective. Program changes are decided on an *ad hoc* basis by management. Conversely, the sequence of events in the context of the alternative, "employee-centered" explanation begins with employees voicing their demand for workplace programs in intra-firm or sector-wide bargaining. While employees want a workplace program, employers try to keep social policies in general to a minimum. The employees, however, prevail in this conflict, so that the negotiation results in an agreement over a workplace program, which is then implemented, whereby employees will try to prevent employers from reneging on the agreement.

If the "employer-centered" explanation were to hold, we would thus expect with respect to the sequence of events that:

- the programs were *not* a result of intra-firm or sector-wide bargaining, and their emergence in general did *not* involve any conflict between employers and employees;
- the programs were instead initiated and created by management;
- implementation problems, if any, would arise on account of the lack of acceptance of workplace programs on the part of employees (whom the program addresses).

If the "employee-centered" explanation were to be confirmed, we would expect with respect to the sequence of events that:

- the programs could be traced back to employee demands;
- the programs would emerge as a result of intra-firm or sector-wide bargaining and conflicts between employers and employees; employers and employees would continue fighting about the quality, range and extent of services offered in the context of HIV/AIDS programs while the program is implemented;
- implementation problems, if any, would arise on account of management trying to renege on the bargaining agreement establishing the workplace program.

These observable implications can be reasonably expected for cases that illustrate a minimum level of asset specificity. In the absence of asset specificity, management will not take the initiative to set up a workplace program; likewise, employees will either have no interest in pressing for HIV/AIDS programs or lack bargaining power to push such programs through. The observable implications will thus be most profound in the cases of Sä, Sh, FE, and Crossley Carpets, which are characterized by high levels of asset specificity (see Figure 4.2). They should also be present in the cases of V, AL, and Fe – the cases that illustrate medium to low levels of asset specificity. The observable implications do not apply to CS and DBA – the cases that exemplify low levels of asset specificity.

The second set of observable implications (2) concerns differential effects, which these two alternative causal mechanisms can be predicted to have in the dependent variable. More specifically, they concern the institutional design of HIV/AIDS programs (Abbot *et al.* 2000; Crawford and Ostrom 1995; Koremenos *et al.* 2001). According to the "employer-centered" explanation, the creation of HIV/AIDS programs does not involve conflict. In consequence, there is no need for management to formulate concise and obligatory program goals. Such would only create the risk of being held accountable for these goals by some external actor or stakeholder in the future. However, management will want to remain flexible in its ability to react to new situations and learn from past experiences and mistakes. Hence, in the context of the "employer-centered" explanation, we expect HIV/AIDS programs to be weakly institutionalized, i.e. to be rather informal, non-specific, non-obligatory, and flexibly formulated. Conversely, the "employee-centered" explanation expects a highly institutionalized program design. HIV/AIDS programs are here the result of bargaining processes and conflict. Employees may have prevailed over employers in making HIV/AIDS parts of the firms' responsibilities. However, in putting this negotiation outcome into practice, the employer side may renege on the agreement. To preempt such shirking, employees will insist on concise, obligatory, and formalized policy formulations.

The third set of implications (3) concerns the interpretative frames of management and employees within which they make sense of the emergence and persistence of the HIV/AIDS programs. In the context of the "employer-centered" explanation, the interpretation of events leading to the decision for HIV/AIDS programs will emphasize the skills-based business model of the firms and the function of the programs to protect this model against the negative effects of HIV/AIDS. The "employee-centered" alternative gives rise to different interpretations: employees will emphasize that the program is an achievement of the unions/employees and thereby point to the importance of workers' interests and organized labor for the solution of social problems. Employers, on the one hand, will mention the programs in the context of the strong role of unions and organized labor in general in South

Africa, and, on the other hand, portray the program as part of their general contribution to governance and the solution of social problems in South Africa. Table 4.6 summarizes these observable implications. What do the empirical cases reveal?

(1) Considering the sequence of events (Implication 1), the cases strongly support the "employer-centered" explanation and disconfirm the "employee-centered" one. The clear-cut "positive" cases – the cases that illustrate the positive relation between high levels of asset specificity and strong HIV/AIDS workplace programs – are the clutch maker Sä, the car glass manufacturer Sh, the precision engineering firm FE, and the textile firm Crossley Carpets (see Figure 4.2). Who initiated the strong HIV/AIDS workplace programs in these firms – management or employees? Was the decision for these programs associated with conflict or was it a "quiet," top-down decision by management? Do implementation problems exist and, if so, what are these problems?

The analysis begins with Sä, Sh, and FE. Managers of Sä, Sh, and FE say, when asked how the unions or employees in general were involved in setting up the firms' workplace program, that "they have not been involved at all and are still not involved at this stage."[133] This statement was made by a manager of Sh, but is also confirmed by managers for FE and Sä.[134] Union and worker representatives validate it as well. A labor council representative says, for example, that generally "on the HIV/AIDS issue, I don't think there has ever been any sort of demand from our side."[135] The issue appears in the context of neither intra-firm nor sector bargaining: "the function of bargaining is to resolve conflict ... and there are many issues that sit in there, in our bargaining rounds ... HIV/AIDS is not one of them."[136] Hence, the creation of HIV/AIDS programs at Sä, Sh, and FE does not trace back to employee interests and/or bargaining power. This finding is remarkable. Not only is asset specificity high in all three cases, but also

---

[133] Interview with the Product Engineering and Corporate Quality Assurance Manager of Sh, September 22, 2008, Port Elizabeth.

[134] Interviews with the Manager of Integrated Systems of Sä, September 22, 2008, Port Elizabeth and the Human Resources Manager of FE, September 23, 2008, East London.

[135] Interview with two union representatives of SACTWU and NAAMSA, March 30, 2007, Bellville.

[136] Ibid.

Table 4.6 *Tracing the process: employer- or employee-driven?*

| | | Who pushes for HIV/AIDS programs? Employer vs. employee-based explanations | | |
| | | | Observable implications | |
	Mechanism	(1) Sequence of events	(2) Institutional design	(3) Interpretation of events
Employer-centered	Managerial dilemma: management mitigates risks associated with asset-specific investments through HIV/AIDS programs	HIV/AIDS programs not an issue of intra-firm or sector-wide bargaining or conflicts; initiated and driven by management; Compliance problems on the side of employees	Weakly institutionalized design of programs (to remain flexible)	Emphasis on risk mitigation in relation to skills-intensive business model (both employers and employees)
Employee-centered	Employees have a strong bargaining position vis-à-vis management and can therefore push for HIV/AIDS programs	Employees raise issue of HIV/AIDS in negotiations with employers; conflicts between employer and employees about the quality, range and extent of services of HIV/AIDS programs; main implementation problem: management reneges on agreement	Highly institutionalized design of programs (so that labor can hold management accountable)	HIV/AIDS programs are a main achievement for workers vis-à-vis employers' interests; programs demonstrate the importance of workers' interests and organizations for the solution of social problems in the country

the degree of organization among workers in unions.[137] Conflicts between employers and employees are frequent and concern diverse issues. Hence, in other issue areas, employees seem to make use of their strong bargaining position vis-à-vis management. However, the cases do not indicate any "employee-centered" mechanisms in relation to HIV/AIDS workplace programs.

Instead, they illustrate the "employer-centered" explanation: the workplace programs were initiated, developed, and planned by human resources managers on behalf of top management. The human resources manager of Sh says that he planned the workplace program with strong support of the CEO.[138] He is also the one who, together with higher-level management, implements changes and develops ideas for new program parts. The situation is very similar in this respect at Sä and FE. The human resources manager of FE, for example, explains how the workplace programs in her firm evolved: "We [management] constantly look for ways to improve our policy. Wherever we can facilitate additional help we will do it and make it a program part – for example, recently we found that we can help our employees by providing some form of medical assistance to their families. So we decided to do this. This is how our program continuously develops."[139]

While FE, Sä, and Sh thus confirm the "employer centered" explanation for workplace programs as regards the sequence of events triggered by asset specificity, the hotel carpet maker Crossley Carpets is a case that involves employees' interests. Unlike Sä, FE, and Sh, who are unionized by NUMSA, Crossley Carpets is a textile firm and therefore organized by SACTWU. SACTWU is generally more active in regard to the fight against HIV/AIDS than NUMSA.[140] The union offers basic HIV/AIDS programs in all firms that are SACTWU-unionized.

---

[137] Interviews with the Product Engineering and Corporate Quality Assurance Manager of Sh, September 22, 2008, Port Elizabeth, the Manager of Integrated Systems of Sä, September 22, 2008, Port Elizabeth, and the Human Resources Manager of FE, September 23, 2008, East London.

[138] For the following, see ibid.

[139] Interview with the Human Resources Manager of FE, September 23, 2008, East London.

[140] Even the websites of the two unions are evidence of this. Whereas SACTWU prominently features worker health programs, no such programs are advertised on the website of NUMSA. See http://numsa.org.za/page/achievements-and-challenges and www.sactwu.org.za/worker-health-program (January 3, 2013).

However, while remarkable, the activities of SACTWU cannot explain the relation between asset specificity and HIV/AIDS workplace programs. In comparison with car firms, textile and clothing firms usually operate on much lower levels of asset specificity. For example, automotive supplier firms spend on average 3–7 percent of their labor costs on training in South Africa, whereas textile firms pay less than 1 percent.[141] Hence, if it were asset specificity that motivated and allowed employees to push for HIV/AIDS policies, we would rather expect NUMSA – the union which organizes workers in the car industry – to run strong programs, and not SACTWU.

Besides, the contribution of SACTWU to the workplace program of Crossley Carpets is on a very basic level only. The union organizes the same program parts at Crossley Carpets as in other firms, including the textile manufacturer DBA. DBA was the comparative case of Crossley Carpets in the controlled, pair-wise analysis above. This analysis identified DBA as a negative case of HIV/AIDS workplace programs and asset specificity (see Figure 4.2) and Crossley Carpets as a positive case. Which mechanisms account for the difference between the two firms? The interviews reveal that those parts of the workplace program at Crossley Carpets that go beyond DBA's were initiated neither by SACTWU nor Crossley Carpets' employees but by management. This assertion does not only reflect the interpretation of events by managers of Crossley Carpets, who say that they were the ones pushing for an HIV/AIDS workplace program beyond the union-run components.[142] It is also confirmed by a SACTWU representative who says that these strong "AIDS policies are initiated by the managers" and not the unions.[143] Both sides – employers and employees – confirm that there has never been any specific demand from the employee side or the union concerning HIV/AIDS that would go beyond allowing SACTWU to run its basic program parts. Hence, while the case of Crossley Carpets is more complicated than the cases of Sä, Sh, and FE on account of its involvement of SACTWU, it nonetheless shows that the relation

---

[141] Interview with the Human Resources Manager of Monviso, September 16, 2008, Cape Town.
[142] Interview with the Director of Human Resources and the Assistant of the Managing Director of Crossley Carpets, September 28, 2007, Durban.
[143] Interview with two union representatives of SACTWU, March 30, 2007, Bellville.

between high levels of asset specificity and strong HIV/AIDS workplace programs is explained by the "employer-centered" mechanism.

This conclusion gains additional support from the analysis of the implementation problems the workplace programs of the four firms – Sä, Sh, Crossley Carpets, and FE – confront. The main problem according to interview partners is that employees tend to stay away from these programs. The Human Resources director of Crossley Carpets, for example, explains when asked about the effectiveness of the program he runs that "it is really hard ... it's very, very difficult to convince the people to accept the offers we make them."[144] This statement is confirmed by basically all managers in charge of workplace programs. It shows that the programs are obviously not something the workers fought for – a fact that is in line with the "employer-centered" explanation, but not with the "employee-centered" one. In summary, the four positive cases of the clutch maker Sä, the car glass manufacturer Sh, the precision engineering firm FE, and the hotel carpet maker Crossley Carpets indicate that "employer-centered" mechanisms lead from asset specificity to HIV/AIDS workplace programs; they also show that "employee-centered" mechanisms are largely absent and even in the cases where they are present – as at Crossley Carpets and DBA – they do not contribute to HIV/AIDS programs beyond a very basic level.

These assertions gain additional support from the manufacturer of auto body parts AL, the vacuforming firm V, and the car carpet maker Fe. These firms illustrate lower levels of asset specificity and HIV/AIDS workplace programs when compared to Sä, Sh, Crossley Carpets, and FE. The findings, however, are analogous to the cases of Sä, Sh, Crossley Carpets, and FE: the cases do not provide for any support of the "employee-centered" mechanism, but point to the validity of the "employer-centered" one. The human resources manager of AL says, for example, with respect to the role of the unions in the development of the firm's workplace program (and employee interests in general) that "HIV/AIDS is not really a thing that they [the unions and employee representatives] approach us for. They never say that we have to put certain things in place with respect to HIV/AIDS."[145] Employees can

---

[144] Interview with the Director of Human Resources of Crossley Carpets, September 28, 2007, Durban.

[145] Interview with the Human Resources Manager of AL, September 13, 2007, Rosslyn.

thus be excluded for these cases as a decisive driving force in support of the firms' HIV/AIDS workplace programs.[146]

It is worth mentioning, though, that Fe's workplace program, as a car carpet maker, is partly organized by SACTWU (while SACTWU has a strong presence at Fe, the employees of V and AL are organized by NUMSA). The union runs the same program parts at Fe as it does at Crossley Carpets and DBA. However, the same applies here as in case of Crossley Carpets: those program parts that make Fe a relatively strong case of HIV/AIDS workplace programs have been developed by management and not by employees or unions. The assertion that management drives HIV/AIDS programs applies in the same way for V and AL. For example, the Director of V says that he is currently in the process of developing the idea of mobile clinics in the context of NAACAM – the car supplier association of South Africa – with other firms. Mobile clinics could provide anti-retroviral medication on-site and would thus improve access to medication for the employees. When asked how this idea emerged, he said that he developed it together with other managers at a recent NAACAM meeting.[147] He furthermore regretted that the unions and his employees are passive with respect to HIV/AIDS so that he, together with other managers, has to drive policies. If it were not for them, no one else would, according to the director. Managers of V, AL, and Fe confirm this.

Beyond this confirmative evidence for the "management-centered" mechanism, the three firms report the same difficulties in implementing the workplace programs as Sä, Sh, Crossley Carpets, and FE. "Our biggest difficulty is that ... when a guy gets identified as HIV-positive, he often does not want to go for our program. Instead, he goes to the local healers, the faith healers. And you can see it, the physical decline is just so rapid and we lose him," says the Director of V – a statement which is highly representative of what the managers of Fe and AL say with respect to the problems they confront in making the HIV/AIDS programs work.[148] As in the cases of Sä, Sh, Crossley Carpets, and FE, the employees of these firms do not seem to have a strong interest in workplace programs. Hence, all cases that illustrate a positive

---

[146] Managers of Fe and V confirm this also for their firms.
[147] Ibid. This is confirmed by the Executive Director of NAACAM; see interview with the Executive Director of NAACAM, September 29, 2008, Johannesburg.
[148] Interview with the Director of V, October 1, 2008, Rosslyn.

relationship between asset specificity and HIV/AIDS workplace programs are cases of "employer-centered" mechanisms. While these assertions alone allow us to reject the "employee-centered" explanation for the effects of asset specificity in the cases analyzed in this chapter, this study will now turn to the analysis of program design (Implication 2) and interpretative frames (Implication 3) to illustrate the theorized "employer-centered" causal mechanism of asset specificity further.

(2) Considering institutional design (Implication 2), the four positive firm cases Sä, Sh, FE, and Crossley Carpets have the policy implied rather than explicated. Hence, the design of these programs is hardly institutionalized at all, even though they exist on a profound level in the practices of the firms. This finding is in line with the "employer-centered" mechanisms. At the same time it clearly indicates the absence of employee interests and power in the processes leading to the policies. If the policies were the result of employee demands, they would be highly institutionalized in order to guarantee that management did not undermine effective implementation.[149] Hence, the observable implications these have with respect to the institutional design of the HIV/AIDS programs of the four firms is evidence contradicting the "employee-centered" explanation. They are at the same time pointing to the validity of the employer centered explanation.

(3) With respect to the interpretative frames used by managers and union representatives to make sense of workplace programs, the findings are additional support or the "employer-centered" explanation. Managers of the positive cases Sä, Sh, FE, and Crossley Carpets interpret the extensive efforts these firms make to fight the disease as a form of risk mitigation in relation to the firms' skills-dependent business models. The Human Resources Director of Crossley Carpets, as mentioned above, pointed out that the skills required are unique to the job as they use specialized machines and are thus not attainable on the labor market. Owing to the high prevalence rate of HIV/AIDS, the firm will lose some of their specialized and experienced employees: "The HIV/AIDS program is one way of trying to

---

[149] Wage agreements and agreements on paid leave are examples in which employees have negotiated their interests for high wages with the employer side in the context of intra-firm and sector-wide bargaining. They are usually highly formalized in a concise and obligatory contract between employers and employees.

retain these skills."[150] This interpretation of events illustrates the rationale of management for creating strong HIV/AIDS workplace programs. Managers of Sä, Sh, and FE have made similar statements. Explaining why the precision engineering firm FE has, despite being a rather small firm, a relatively comprehensive workplace program: "it all started after the very first black tool maker we qualified, unfortunately, died of AIDS. We were so proud of him: he was chosen for an exchange program with India for talented engineers by a foundation. We trained him for three years. Then he died."[151] Since the firm confronts a "huge skill shortage" and therefore has to train its own engineers in order to remain productive, she maintains that she does everything she can to make medical care available for employees who have contracted HIV in order to protect her firm against the threat of HIV/AIDS. Similarly, a representative of Sh explains: "you could take an employee out of General Motors and put him into Volkswagen. He would transfer his skills. We in the glass industry are different. We are unique in South Africa as we do not have any competition. This uniqueness makes AIDS a huge problem, and we try to make it less severe and so always look for opportunities to offer [HIV/AIDS related medical] services."[152]

While these examples are clearly in line with the "employer-centered" explanation of the relation between asset specificity and HIV/AIDS programs, they do not support the "employee-centered" one. With the exception of the interviews held with managers and employee representatives of DBA, none of the interviewed representatives of the firms or unions mentioned interpretative frames that would point to the "employee-centered" explanation.

The employee representatives of DBA, however, made clear that they consider it the achievement of SACTWU that the firm has a workplace program. However, the case illustrates low levels of asset specificity and is a negative case of workplace programs in the context of this study. Hence, this exception does in no way disconfirm the

[150] Interview with the Director of Human Resources of Crossley Carpets, September 28, 2007, Durban.
[151] Interview with the Human Resources Manager of FE, September 23, 2008, East London.
[152] Interview with the Product Engineering and Corporate Quality Assurance Manager of Sh, September 22, 2008, Port Elizabeth.

theorized mechanism of asset specificity in this book, which is "employer-centered". Table 4.7 summarizes the findings.

Conclusion

This chapter showed that:

- everything else being equal, asset-specific investments in employee skills cause HIV/AIDS workplace programs;
- internal driver 1 is able to solve important empirical puzzles of labor-related corporate social responsibility in different contexts, such as the textile and car industries, and on different levels of intensity of asset specificity;
- the causal processes unleashed by asset specificity consist of management creating HIV/AIDS workplace programs in order to protect previous investments in rare employee skills – as theorized in Chapter 2.

What are the wider implications of these findings? First, asset-specific investments in employee skills are an important explanation for the diffusion of labor standards through international trade. On the firm level, they explain why some businesses drive "race to the bottom" dynamics while others push to spread global standards. The findings suggest an additional – complementary – explanation for trade-based diffusion: trade relations that involve a skills gap between highly regulating countries and weakly regulating ones so that skills have to be created in-house by businesses in weakly regulating countries will be associated with the emergence of labor standards in the weakly regulating country.

Second, the process tracing analysis in this chapter allows us to draw conclusions with respect to the mechanisms that ultimately bring about social policies. We can identify all in all three such processes, two of which are related to asset specificity. Asset specificity may motivate and empower employees to push for social policies (Iversen 2005; Iversen and Soskice 2001, 2009); asset specificity may, alternatively, motivate managers to create such policies to protect their investments (Hall and Soskice 2001, and the approach in this study). Finally, employees may press successfully for social policies for reasons entirely unrelated to asset specificity (Esping-Anderson 1990; Korpi 2006) – as in the cases in which the textile union SACTWU provided HIV/AIDS-related services,

Table 4.7 *Process tracing: summary of the findings*

	Mechanism	Managerial dilemmas cause HIV/AIDS programs		
		Observable implications		
		(1) Sequence of events	(2) Institutional design	(3) Interpretation of events
Employer-centered	Managerial dilemma: management mitigates risks associated with asset-specific investments through HIV/AIDS programs	Confirming evidence: Sä, Sh, Crossley Carpets, FE, AL, V, Fe Does not allow for inference: CS Disconfirming evidence: none (DBA is negative case of asset specificity and workplace programs and does therefore not conflict with the "employer-centered" explanation)	Confirming evidence: Sä, Sh, Crossley Carpets, FE Does not allow for inference: CS, AL, V, Fe, DBA Disconfirming evidence: none	Confirming evidence: Sä, Sh, Crossley Carpets, FE Does not allow for inference: CS, AL, V, Fe, DBA Disconfirming evidence: none
Employee-centered	Employees have a strong bargaining position vis-à-vis management and can therefore push for HIV/AIDS programs	Confirming evidence: none (DBA is a negative case and thus does not support "employee-centered" explanation) Does not allow for inference: CS Disconfirming evidence: Sä, Sh, Crossley Carpets, FE, AL, V, Fe	Confirming evidence: none Does not allow for inference: CS, AL, V, Fe, DBA Disconfirming evidence: Sä, Sh, Crossley Carpets, FE	Confirming evidence: none Does not allow for inference: CS, AL, V, Fe, DBA Disconfirming evidence: Sä, Sh, Crossley Carpets, FE

despite the very low level of asset specificity of the workers the union represents (see analysis above).

Overall, the findings in this chapter provide clear evidence for the second mechanism: it is managers who drive HIV/AIDS workplace programs. This is a remarkable finding. In light of the literature on welfare state development, which points to the importance of workers' interests and power resources, it may even seem ahistorical (Esping-Anderson 1990; Korpi 2006). However, is it really? An area of limited statehood such as South Africa is, in a way, a natural experiment in welfare state development. Hence, this finding should not be too easily discarded. This assertion gains additional support from research that shows that asset specificity motivates firms to contribute to the fight against the disease in South Africa also beyond workplace programs on a general societal level and even approach government to lobby for a better service provision (Börzel and Thauer 2013; Thauer 2013a and 2013b; von Soest and Weinel 2006). At the same time, however, these conclusions have also to be treated with caution: in other industry sectors and in issue areas less stigmatized than HIV/AIDS in South Africa, the other two mechanisms may as well be important – or we find, when asset specificity and worker empowerment are both absent, no mechanism for social policies at all.

This study will now turn to an assessment of asset-specific investments in production technology (internal drivers 2 and 3), which motivate firms for environmental policies. Are internal drivers as important for environmental policies as they are for labor-related corporate social responsibility?

5 | *Internal drivers 2 and 3: the* technological specialization *and* foreign direct investment dilemmas

While the old triad Europe, the US, and Japan is facing a time of economic stagnation, emerging markets such as Brazil, Russia, India, China, and South Africa (the BRICS; Armijo 2007) have become the main engine of growth for the international car industry.[1] It is in the context of this development that the automotive industry has invested substantially in South Africa over the past one and a half decades (see Chapter 3). This investment grants the industry access to the South African growth market; it also provides car firms with export opportunities to the US under the African Growth and Opportunity Act (AGOA) and to Europe under similar preferential trade agreements. The investments that allow car firms to profit from these benefits are substantial and long-term. The case of the German originating multinational car company M is illustrative in this respect.[2] The firm decided in 2006 to produce parts of its new entry-level model in South Africa. For this task, it had to construct a whole new factory in East London in the Eastern Cape province of South Africa, which took about one and a half years. It then had to set up and implement production processes, which required another six months of preparation before the first models "made in South Africa" were sold. After that, the factory produced and sold cars for two years until the investment in South Africa actually began to pay off for M in Germany.

---

[1] Thauer 2013b; BBC News, "Globalizing the Car Industry" (by Steve Schifferes: http://news.bbc.co.uk/2/hi/business/6346325.stm, January 22, 2012). Growth rates of 20–25% (between 2004 and 2011) make South Africa one of the fastest growing car markets worldwide (see NAAMSA 2011).

[2] Interview with the Manager: Quality Manager and Integrated Management System of M South Africa, September 23, 2008, East London.

The Director of Public and International Affairs of another German multinational car company explained upon being asked about the comparative cost advantages of producing in South Africa that "the industry is in general less over-regulated than in Germany. Also, energy, water, and waste management costs are significantly lower."[3] However, in light of the firm's long-term business model "there is absolutely no way that we organize production in the country based on the assumption that the costs for using these resources [energy, waste disposal, water etc.] are negligible. We cannot know how the situation in South Africa will be in the future. We need to be prepared for all kinds of scenarios. We therefore apply exactly the same [environmental] standards in South Africa as we do in our mother plant in Munich."[4]

Apart from uncertainty about the development of basic cost factors, another reason for the adoption of high environmental standards in the event of long-term investments concerns *intra-organizational* management. A top production manager of M in Germany, for example, says, "of course, we do not just transfer €200 million–€300 million to South Africa and then wait two and a half years to see what kind of cars roll out of the factory."[5] Such investment decisions are accompanied by extensive supervisory measures. M immediately dispatched around thirty production and environmental engineers from the mother plant in Stuttgart to the plant in South Africa once it had made the decision to produce parts of its entry-level model in the country. Upon arrival, the engineers took control of the factory, reimplemented production processes, and continued supervising the investment process over the whole period of two and a half years. The engineer from Germany leading this supervision underlined that before any long-term investments can be carried out it has to be made sure that the "house is in order" and that the "right processes are in place when production starts."[6] He specifies that global headquarters in Stuttgart, Germany, requires the production plant in East London, South Africa, to implement "precisely the same

[3] Interview with the Director of Corporate and International Affairs Management of B, August 2, 2007, Munich. Statements were made in German: translation by author.

[4] Ibid.

[5] Interview with the Production Quality and Integrated Management System Manager of M, September 23, 2008, East London.

[6] Interview with the Manager: Quality Manager and Integrated Management System of M South Africa, September 23, 2008, East London.

standards and processes that we have in our plants in Germany."[7] This allows management in Stuttgart to know, control and verify the procedures at the branch in South Africa.

These examples illustrate the *technological specialization* and *foreign direct investment dilemmas*: investments in production facilities with long pay-off periods are for the aforementioned multinational car companies potentially beneficial. At the same time, they create uncertainties as concerns the socio-political development of the investment environment and raise issues of managerial control thus bearing significant risks. Environmental (process) standards help managers confronting such dilemmas to reduce these uncertainties and regain managerial control, and thus to mitigate the risks inherent in asset-specific investments. Environmental standards are therefore part of the economic organization that emerges when investments are asset-specific.

This argument for internal drivers of environmental standards allows us to address important empirical puzzles of corporate social responsibility and the spread of global standards. We know from studies inspired by diffusion theory (DiMaggio and Powell 1991; Shipan and Volden 2008; Simmons *et al.* 2006) that business standards may diffuse through multinational corporations from highly regulating "home" to weakly regulating "host" countries with foreign direct investment.[8] The international environmental management system ISO 14001, for example, has proliferated this way (Prakash and Potoski 2006, 2007). These studies point to an international version of the "California effect" (Vogel 1995; see Chapter 4), i.e. to a conversion of standards on a high level or even a regulatory "race to the top" (Börzel and Thauer 2013). However, we also know that firms investing in overseas markets often do so to profit from "pollution havens" and generally lax standards (Collingsworth *et al.* 1994; Mani and Wheeler 1998; Xing and Kohlstadt 2002). In such cases, foreign direct investment can have the opposite effect, forcing states into a regulatory "race to the bottom" – competitive downsizing of regulation or regulatory "freeze" (Madsen 2009: 1298) for comparative cost advantages (Bohle 2008; Chan 2003; Singh and Zammit 2004).

---

[7] Ibid.

[8] Blanton and Blanton 2007; Garcia-Johnson 2000; Greenhill *et al.* 2010; Börzel *et al.* 2011; Mihalache-O'keef and Li 2011; Prakash and Potoski 2007; Sethi and Elango 1999; Skjaerseth and Skodvin 2003; van Tulder and Kolk 2001; Zeng and Eastin 2007.

The literature is still at an early stage in terms of defining the relationship between foreign direct investment and regulatory standards in this respect. Some authors make the case for the importance of distinguishing between different categories and types of foreign direct investment (Alfaro 2003; Aykut and Salek 2007; Chakraborty and Nunnekamp 2008). Sector characteristics, for example, may help us to understand better the relationship between foreign direct investment and high standards (Blanton and Blanton 2009; Mihalache-O'keef and Li 2011) and why, for example, the textile industry is associated with "race to the bottom" dynamics, while the auto industry is thought to be driving standards up (Börzel and Thauer 2013; Lorentzen 2006).

These specifications have enhanced our understanding of the relationship between environmental standards and economic globalization. However, they are mainly based on external driver-oriented explanatory models. As in the case of labor standards, these models presume non-governmental organization (NGO) and consumer induced California effects (see Chapter 4). As in Chapter 4, I argue here that this focus on external drivers does not give us the full picture of the relationship between firm behavior and voluntary standards under conditions of economic globalization. Taking the example of ten cases of multinational car companies in South Africa, this chapter shows, first, that important empirical puzzles are yet to be solved in relation to the phenomenon of environmental standard diffusion. Second, it specifies the argument on the diffusion of business standards further in order to resolve some of these puzzles. The chapter argues that it is not only important where foreign direct investments come from in terms of country of origin and industry sector (as argued in literature, see above), but also of what quality it is: *intra*-firm asset-specific (foreign direct) investments cause the spread of global standards. Third, the chapter traces the *intra*-organizational processes and rationales of standard diffusion. This approach to diffusion allows us to address the following questions: which attributes of foreign direct investment cause standard diffusion, and why? Under which conditions will a cross-country diffusion of standards take place within a firm? Which firms in an industry sector through which standards diffuse will be more or less affected at distinct points in time? What is the causal mechanism that links foreign direct investment to high standards?

Finally, this chapter then looks beyond the multinational car industry at two cases from the South African textile industry in order to establish the *technological specialization dilemma* as a general explanation for voluntary environmental standards of firms – irrespective of the firm's country of origin and whether it is based on foreign direct investment or not.

The *foreign direct investment dilemma*: multinational car companies in South Africa

The ten cases of South African branches of multinational car companies are chosen from among the same large multinational firms that also dominate the global car market: BMW, Ford, General Motors, Mercedes, Nissan, Toyota, and VW. The South African branches of these seven firms are generally very similar to each other (see Chapter 3). They are instances of foreign direct investment, making South Africa their host country while they originate from home countries (the US, Germany, and Japan) that tightly regulate the industry with respect to environmental standards. The seven firms also resemble each other in terms of size, as each of them generates revenues worth $50 billion to $200 billion a year. In terms of finances, these companies' budgets are more extensive than those of some African states. The seven branches also have in common the fact that they operate production sites that are technologically highly advanced and complex in the context of South Africa; and that they are export-oriented: most of the production output is sold abroad. However, while highly similar in such respects, the firms show some remarkable differences concerning the level of environmental standards they operate on.

Some firms run operations in their host country South Africa on the basis of the same high environmental standards they have at home. B, for example, a German high-end car manufacturer, has fully implemented the German environmental law with regard to water usage, energy consumption, waste management, and emissions in South Africa. This is remarkable as the German standards are much stricter than required by South African law. M of South Africa, also a high-end market car producer from Germany, is another case in point. This firm has also implemented German environmental standards in its South African production site. However, while B had already transferred the high standards from home to its operations abroad in the late 1990s, M did not do so until recently. The firm upgraded the plant in East London in the Eastern Cape only in 2006/07. Prior to this, production in South Africa was disproportionately energy and water intensive compared to a German production site. In addition, it did not have a comprehensive waste management system, nor would it control emissions and effluents released into the environment. Hence, while the firm has environmental policies in place today, it did not before. What explains M's time lag? Why did B feel the urge to operate on the highest attainable standards in South Africa already in the 1990s, while M was still making use of the lax environmental laws in South Africa at the time?

While M and B have now implemented very high environmental standards, other firms such as F – a US American car manufacturer – operate on low environmental standards to this day. A production manager of F, for example, says that it takes much more energy to make a car in the Sylverton plant in Gauteng than in a comparable plant in the US or in Europe.[9] In addition, F's plant in South Africa does not manage its waste output effectively, does not account for its emissions, and makes excessive use of water during the production process. Only recently has F started to improve the practices in its plant. Why is it that some firms such as M and B produce in a resource-efficient way based on high environmental standards, while F and other firms make cars in a comparably resource-intensive way?

To systematically compare these differences, the analysis takes into account five firms producing in South Africa: the German manufacturers of high-end cars M and B; US mass producer F; V, a German mass producer; and N, a Japanese producer of mass-market cars.[10] The comparative analyses include a cross-sectional and a longitudinal perspective. In the longitudinal perspective, the analysis subdivides the cases according to points in time at which the level of implemented standards and practices change. The five firms provide ten cases in total. I focus, on the one hand, on procedural standards such as management systems – an example is ISO 14001 – and, on the other hand, on substantive standards that specify reduction targets or the maximum of resources that can be used over a certain period of time.

Figure 5.1 illustrates levels of environmental policies in the South African automotive industry in comparative perspective across firms and over time. The trend in the industry is towards higher standards

---

[9] Interview with the Quality and Environmental Systems Engineer of F South Africa, September 30, 2008, Sylverton.

[10] Unfortunately, two of the seven multinational car companies with plants in South Africa were not willing to contribute to this study.

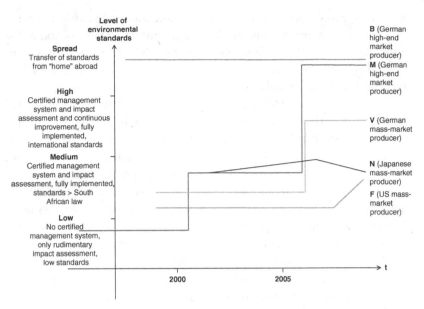

Figure 5.1 Environmental standards in the South African automotive industry over time

(with the exception of N). This is certainly in line with arguments about the diffusion of standards through multinational corporations. However, the illustration also reveals that there are important questions which are yet unanswered: what accounts for the striking differences in environmental policies in the South African car industry across cases and over time? Under which conditions will a cross-country diffusion of standards take place within a firm, and what motivates this? Which multinational firms in a given industry sector will be more or less affected by diffusion dynamics at distinct points in time?

In search for an explanation: a literature review

The literature suggests a number of factors and drivers pushing firms to adopt high standards voluntarily. Can any of these explain the different environmental policies among South African carmakers? An important factor for environmental standards is the institutional context, and an important feature of this institutional context, according to the literature on governance in areas of consolidated statehood (Halfteck 2008; Héritier and Lehmkuhl 2008; Scharpf 1997), is the regulatory threat by state agencies (the "shadow of hierarchy," see Chapter 4). However, the shadow of hierarchy cannot explain the variation illustrated above (Figure 5.1).

In the policy field of the environment South Africa has had fairly well developed legal standards on an abstract, national level ever since the mid-1990s. However, details pertaining to the behavior of firms are often not specified on a local level (Hönke *et al.* 2008; Lund-Thomsen 2005). Overlapping responsibilities of several government departments lead to regulatory confusion, contradictory requirements, and implementation gaps. Most importantly, the enforcement of regulations is in many cases deficient since local state agencies lack the capacity to effectively monitor and sanction corporate malpractice. Hence, the shadow of hierarchy is absent in our cases on account of limited statehood in South Africa in the field of the environment. The cases confirm this: for example, the South African plants of the German manufacturer of high-end cars B, of the US car company F, and of the automotive firm N from Japan, are located in the same area close to Pretoria in Gauteng. According to the firms' representatives, one and the same environmental agency in Johannesburg is responsible for regulating this area in theory, although alas it does not do so in practice. Regulatory pressure is thus a constant (constantly absent, that is) among the three firms.[11] Nonetheless, they reveal stark differences in the level of environmental policies on which they operate (see Figure 5.1).

While a South African "shadow of hierarchy" is thus excluded as a potential explanation, we can also exclude extraterritorial regulation and regulatory threats as explanations for the firms' different levels of environmental standards. In some industries, such as mining, the home market countries of multinational corporations can effectively impose regulation on offshore business operations (Ladwig and Rudolf 2011; Hönke and Kranz 2013; Szablowski 2007). However, the standards of concern here are not part of any such extraterritorial regulatory approaches. Standards regulating the process of production ("process standards") – on which this chapter focuses exclusively – cannot be regulated extraterritorially under the World Trade Organization (WTO)/General Agreement on Tariffs and Trade (GATT) regime.

---

[11] Interview with the General Manager Corporate Planning of B South Africa, February 20, 2007, Midrand.

However, home market regulations can also influence firm behavior in other ways than through an external "shadow of hierarchy." Studies show that firms often transfer the regulatory standards from their home markets to host countries, as this allows them to apply the same organizational routines and standard operating procedures in different contexts.[12] Hence, the differences among the ten cases may simply reflect the different levels of environmental regulation in the home countries of the five firms. Germany, for example, has in many ways developed stricter environmental regulations in the past years than the US.[13] Do differences in the strictness of regulation in the home markets of the five firms thus explain their different levels of environmental standards over time? They do not: the German originating firms account for much of the overall variation illustrated in Figure 5.1. They have, however, all been exposed to the same home country regulation over the past years. In addition, only two of the five companies – M and B – decided to implement the same high standards in South Africa that they have in their home market. The other three firms – German originating V, American F, and Japanese N – have not made any such decision as they still operate on South African and international voluntary standards. This means that they still operate on levels way below their home country regulations, and have thus not (yet) reached a level of standards on which the differences in the strictness of home market regulation may become important.[14]

While the strictness of home market regulations is thus excluded as a potential explanation, another important argument for environmental policies pertains to reputational concerns. Campaigns and disclosures organized by NGOs are a factor in this respect (Hendry 2006; Schepers 2006; Spar and La Mure 2003). Generally, the five large multinational

---

[12] Blanton and Blanton 2007; Garcia-Johnson 2000; Greenhill *et al.* 2010; Börzel *et al.* 2011; Mihalache-O'keef and Li 2011; Prakash and Potoski 2007; Sethi and Elango 1999; Skjaerseth and Skodvin 2003; van Tulder and Kolk 2001; Zeng and Eastin 2007.

[13] See Manheim 2009; however, this does not automatically mean that the level of achievements in environmental pollution reduction is higher in Europe than in the US, see Freeman and Kolstad 2007; Harrington *et al.* 2004.

[14] Note that all three home markets' environmental regulations are significantly stricter than South Africa's (Börzel and Thauer 2013). Hence, we can also exclude the possibility that in the cases of the American and Japanese firms the host market regulation of South Africa exceeds the home market regulation.

car firms featured in the analysis above are under pressure from NGOs, especially for their cars' emissions levels. They are not usually targeted for their production processes. This is confirmed by managers of the five firms, who say they do not feel under attack from NGOs regarding production processes.[15] Furthermore, an NGO representative says, "regarding their production processes, I fully trust them. In this respect, they are way above anything in South Africa. So we do not target them in this area. We only have problems with their products."[16] Hence it is not NGO pressure that motivates car companies to adopt environmental standards; this factor does not explain the observed variation between the ten firm cases.

More reputational concerns derive from the market orientation of firms and corresponding consumer expectations and pressure (Héritier *et al.* 2009; Smith 2008; Spar and La Mure 2003). Whereas the German producers B and M are high-end market firms, Japanese N, German V, and American F target the mass market. However, this difference in market orientation cannot explain the asserted variation either. The high-end market firm M for a long time operated on environmental standards that were on a similar level to those of the mass-market producers V and F – and even below those of the mass-market firm N. Differences in the target market of the firms cannot explain either why the high-end market firm M in 2006/7 began to upgrade its operations with respect to environmental standards, or why the mass-market manufacturer N's environmental policy declined recently.

Other potential drivers for firms to engage in environmental concerns are governance institutions and their institutional design. Institutionalized cooperation can be established among firms in an industry sector or

[15] Interview with the Manager: Quality Management and Integrated Management System of M South Africa, September 23, 2008, East London; with the Senior Manager Corporate Social Responsibility of M Germany, August 6, 2007 (phone); with the Project Leader VPS and SHE Representative, and the General Manager, Corporate Planning of B South Africa, February 20, 2007, Midrand; with the Corporate and Intergovernmental Affairs Manager, the Department Manager Corporate Messages, the Manager of Group Publications, and the Manager of Sustainability and Corporate and Intergovernmental Affairs of B Germany, August 2, 2007, Munich.

[16] Interview with the Trade and Investment Advisor and Automotive Sector Specialist of the World Wide Fund for Nature (WWF) South Africa, September 29, 2008, Johannesburg.

between firms and government and/or NGOs. For example, business associations can facilitate self-regulation (Ronit and Schneider 2000). "Green clubs" (Prakash and Potoşki 2006) such as ISO 14001, public–private parnerships, and other "civil regulation" (Vogel 2010) can provide firms with incentives to adopt environmental standards. However, these cannot account for the asserted variation either. The five firms featured in Figure 5.1 resemble each other very much with respect to their membership and participation in such governance institutions. They are members of the same associations in South Africa, and are to the same extent exposed to the diffusion of ISO 14001 internationally. They usually do not cooperate with state agencies in the context of public–private partnership in terms of their processes of production. Therefore, this explanation cannot account for the finding of differential environmental policies in the South African car industry either. What, then, is the explanation?

Asset specificity: *driving the transfer of environmental standards?*

I shall argue in the following that *intra*-organizational asset-specific investments account for the differences among the firms in their decision to diffuse high environmental standards from highly regulating home to weakly regulating host country operations. Analogous to the procedure in Chapter 4, the analysis will now conduct controlled pair-wise comparisons to argue for the importance of asset-specific investments for the emergence and spread of environmental standards in a stringent way. The analysis will therefore divide the ten firm cases into two groups, analyzing the four cases pertaining to the high-end market firms M and B first, before turning to the six cases relating to the mass-market producers V, N, and F. This procedure allows the analysis to conduct the assessment in a way consistent with the *ceteris paribus* clause: comparisons that neutralize potential other explanations (such as the market orientation of firms) so as to assess the isolated effects of *intra*-organizational investments in production technology. While this analysis assesses the plausibility, applicability, and validity of the *foreign direct investment dilemma* it also allows us to infer from the results the validity of the *technological specialization dilemma*: the former is a specific instance of the latter; hence the findings pertain to both in the same way.

Measuring internal drivers 2 and 3: the *foreign direct investment* and *technological specialization dilemmas*

How can we gauge asset specificity in terms of investments with long pay-off periods? The *technological specialization dilemma* refers to the commitment that is made by management to support the task delegated to a subunit to start up and run production. Hence, it refers to asset-specific investments in the production unit. The *asset*-dimension refers to the relative quantity of resources delegated to the production unit to set up and run production.[17] The *specificity* dimension entails a commitment, i.e. the period before envisioned return of investment, because throughout that period management cannot redirect resources to support another task or to build up production capacities somewhere else. To measure these dimensions, *indicator 1* relates the amount of annual investments in production facilities, machines, and technology to the total annual turnover of a firm or the total global investment volume. The higher the proportion of the resource allocation, the higher the score on this indicator.

Indicator 2 refers to the envisioned duration before return of investment. The more resources are dedicated and the longer the commitment of resources, the higher the degree of "production specific assets," and vice versa. The absence ("zero" score) in any of the two dimensions indicates the absence of asset-specific allocation of resources and, hence, the absence of a managerial dilemma. If *indicator 1* scores low, this means that only few resources are allocated to support the start up of a new production facility. Consequently, management is not dependent on the production unit and the intra-organizational mode of social coordination is not transformed. Wherever the measurement of *indicator 2* scores low, this implies that the resources can easily be redirected to support the creation of production capacities somewhere else. Therefore, resource allocation in this case would not be asset-specific. Asset-specific allocation of resources in production instead requires positive scores in both dimensions. The more resources are allocated to support the creation of production facilities and the longer the period in which these resources cannot be transferred due to a long commitment, the higher the degree of asset specificity and the more severe the managerial dilemma the case illustrates, and vice versa (Table 5.1).

---

[17] Relative as measured in proportion to the size of the firm or its overall investment volume.

Table 5.1 *Indicators for the* technological specialization dilemma

Concept: asset specificity	Indicators	Assessment	
Dimension 1: asset creation Resources allocated to subunit to start up and run production	**Indicator 1:** amount of annual investment in production facilities, machines, and technology as a proportion of annual turnover	**High vs. low**	High
Dimension 2: specificity Duration of commitment of resources	**Indicator 2:** period before envisioned return of investment	Long vs. short	Low

As a specific instance of the *technological specialization dilemma*, the *foreign direct investment dilemma* is assessed accordingly. It assumes, however, a cross-border element and the existence of a gap between regulatory contexts. The asset-specific investments in the production unit originate from a highly regulating home country and a host country marked by weak regulation (Table 5.2).

The *foreign direct investment dilemma*: high-end market multinational car companies (cases 1–4)

The first set of comparative analyses features the two South African branches of the high-end market original equipment manufacturers (OEM) M and B originating in Germany. As South Africa is a weakly regulating country with respect to environmental regulation, whereas Germany is a strongly regulating country, the cases exemplify the creation of the *technological specialization dilemma* on account of foreign direct investments. The analysis of the two firms is therefore able to draw conclusions on the validity of internal drivers for corporate social responsibility with respect to two dilemmas: the *technological specialization dilemma* and the *foreign direct investment dilemma*.

The first branch, M, entered the South African market in 1958, but remained largely independent from M Germany during apartheid. In

Table 5.2 *Indicators for the* foreign direct investment dilemma

Concepts: asset specificity and FDI	Indicators	Assessment	
Asset specificity	**Dimension 1: asset creation** Resources allocated to subunit to start up and run production	**Indicator 1:** amount of annual investment in production facilities, machines, and technology as a proportion of annual turnover	**High vs. low**	High ⎫
	Dimension 2: specificity Duration of commitment of resources	**Indicator 2:** period before envisioned return of investment	Long vs. short	Low ⎬
Foreign direct investment (FDI)	**Assumption 1:** investment originates from highly regulating "home" country	**Indicator 1:** level of enforced regulation in "home" country	**High vs. low**	⎫ FDI
	Assumption 2: investment in branch located in weakly regulating "host" country	**Indicator 2:** level of enforced regulation in "host" country	**High vs. low**	⎭

1984, however, the global headquarters of M decided to take control of its South African operations. In consequence, M Germany bought 50.1 percent of the shares of the South African operations. Ownership augmented to 76.6 percent in 1992 and to 100 percent in 1998. Turnover in 2000 was ZAR8.46 billion. In 2007 the branch with local headquarters in East London had a turnover of ZAR37 billion and about 3,800 employees.[18] The second firm, B, entered the South African market in the early 1970s by buying shares from Praetor Monteerders, a Pretoria-based local car factory.[19] B gained full owner-ship of this factory in 1975, thereby founding the first production site for vehicles of B outside of Germany. Unlike other OEMs such as General Motors or Ford, that had to disinvest from the country as a consequence of the public protests against their collaboration with the racist regime, B remained fully active in South Africa during apartheid times. Today, B has 3,400 employees who, like the employees of M, produce expensive, high-end cars for the South African market. Most of the South African-produced cars by B and M, however, are exported to the Asia-Pacific region and the US.

The analysis adopts a longitudinal and a cross-case comparative per-spective. In the longitudinal perspective, M makes up for three cases: case 1 is M at t1 during the late 1990s (1995–1999/2000), case 2 is the firm at t2 between 2000 and 2005/06, and case 3 at t3 from 2006 onwards. In total, the analysis features four cases: case 1 (M t1) represents a rather weak managerial dilemma. Case 2 (M t2) exemplifies medium levels of asset specificity. Case 3 (M t3) illustrates a rapid increase of non-transferable investments in the production unit, on account of which the *foreign direct investment dilemma* emerges as important.

---

[18] Interview with the Manager: Quality Management and Integrated Management System of M South Africa, September 23, 2008, East London; with the Senior Manager Corporate Social Responsibility of M Germany, August 6, 2007 (phone); additional information drawn from the website of M (February 1, 2009).

[19] Interview with the Project Leader VPS and SHE Representative, and the General Manager, Corporate Planning of B South Africa, February 20, 2007, Midrand; with the Corporate and Intergovernmental Affairs Manager, the Department Manager Corporate Messages, the Manager of Group Publications, and the Manager of Sustainability and Corporate and Intergovernmental Affairs of B Germany, August 2, 2007, Munich; additional information drawn from the website of B South Africa (February 1, 2009).

Case 4 deals with B, a case defined by high levels of asset-specific investments throughout t1, t2, and t3, that is, a constantly severe *foreign direct investment dilemma*-situation. This fourth case (that is, B t1–t3) is the control case for the longitudinal analysis of M. The expected greater engagement in environmental policies of M between t2 and t3 could be the result of a general historical trend in the industry, as "diffusion theory" (see Prakash and Potoski 2006, 2007; Simmons *et al.* 2006) would suggest – and turn out not to be the outcome of higher degrees of asset specificity.[20] However, if B's environmental policy is constant throughout t2 and t3, this alternative explanation can be dismissed. The analysis will focus on the three cases of M first, and then turn to case 4, which features B.

Case 1: M t1

M at t1 illustrates no particular degree of asset specificity as concerns the investments made in the South African branch. During the 1990s the firm assembled the full global product range of M for the South African consumer market in "completely knocked down" (CKD) mode – from Freightliner Trucks to passenger cars.[21] "CKD-mode" denotes a process according to which new cars made in Germany are disassembled and shipped to South Africa only to be reassembled again in M's East London plant in order to be sold there.[22] The assembly line required some ongoing investments of up to $10 million per year, which equals about 0.5 percent of the total annual investment volume of M globally

[20] For example, ISO 14001 certification for environmental management systems begins in the late 1990s. In a "first wave" of certifications, the main factories of the OEM implemented the standard. Afterwards, ISO 14001 was also diffusing down the supply chain and certification numbers have been growing worldwide ever since.

[21] Interview with the Manager: Quality Management and Integrated Management System of M South Africa, September 23, 2008, East London.

[22] "CKD-mode" production is a common practice of globally operating car companies. The reasons for the dis- and reassembly are threefold: first, the South African market is not yet fully liberalized. Import restrictions and local content requirements force OEM to relocate some value added processes (i.e. the assembly) to the country, on the one hand, and to add some local content (usually of minor importance) to the vehicle, on the other. Second, there are a number of countries that grant Africa preferential access to their markets. To have an African production base allows auto firms to enter these markets on lower duties. Third, the global car sales market is restricted by import and export quotas. A CKD site in South Africa enables a German firm, for example, to export more to Asia by using South Africa's export quotas in addition to the German ones.

at that time.[23] In comparative perspective, these investments are on a smaller scale than at t2 and t3 (see below). Most importantly, however, the duration before these investments were supposed to pay off was rather short during that time.[24] They led to immediate increases in assembly capacity, which directly translated into bigger sales capacities. Hence, they generated higher returns at once. These investments were therefore not very asset-specific; the dependence of M Germany on the South African branch was accordingly low. An additional indication for this assertion is that production depth, which refers to the added value of production processes to the end product, was flat (about 4–5 percent value added) during that time. Moreover, the proportion of cars sold in South Africa accounted for a negligible proportion of the total global sales of M (less than 0.5 percent).[25]

Over time, however, the South African branch emerged as an increasingly important export hub for the mother company's headquarters. In the context of this development, the operation in South Africa was developed in two major steps from a mere assembly plant into a full production site with significant production depth. For these upgrades, the German headquarters had to make significant investments into its South African production branch with long periods before returns were expected. So the level of asset specificity increased.

Case 2: M t2
In 2000 M of South Africa secured a contract with the global headquarters in Germany over the assembly of the new entry-level model of M for the left-hand drive markets.[26] This contract demarcates case 2. The decision was made to upgrade the assembly plant of M in South Africa to a factory with production components for the required task. To this end, investments of about $30 million were made on average each year.[27] M usually invests between €1.5 billion and €2 billion per

---

[23] Measuring *Indicator 1*. For data see email questionnaire answered by the Quality and Integrated Systems Management of M South Africa.

[24] Hence, M t1 scores low on *Indicator 2*.

[25] Email questionnaire answered by the Quality and Integrated Systems Management of M South Africa.

[26] Left-hand drive markets are, for example, South Africa, the UK, Australia, and Japan. Overview of the history of M in SA on the website of the company (February 4, 2009).

[27] Interview with the Manager: Quality Management and Integrated Management System of M South Africa, September 23, 2008, East London; email

annum in its production facilities worldwide.[28] Hence, the South African branch accounts for 1 to 1.5 percent of the total *intra*-organizational investment volume of M during t2. Thus, in the *intra*-organizational distribution of resources, the South African production-unit is still not a top priority during t2, but nonetheless slightly more important than during t1.

However, these investments had longer pay-off periods.[29] Most of the $30 million spent annually paid off within about one year.[30] Product cycles in the automotive industry are in general extremely long and often require firms to invest for up to seven years in the development and making of new models before the first units are sold. Calculated return of investment for generation models is about eight to nine years. In the light of these long investment periods, commitments with durations of less than one year do not seem too significant. An exception in this respect is, however, a larger investment in a new paint shop in 2002. Calculated return of this investment was two to three years. On account of this latter long-term commitment case 2 illustrates in total short to medium-long durations before calculated return of investment.

In summary, case 2 (M t2) is characterized by relatively low levels of investment made by the global headquarters in the South African branch and by short to medium-long pay-off times. Hence, the case illustrates the *foreign direct investment dilemma* on a rather low to medium level of intensity. However, when compared to t1, the case of M is at t2 marked by higher levels of asset specificity. Additional evidence for these assertions is that when compared to t1 the value added by the South African branch increased during t2 on account of the yearly investments to about 15 percent production depth.[31] At t2 M

questionnaire answered by the Quality and Integrated Systems Management of M South Africa.
[28] Annual Report of M, 2000.
[29] The analysis thus turns now to a measurement of *Indicator 2*.
[30] Interview with the Manager: Quality Management and Integrated Management System of M South Africa, September 23, 2008, East London; email questionnaire answered by the Quality and Integrated Systems Management of M South Africa; additional information drawn from website of M South Africa (February 3, 2009) and from press releases of M Germany. See also Lorentzen 2006; Lorentzen and Barnes 2004; Lorentzen *et al.* 2004.
[31] Interview with the Manager: Quality Management and Integrated Management System of M South Africa, September 23, 2008, East London; with the Corporate Health Manager of M South Africa, February 26, 2007, East London; email questionnaire answered by the Quality and Integrated Systems Management of

thus started off as a CKD-mode assembly plant, but developed subsequently into a hybrid consisting of an assembly plant and a manufacturing site during this period. Two million units of the third-generation of the entry-level model of M were sold between 2000 and 2006, out of which 250,000 originated from East London.[32] Hence, about 12.5 percent of this generation model was made in South Africa, which equals about 4 percent of the more than six million worldwide units sold of all models of M during that time.

Case 3: M t3

Case 3 (M t3) begins, on the one hand, with the expiration of the contract demarcating t2 in late 2006. On the other hand, t3 starts in 2005 with M of South Africa winning an internal tender for the production of the next generation of the entry-level model of M.[33] The new contract was settled with central management in Germany and triggered unprecedented investments for the South African branch. A new factory was built specifically for the production of the new generation model, with 250 robots (the old plant had only 6 robots) and a renewed paint shop (the ovens that dry and harden the paint were technically upgraded). Thereby, the branch was transformed from an assembly plant with some manufacturing components (t2) into an OEM site marked by high degrees of asset-specific investments (t3). To this end, headquarters invested about $300 million to $350 million in 2006/07 in the branch.[34] Global headquarters of M spent about €1.75 billion on average on "property, plant, and equipment" in 2006 and 2007.[35] Considering that the annual investment in the South African plant is about $100 million to $150 million, about 10 percent of the total global investments of M went into the South African production unit. Hence the proportion of total global investment that went into the South African plant is during t3 eight to ten times higher than at t2.[36]

M South Africa; additional information was drawn from website of M South Africa (February 3, 2009).

[32] Information drawn from press releases of M Germany and the website of M South Africa (February 4, 2009).

[33] Interview with the Manager: Quality Management and Integrated Management System of M South Africa, September 23, 2008, East London; additional information drawn from website of M South Africa (February 5, 2009).

[34] Ibid. The analysis thus considers now *Indicator 1* for M t3.

[35] Annual Report of M, 2007.   [36] Annual Reports of M, 2006 and 2007.

Similar differences between t2 and t3 exist as concerns the average period before envisioned return of investment.[37] Pay-off periods were between one year and three years during t2, while it is on average three to four years during t3. The $300 million to $350 million invested in the South African branch in 2006 and 2007 did not generate revenue in the first two years – during which the new factory was built and processes were implemented before production started. Only in late 2007 did production in the new facilities and, consequently, generation of revenues, begin. According to a production manager it took another 18 to 24 months from that point to reach return of investment.[38]

In conclusion, the amount of annual investments are much higher at t3 than at t2 and t1 and the period before the investments are envisioned to pay off is much longer in case 3 than in cases 2 and 1. Hence, the level of asset-specific investments is much higher in case 3 than in case 2 and 1.[39] Accordingly stronger is the *foreign direct investment dilemma*. Additional evidence confirms these assertions. According to a production manager of M South Africa, "one of the big changes that were brought about with the new contract for producing the new model of 2006 was the increase in production depth."[40] More precisely, the value added generated by the South African operations increased from an average 3–4 percent during t1 to about 15 percent during t2 and to 30–40 percent during t3.[41] According to the same manager, "the production depth is as high as you would find it in the parent plant in Germany. As a matter of fact, there are only three plants of M outside of Germany that qualify as true manufacturers today. One of them is in Tuscaloosa [Alabama, US]; then there is a Chinese plant that is being developed into a full manufacturing plant. The only other one I can think of is East London."[42] The number of units produced per day

---

[37] I thus turn now to an evaluation of *Indicator 2*.

[38] Interview with the Manager: Quality Management and Integrated Management System of M South Africa, September 23, 2008, East London.

[39] In fact, in case 3 M of South Africa scores the highest a foreign operation of a German-based car manufacturer can possibly score – and is therefore not only ahead of M t2 but also of most developing country operations of Western OEMs worldwide.

[40] Interview with the Manager: Quality Management and Integrated Management System of M South Africa, September 23, 2008, East London.

[41] Ibid.

[42] Ibid. M operates many more plants around the globe. However, most of them operate in CKD-mode, just as M of South Africa before and during t1.

increases to 160 as well; East London accounts for roughly one-fourth to one-third of the total worldwide production of the new entry-level model today – and for three times the production output during t2. Hence not only did production depth increase between t1, t2 and t3, but also South Africa's share of production worldwide. These additional facts support what the analysis of asset specificity revealed: the dependency of M's global operation on South Africa continuously increases between t1, t2, and t3.

Case 4: B (t1–t3)
B of South Africa, case 4, ranges from 1998 – that is, in the middle of the period t1 of M – to 2008. The case resembles case 3 (M t3) closely. As early as 1994 (hence, even before t1) the South African branch of B closed a contract with the German headquarters over the making of B's high-volume, entry-level model for the left-hand drive markets.[43] Production consisted, similarly to M t2, in a combination of assembly and manufacturing. In 1998/9 (that is, during M t1), however, the branch won a second bid for the making of B's next generation of the high-volume, entry-level model for the left-hand drive market. Analogous to M at t3 B was henceforth transformed into a full-fledged manufacturing plant in order to fulfill the stipulations of this renewed contract: "B South Africa has moved from operating as a CKD vehicle production plant, assembling vehicles with limited customization possibilities for the local market, to a world class plant capable of producing customized cars for discerning customers across the globe."[44] Finally, in 2004 B South Africa was entrusted again with the manufacturing of the renewed fifth generation of the entry-level model of B. Hence, in comparison with M, B's development is more than one generation ahead in terms of manufacturing the respective entry-level model in South Africa. This is why the firm displays constantly high levels of asset specificity throughout the period in which M transformed itself (that is, between mid M t1 throughout M t2 and M t3).

For example in 1998 and 1999 B invested €150 million to €200 million in a new production facility with robots and a new paint shop for the

---

[43] In addition to left-hand drive markets B of South Africa exports to the US, which grants Africa preferential market access through the African Growth and Opportunity Act (AGOA).
[44] Website of B South Africa (February 5, 2009).

making of the fourth generation of the entry-level model.[45] In 2004 and 2005, another \$300 million to \$350 million were invested to support the manufacturing of the fifth generation of the same model.[46] In between these major investments, about €30 million to €35 million were spent annually on plant Rosslyn for continuous upgrading. Considering that the annual turnover of B is half of M's at t2 (about €55 billion) the proportion of turnover invested is identical for B since 1998/9 and M at t3, but much higher for B than for M at t2.[47] The envisioned pay-off period is analogous to M t3 at about three to four years, whereby the first 18–24 months were dedicated to the construction of new production facilities.[48] After construction another 18–24 months of production were calculated before return of investment was achieved. Hence, the assertion for case 4 is that asset specificity is as high or even higher than in case 3 – and much higher than in cases 2 (M t2) and 1 (M t2).

These assertions are also reconfirmed by additional sources of evidence. A production manager of B remarked that "it is basically just the engine and the gearbox that is being imported, everything else is made locally" in order to describe the extent of production in South Africa.[49] As M at t3, B South Africa accounts for 30–40 percent of the value added. Also the share B South Africa has in B's global production is similar to that of M at t3. M t3 has a daily production capacity of 160 units, B of 170 units.[50] As M t3, B manufactures an estimated one-quarter to one-third of the total sales of the fourth and fifth generation of the entry-level model.[51]

The *foreign direct investment dilemma*: mass-market multinational car companies (cases 5–10)

The second set of cases that will be analyzed features German-originating V, American F, and Japanese N: three large car producers that – unlike

[45] Interview with the Project Leader VPS, the SHE Representative, and the General Manager Corporate Planning of B South Africa, February 20, 2007, Midrand; with the Occupational Health Manager of B South Africa, February 14, 2007, Rosslyn; additional information drawn from the website of B South Africa (February 5, 2009).

[46] Ibid.   [47] The analysis thus turns to the assessment of *Indicator 1*.

[48] Turning to the analysis of *Indicator 2*.

[49] See interview with the Project Leader VPS of B South Africa, February 20, 2007, Midrand.

[50] Website of B South Africa (accessed February 5, 2009).

[51] See Press Release, B Germany, January 9, 2008.

the high-end market firms B and M of the previous comparison – target the mass consumer market. As South Africa is a weakly regulating country with respect to environmental regulation, whereas Germany, Japan, and the US are strongly regulating countries, the cases exemplify the creation of the *technological specialization dilemma* on account of foreign direct investments.

The first models of V were produced in South Africa in 1961 in Uitenhage, where the company still has its main operations. Today, V South Africa employs 6,000 people. The German OEM is one of the few in the country with a domestic market strategy.[52] Until recently, 60 percent of sales went into the South African market while exports accounted for only 40 percent. However, this is currently changing as V has won a new bid from V Germany. The South African branch's production consists of a mix of CKD-mode assembly and OEM. V's manufacturing mainly pertains to a model that is outdated in Europe and made and sold exclusively in South Africa. F has had operations in South Africa since the 1920s, when the brand was the most popular carmaker in the country.[53] During apartheid, however, F pulled back business as a consequence of public protests against American firms' relations with the racist regime (see Chapter 3). In 1994 F reentered South Africa by buying an old CKD assembly plant in Silverton on the outskirts of Pretoria that was founded by Chrysler in the 1960s.[54] Besides, F operates an engine plant in Struvendale near Port Elizabeth. F employs about 4,500 people in the country and exports under AGOA either to the US consumer market or to the US military around the world.[55] N has been making cars in South Africa for forty years now.[56]

---

[52] Most South African OEMs are export-driven.

[53] See interview with the Manager for Employee Wellness and Occupational Health of F South Africa, September 14, 2007, Silverton; the Manager for Environmental and Safety Engineering of F South Africa, February 20, 2007, Silverton; the Quality and Environmental Systems Engineer of F South Africa, September 30, 2008, Silverton; additional information drawn from the website of F South Africa (February 1, 2009).

[54] As Chrysler disinvested as well in the 1980s, the factory changed ownership a number of times and was temporarily in the hands of Sigma, Ampol as well as Renault and Citroen before Ford bought it.

[55] F of South Africa recently won a bid to make the company's next generation compact pickup truck and a diesel engine, which will lead to changes to the assembly line. However, given the current financial problems of F in the US, there are fears that the ZAR1.5 billion investment to support the contract will never be made.

[56] See website of N of South Africa (December 6, 2012).

The firm started an alliance with France's Renault Group in 1999 on a global level. This alliance accounts for N South Africa also producing Renault cars. N's factory in Rosslyn near Pretoria employs about 1,900 people today. As many other carmakers, N reinforced its engagement in South Africa with the end of apartheid and the beginning of economic liberalization. In the 1990s, N global still held only minority shares in its South African factory, which subsequently have been increased so that today N owns 98.7 percent of the operations in South Africa.

The analysis adopts a cross-case comparative perspective and complements it with longitudinal elements. I begin looking at German V and the American F. The two mass-market producers make four cases if we include the longitudinal perspective. I will then turn to a consideration of N, which is a particularly interesting case as it is the only one that features an investment level which decreased with time; the case thus illustrates a decline of asset-specificity levels.

Cases 5 and 6: V before 2006 and F before 2007/8

Up until 2006, the German multinational V manufactured in South Africa mainly a model outdated in Europe and the US with an old production line from Europe dating back to the 1980s. Apart from this, V South Africa assembled mainly in CKD-mode, just as F did up until 2007/8. As the old production line of V, CKD-mode production required constant investments from both firms – but on a rather low level and with short periods before return of investment. As mentioned above, investments in assembly plants usually translate directly into higher and more efficient production output – and, hence, higher sales volumes.[57] The same is true for the old manufacturing line of V. Hence, the level of asset specificity that characterizes the two cases is rather low.

The global revenues of F and V are almost identical between 2005 and 2007. F's amount to $170 billion in 2007, V's to €110 billion in the same year. Hence, we can easily determine the relative investment level of the two firms in South Africa in comparative perspective by looking at the absolute investments both firms make in the country.[58] As

---

[57] Interview with the Manager for Environmental and Safety Engineering of F South Africa, February 20, 2007, Silverton; the Quality and Environmental Systems Engineer of F South Africa, September 30, 2008, Sylverton; interview with the Environmental Controller for Manufacturing Planning of V South Africa, September 22, 2008, Uitenhage.

[58] The analysis thus assesses now *Indicator 1*.

concerns F, the assembly plant has not changed much since it was bought in 1994 and basically still consists of old Chrysler equipment and machinery from the 1960s. The production engineer of F in South Africa concedes "most other Ford factories have newer plants with newer technology."[59] For example, the paint shop is still the same as the one installed in the 1960s operating with coal ovens and coal boilers – technologies that were replaced in Europe and in the US in the late 1980s.[60] The old production line is complemented by new tooling instruments and some newer machinery necessary for the assembly of recent models of F. Such partial upgrading incurred costs of ZAR1.2 billion to ZAR1.5 billion between 1998–2007.[61] Hence, the average investment ratio for that period is ZAR120 million to ZAR150 million per year.

The situation was highly similar in this respect at V before 2006. The firm operated mainly old manufacturing lines from the early 1980s, which were shipped over from Germany to South Africa for the symbolic price of €1.[62] V had to make minor investments similar to those of F (between €1 million and €1.5 million per year) in this production line in order to keep it operational. In addition to this manufacturing line, V operated an assembly plant in which most of the models of V were made in CKD-mode. Also this assembly line required some ongoing investments on a similar level as F's. Apart from this, no major investments were made in the South African plant. The minor investments both firms made were either paying off immediately or committed management in Germany for less than one year.[63] Hence, the extent to which both cases exemplify asset specificity is rather limited, with V being slightly more asset-specific on account of the relatively higher investments the branch in South Africa received on average per annum.

---

[59] See interview with the Quality and Environmental Systems Engineer of F South Africa, September 30, 2008, Sylverton.

[60] Paint shop boilers make steam for humidity to keep the paint fluid. The ovens dry and harden the paint after the painting process.

[61] See interview with the Manager for Environmental and Safety Engineering of F South Africa, February 20, 2007, Silverton; the Quality and Environmental Systems Engineer of F South Africa, September 30, 2008, Silverton; additional information drawn from the website of F South Africa (February 1, 2009).

[62] Interview with the Environmental Controller for Manufacturing Planning of V South Africa, September 22, 2008, Uitenhage; additional information drawn from the website of V South Africa (February 1, 2009).

[63] Measuring *Indicator 2*.

Cases 7 and 8: V from 2006 on, and F after 2008
At V this started to change in 2006, after the South African branch won a new bid from V Germany to produce parts of a new generation model of the firm for the global markets. The South African branch was subsequently upgraded through major investments. For example, a new paint shop and a whole new production line were installed in 2007.[64] In the context of these investments, the plant was developed from a purely CKD-mode assembly plant to a factory with a production mix of CKD-mode assembly and OEM.[65] From then on, V is marked by significantly higher levels of asset specificity than before – and also higher than F shows before 2007/8. The new paint shop, for example, cost about ZAR750 million (about $10 million) and is part of a $60 million to $70 million investment-package V Germany spent in 2006/7 to technologically upgrade and enlarge the South African branch.[66] The average time before returns of this investment is about two years, and three to four years for the new paint shop.[67] This constitutes a substantial commitment, as the CEO of V of South Africa in the roof wetting speech for the paint shop indicates: "to justify an investment in a process such as painting motor cars, you have to be confident about the future," which implies that only if the branch functions as efficiently as planned is a return of investment achieved.[68]

A similar development started at F from 2007 onwards. The branch won a bid from F America, which requires the headquarters in Detroit to make asset-specific investments in South Africa. More specifically, F has announced annual investments of up to $70 million from 2008 until 2010/11 in new technology, a new paint shop, and for an installation of a new production line.[69] These investments have a time to return of

---

[64] Interview with the Health and Safety Manager, and the Environmental Controller for Manufacturing Planning of V South Africa, September 22, 2008, Uitenhage, the Occupational Health, Employee Wellness and HIV Manager, September 25, 2007, Uitenhage; additional information drawn from the website of V South Africa (February 1, 2009).
[65] Interview with the Health and Safety Manager, and the Environmental Controller for Manufacturing Planning of V South Africa, September 22, 2008, Uitenhage.
[66] Measuring *Indicator 1*.
[67] Measuring *Indicator 2*. Interview with the Environmental Controller for Manufacturing Planning of V South Africa, September 22, 2008, Uitenhage.
[68] Quote from the website of V South Africa (February 7, 2009).
[69] This data concerns the assessment of *Indicator 1*; the pay-off period – *Indicator 2* – is the same as for V after 2006.

investment similar to the investments of V from 2006 onwards and thus raise the level of asset specificity of F significantly. In summary, V after 2006 and F after 2008 are cases that illustrate the *foreign direct investment dilemma* on a higher level than V before 2006 and F before 2008.

Cases 9 and 10: N before and after 2005/6
N makes up for a particularly interesting set of cases. The South African branch of this producer of mass-market cars was in the process of securing a larger asset-specific investment from its Japanese head offices in 2005. However, this investment was cancelled in 2006 as a consequence of intra-firm economic austerity measures: the firm experienced a major crisis in sales during that time.[70] Since then, the general level of continuous investment in the South African branch declined for some time. Hence, the two cases of N before and after 2006 exemplify – unlike the previous eight cases – a decline in and even failure to make asset-specific investments.

Economic austerity measures often make firms unwilling to disclose information. As in case of N, interview partners said they were not authorized to share exact data with regard to the amount of investments N South Africa received from N's global headquarters.[71] However, they were willing to draw analogies with other multinational car companies at different points in time. More specifically, they confirmed that before 2005/6, the firm assembled the global product range of the firm – as well as of Renault – in its Rosslyn plant in CKD-mode. During that time, N received continuous investments in order to keep the assembly line running. While interview partners were unable to disclose exact data with regard to these continuous investments, they said that the level of investment the firm received – and the pay-off times of these investments – were more or less identical with those of other multinational car companies producing in CKD-mode. When specifically asked, the interviewed

---

[70] Renault took over N in 1999, when the firm was close to bankruptcy; Carlos Ghosn, who also leads Renault, subsequently also became the CEO of N (in 2001). He managed to turn the company around and generate profits within two years. However, in 2004 and 2005 N was yet again hit by a sales crisis and had to restructure and implement economic austerity measures. See for example: "Carlos Ghosn im Spagat" *Frankfurter Allgemeine Zeitung* (September 12, 2005: www.faz.net/aktuell/wirtschaft/renault-und-nissan-carlos-ghosn-im-spagat-1257237.html, January 15, 2013).
[71] Hence, systematic data for an evaluation of Indicators 1 and 2 is not available.

managers confirmed that these levels were similar to V before 2006 and F before 2007/8.[72] As many other OEMs in the country, N planned from 2003 onwards to upgrade its operation from a basic assembly plant to one with some production components, in which processes would actually add significant value to the cars made in South Africa – just like V since 2006 and F since 2007/8.[73] To this end, the branch was in 2005 in the process of securing a major investment from Japanese head-quarters and was therefore busy preparing this technological upgrade. The investments were meant to go into a new paint shop and a whole new production line and would have had return of investment periods of two to three years.[74]

However, in the end, the envisioned investments were never made. In the face of a sales crisis which N confronted between 2004 and 2005, Carlos Ghosn, who has led the firm since 1999, pursued the plan to make N as quickly as possible profitable again.[75] N had to let go employees in Japan to meet this target, which caused a public outcry. In the context of these measures, investments in South Africa could not be justified at home in Japan, and were therefore put on hold in 2005 and then scrapped altogether in 2006.[76] More severely, also N South Africa was forced to let employees go and reduce production output. According to managers of N, the annual investment volume of the company shrunk at that time, too. The two cases – case 9 (before 2005/6) and 10 (after 2005/6) in the analysis – of N South Africa thus illustrate, on the one hand, decreasing investment levels and, on the other hand, a firm that prepared for major asset-specific investments which in the end were never made.

[72] Interviews with the CSR Manager, the Manager Integrated Systems and the Senior Manager in Corporate Affairs, N South Africa, February 14, 2007, Rosslyn.
[73] Ibid.
[74] See for example: "Nissan–Ford vehicle export deal could earn SA billions." *Business Day Online*. March 7, 2003 (available at www.businessday.co.za) or "Nissan predicts strong growth." *Business Day Online*. February 17, 2003 (available at www.businessday.co.za).
[75] Interviews with the CSR Manager, the Manager Integrated Systems and the Senior Manager in Corporate Affairs, N South Africa, February 14, 2007, Rosslyn.
[76] See www.nissan-global.com/EN/DOCUMENT/HTML/FINANCIAL/SPEECH/2007/fs_speech20070620.html.

Table 5.3 summarizes the ten cases just analyzed with respect the *foreign direct investment dilemma*.

Firm characteristics and control variables

Controlled comparisons imply a case selection of highly similar cases. Case selection for the evaluation of the effects of the *foreign direct investment/technological specialization dilemma* must therefore take into account a number of control variables. These are

- CV 1: firm size – indicator: number of employees of the firm;
- CV 2: the *human resources dilemma*;
- CV 3: collaboration with associations and/or corporate social responsibility initiatives – indicator: active participation in meetings, exchange of minutes and notes, and presentation of progress to the association (public–private partnership, multistakeholder forum or otherwise) in the issue area of the environment;
- CV 4: NGO pressure – indicator: campaigns of NGOs targeting a specific firm;
- CV 5: problem pressure – indicator: intensity of the problem mitigated through corporate social responsibility (i.e. of environmental pollution);
- CV 6: supply chain regulation – indicator: the extent to which a firm is controlled and regulated by buyer firms;
- CV 7: brand name/target market – indicator: marketing expenses of a firm or the end-consumer target market (high-end vs. low-end);
- CV 8: level of industry regulation in home country – indicator: strictness of environmental regulation in the country of headquarters;
- CV 9: shadow of hierarchy (South African and external).

Table 5.4 establishes the ten cases with respect to these control variables. For the causal arguments underlying these control variables see the section in this chapter on "In search for an explanation: a literature review."

Environmental standards and corporate social responsibility

I will now turn to the analysis of the level of environmental policies that the ten firm cases display. This evaluation will concentrate, on the one

Table 5.3 Empirical cases, illustrating (variance of) the foreign direct investment dilemma

Indicators	Comparison 1: multinational car companies targeting a high end of the market				Comparison 2: multinational car companies targeting a mass market					
	M (German high-end market producer)			B (German high-end market producer)	V (German mass-market producer)		F (US mass-market producer)		N (Japanese mass-market producer)	
	Case 1: t1 (1996–2000/1)	Case 2: t2 (2000–2005/6)	Case 3: t3 (from 2006 on)	Case 4 (1998–2008)	Case 5: t1 (1997–2006)	Case 7: t2 (from 2006 on)	Case 6: t1 (1990s–2007/8)	Case 8: t2 (from 2007/8 on)	Case 9: t1 (before 2005/6)	Case 10: t2 (from 2006 on)
Indicator 1: amount of annual investments in production facilities, machines, and technology as a proportion of annual turnover or total investments	$10m/year 0.5% of global investments	$30m/year 1–1.5% of global investments	$300m–$350m/year 9–10% of global investments	$150m–$200m/year 9–12% of global investments	ZAR0.15bn/year (about $2m)	c. ZAR0.5bn ($60m–$70m)	ZAR0.12bn–ZAR0.15bn/year (about $1.5m–$2m)	Anticipated investment: c. ZAR0.6bn ($70m)	Estimated ZAR0.1bn–ZAR0.15bn/year (about $1m–$2m) anticipated major investment	Estimated ZAR0.1bn/year
(asset specificity)	Low/insignificant levels of asset specificity	Low/medium levels of asset specificity	High levels of asset specificity	High levels of asset specificity	Low levels of asset specificity	Medium levels of asset specificity	Low levels of asset specificity	(Anticipated) medium levels of asset specificity	Anticipated increase in levels of asset specificity	Decreasing levels of asset specificity
Indicator 2: period before envisioned return on investment	Immediate return on investment	Less than 1 year on average Some larger investments (e.g. paint shop) 2–3 years	3–4 years	3–4 years	Immediate return on investment/less than 1 year	2 years on average Some larger investments (paint shop) 3–4 years	Immediate return on investment	Anticipated 2 years on average Some larger investments (paint shop) 3–4 years	Immediate return on investment Anticipated 2–3 years	Immediate return on investment

Table 5.4 *Empirical cases, analyzed with respect to control variables*

| | Control variables: analysis of the *foreign direct investment dilemma* | | | | |
| | Comparison 1 High-end market multinational car companies | | Comparison 2 Mass-market multinational car companies | | |
Control variables	Cases 1, 2, and 3 M	Case 4 B	Cases 5 and 7 V	Cases 6 and 8 F	Cases 9 and 10 N
CV 1 Firm size	Large (3,800 employees)	Large (3,400 employees)	Large (6,000 employees)	Large (4,500 employees)	Large (1,900 employees)
CV 2 The *human resources dilemma*	High investments in skills development	High investments in skills development	High investments in skills development	High investments in skills development	High investments in skills development
CV 3 NGO pressure	Not with respect to production processes	Not with respect to production processes	Not with respect to production processes	Not with respect to production processes	Not with respect to production processes
CV 4 Association/PPP initiative	Many, but the same as B	Many, but the same as M	Many, highly similar to F	Many, highly similar to V	Many, highly similar to V
CV 5 Problem pressure	Impact areas: waste, energy, water, effluents, CO_2, fallout	Impact areas: waste, energy, water, effluents, CO_2, fallout	Impact areas: waste, energy, water, effluents, CO_2, fallout	Impact areas: waste, energy, water, effluents, CO_2, fallout	Impact areas: waste, energy, water, effluents, CO_2, fallout
CV 6 Supply chain regulation	No, firm is a regulator of suppliers	No, firm is a regulator of suppliers	No, firm is a regulator of suppliers	No, firm is a regulator of suppliers	No, firm is a regulator of suppliers

	High-end	High-end	Mass-market	Mass-market	Mass-market
CV 7 Brand name/target market					
CV 8 "Home country" regulation	High level of regulation	High level of regulation	High level of regulation	High level of regulation	High level of regulation
CV 9 Shadow of hierarchy and external shadow of hierarchy	Absent	Absent	Absent	Absent	Absent

hand, on the level policy formulation – the degree of obligation and precision as well as depth and scope of policies.[77] On the other hand, it will take into consideration implementation processes and practices concerning intra-organizational compliance mechanisms and resources dedicated to the achievement of policy goals, such as personnel, financial resources, and executive support.[78] In measuring environmental policies in this way, I concentrate on two dimensions of practices of environmental corporate social responsibility.

The first dimension concerns the systematic structuring of work and industrial processes, as, for example in the context of ISO 14001 certification. ISO 14001 is a widely adopted voluntary industry standard sponsored by the International Standardization Organization (ISO) against which environmental management systems are certified. The standard refers to a system of rules defining procedures. At the center is an environmental impact assessment according to which firms define, categorize, and rank order activities with a potential negative effect on the environment. This impact assessment is made internally and verified by an external independent environmental assessor. Based on the results of this assessment, all processes with a potential impact are structured by concise and strict rules, including penalties for non-compliance and escalation procedures in case of process failure. The implementation of these rules of procedure is audited and regularly controlled internally by an environmental manager and externally by the certification agency. On the basis of the external audit the firm attains certification.[79]

The second dimension refers to the substantive goals such processes aim at. The level of these goals can be rather low, as when oriented towards implementing South African local standards (which are usually absent or lax), or can be high, when oriented towards international standards. The more structured the processes according to which management systems are organized, and the more demanding the goals of environmental protection, the stronger the firm's corporate social responsibility, and vice versa.

---

[77] These aspects refer to *Indicators 1a–d* as laid out in Chapter 3.
[78] These aspects refer to *Indicators 2a–e* as laid out in Chapter 3.
[79] Interview with an Environmental Management Systems Certifier of SABS (South African Bureau of Standards), September 12, 2007, Pretoria.

Table 5.5 *Environmental programs*

Corporate social responsibility: environmental programs

Analyzed as outcomes of the *technological specialization* and the *foreign direct investment dilemmas*

Dimension	Features	Measurement/assessment	
Dimension 1 Structuring of work and industrial processes according to environmental aspects	• Impact assessment (yes or no) • Management system, such as ISO 14001, VDA 6.1, or TS 16949, implemented (yes or no, third-party certified or not certified; strictly implemented or implemented on a minimum level)	• **Indicator 1a:** degree of obligation • **Indicator 1b:** degree of precision • **Indicator 1c:** depth • **Indicator 1d:** scope	Weak
Dimension 2 Substantive goals of pollution reduction and resource use efficiency	• Level of standards of environmental protection (weak South African standards or beyond) • Transfer of high standards from highly regulating country operations to branch in South Africa	• **Indicator 2a:** personnel • **Indicator 2b:** material resources • **Indicator 2c:** financial resources • **Indicator 2d:** executive support • **Indicator 2e:** compliance mechanisms	Strong

**High-end market multinational car companies (cases 1–4):
transferring standards from home to abroad?**
Case 1: M t1
The level of environmental standards on which M operated during t1 is
rather low.[80] During t1 M does not have a third-party audited environmental management system in place (as, for example, ISO 14001);
nor does the firm measure its impact in the areas of water and energy
consumption and emissions output, or engage in waste reduction or
recycling. The firm looks to South African local regulations in its conduct, but makes little effort to implement this regulation systematically.
Where implemented, these standards are rather lax and often even do
not exist in important areas. For example, during t1 the firm does not
define maximum effluent levels or any emissions standards. It also does
not have a waste management directive, and operates on high levels of
water and energy consumption.

Hence, the environmental standards of M are during that time covering relevant areas only incomprehensively, and are not particularly
demanding (as they are oriented towards South African regulation).
They are also not very concise and obligatory as the lack of clearly
defined effluent standards shows and generally lack the support of compliance mechanisms.[81] Most importantly, however, M lacks at t1 a third-
party audited management system and thus does not show a serious
commitment to implementation of its policy.

Case 2: M t2
Immediately before the first asset-specific investments were carried out
in 2001, the firm decided to enter the ISO 14001 certification process.
M became certified in 2003.[82] The management system was, according
to representatives of M, not particularly well implemented during that
time (that is, during t2). Nonetheless, ISO 14001 certification means

---

[80] The assessment considers policy formulation (*Indicators 1a–d*) and the
implementation process (applying a combination of *Indicators 1a–d* and
Indicators 2a–e).
[81] I am referring here to *Indicators 1a–d* and *Indicators 2a–e*.
[82] The investment in the paint shop was identified in the analysis above as major
commitment made by management. The length of the ISO 14001 certification
process was almost three years. Interview with the Manager: Quality
Management and Integrated Management System of M South Africa, September
23, 2008, East London; with the Corporate Health Manager of M South Africa,
February 26, 2007, East London.

that, unlike at t1, M had at t2 a third-party audited environmental management system in place. Also, as a condition for certification ISO 14001 requires accredited firms to have passed a third-party audit on compliance with the local and national environmental laws.[83] During t2, M therefore also began to assess its impact in terms of water usage and energy consumption, which it did not during t1. While the firm did not (yet) implement strict reduction targets or transfer water and energy consumption standards from Germany to its South African operation, it systematically ensured that its business practices in these areas were in accordance with the South African law. Assessing the policy goals of M t2, the firm's level of environmental policies is thus in substance on a par with South African law.[84] M t2's policy is therefore more demanding, comprehensive, and strict – and much more strictly implemented – than at t1. Still, the level of substantive standards towards which the environmental policy is oriented is the South African environmental regulation and thus not particularly high: South Africa environmental laws are lax, shallow, and imprecise throughout many important areas compared with environmental regulation in, for example, Europe. M t2's policy, which is oriented towards passing the legal compliance audit, reflects these deficiencies.

For example, M t2 formulates the general goal of emissions reduction in the production process. Specific emissions standards, impact assessments, and reduction goals, however, are not detailed by the policy.[85] The reason for this lack of specificity is that emissions standards are not a requirement for the attainment of a legal compliance certificate in East London, where the plant of M is located. The municipality has never put forward legislation limiting emissions. For the same reason, the policy of M t2 does not envision demanding and strict goals as regards energy reduction, water consumption, and waste reduction, or effluent control. The production lines of car companies, however, with their welding machines and paint shops, are especially energy- and water-intensive and produce potentially toxic effluents, emissions, and

---

[83] The firm thus scores high on *Indicators 2a–e*.

[84] The analysis applies *Indicators 1a–c*, that is, the degree of obligation, precision and depth of policies.

[85] Interview with the Manager: Quality Management and Integrated Management System of M South Africa, September 23, 2008, East London; with the Corporate Health Manager of M South Africa, February 26, 2007, East London.

waste. Hence, the policy of M t2 covers the most important impact areas of automotive production only insufficiently.

This assertion can be further substantiated by looking at the impact area of effluents. The regulation of the municipality dates back to pre-apartheid times. As a consequence, M t2's policy was successfully audited on legal compliance despite lacking provisions on, for instance, a systematic measurement of the storm water that runs through the factory property. Modern regulations and, accordingly, modern firm policies include provisions in this respect to ascertain that spillages or leaks are detected, however.[86] The policy of M t2 regarding effluents prescribes only that the effluents stemming directly from the factory are measured and reprocessed before they are released. Aside from being too limited in scope, the standards that are applied here are far below European, US, or Japanese levels, allowing the firm to severely pollute ground water and rivers, as an environmental manager of M concedes.[87] Hence, the policy of M t2 is not only narrow and imprecise but also shallow and lax. However, ISO 14001 certification implies strict and effective compliance measures on the one hand and that the substantive regulatory standards towards which the environmental processes at t2 are oriented are at least on the level of the South African law, on the other hand. Hence, in comparison with t1, M runs at t2 an environmental policy on a higher level.

Cases 3 and 4: M t3, B

When the investments were made in 2006 to support the manufacturing of the new generation of the entry-level model, the German headquarters of M sent a team of thirty environmental and production managers to the South African branch to thoroughly restructure policies and processes.[88] The environmental policy of M was thereby upgraded to a level identical with its operations in Germany – a level that B has been adhering to since the late 1990s. "All the cars we produce here in South Africa are produced according to EU standards" is what both the managers of M t3 and B declare, whereby the manager of M also emphasized that the level of standards has increased significantly since 2006.[89]

[86] Ibid.   [87] Ibid.   [88] Ibid.
[89] Interview with the General Manager Corporate Planning of B South Africa, February 20, 2007, Midrand; with the Manager: Quality Management and Integrated Management System of M South Africa, September 23, 2008, East London.

For example, the level of emissions and effluents standards in South African law are "ridiculous," "pathetic," "weak," "far too lenient and far too broad," and "allowing the whole world to be ridden by effluents," according to environmental managers of B and M t2.[90] This is why M decided in 2006, just as B had done previously in the late 1990s, to adopt a policy on the basis of German and EU standards. Accordingly, B's and M t3's policies require the production unit to measure and gradually reduce emissions and to guarantee and prove that the level of pollution is never higher compared to those licit in Germany. Effluent control and reduction – including systematic probing of storm water – are dealt with accordingly. Hence, the respective policies are much more concise, obligatory, comprehensive, and demanding than at M at t1 and t2.[91]

Concerning electricity and water consumption B and M t3 have implemented demanding goals as well that strictly oblige the branches to achieve reductions of 17 percent per year.[92] M t1 and t2, in contrast, did not formulate any goals in this respect. An interesting aspect of energy reduction is that the costs for energy are still relatively low in South Africa. Hence, the firms do not see an immediate economic reason for energy consumption reductions. However, the country experiences recurrent energy crises. On the one hand, this bears the risk of an increase in energy costs in the future. On the other hand, crises have repeatedly caused outages and subsequent interruptions of production processes including damage to the machinery. A manager of M South Africa commented that in the light of the massive investments in the new production facilities, these risks became unbearable and therefore had to be mitigated through demanding reduction targets.[93] The comment suggests that the decision to impose stricter environmental policies is, as theorized, made to mitigate risks inherent in intra-organizational asset-specific investments in the production unit.

Summarizing the results as concerns policy formulation, cases 1 and 2 (M t1 and t2) illustrate a weak and a medium to low level of engagement

---

[90] Ibid.   [91] Referring here to *Indicators 1a–d.*
[92] Interview with the Project Leader VPS, the SHE Representative and the General Manager of Corporate Planning of B South Africa, February 20, 2007, Midrand; with the Manager: Quality Management and Integrated Management System of M South Africa, September 23, 2008, East London.
[93] Interview with the Manager: Quality Management and Integrated Management System of M South Africa, September 23, 2008, East London.

in environmental protection, respectively, while cases 3 (M t3) and 4 (B) exemplify environmental policies of the highest level. This assertion is further substantiated by an evaluation of the respective implementation measures, which are delegated to ISO 14001.

ISO 14001 details highly obligatory, concise, comprehensive, and demanding process rules in South Africa according to which accredited and certified firms are held accountable by a commercial certification agency. Hence, ISO 14001 includes third party monitoring.[94] The certification agency also carries sanctioning authority. It is obliged to withhold or withdraw the certificate as a consequence of asserted non-compliance. Obviously, the strictness of monitoring and sanctioning mechanisms critically depends on the degree to which certification agencies comply with the strict and demanding rules detailing the certification process. In this respect, a key factor is the national regulation of the market for certification agencies.[95] In South Africa this market is thoroughly regulated and controlled. Hence, if a firm in South Africa attains ISO 14001 certification, this will indicate successful implementation of the respective environmental policy and, accordingly, policy practices that reflect policy prescription.[96] This implies that for Mt2, Mt3, and B the findings on the level of policy formulations also pertain to the level of implementation: the policy of M t2 shows a medium-strong engagement in environmental protection measures, whereas M t3 and B reveal remarkably strong activities in this respect.

[94] Turning to *Indicators 2a–e.*
[95] While ISO 14001 certification is particularly strict in South Africa it is handled rather loosely in other countries. The Chinese market for certification agencies, for example, is weakly regulated. As a consequence, certification procedures are only weakly defined, monitored, and enforced. According to many observers and experts, ISO 14001 certificates in China do not therefore indicate policy implementation. Interview with the European Union Chamber of Commerce in China (EUCCC), April 16, 2008, Beijing; with The American Chamber of Commerce People's Republic of China (AmCham), April 2008, Beijing; with the Delegation of German Industry and Commerce Beijing (DE International), April 2008, Beijing; Delegation of German Industry and Commerce Shanghai (AHK, DIHK), April 2, 2008, Shanghai.
[96] The South African Bureau of Standards (SABS, a state agency), licenses the certification agencies, thereby applying strict standards that provide incentives for these agencies to be themselves strict on their clients. The SABS also operates its own commercial certification agency, which is the biggest agency on the certification market in South Africa. This agency has, apart from implementing strict certification procedures, also the function to monitor other certification agencies.

Diffusing international standards? Mass-market multinational car companies (cases 5–10)

Cases 5 and 6: V before 2006 and F before 2007/8

The assertion that the level of policy formulations also pertains to the level of implementation applies to the cases of V before 2006 and F before 2007/8, too: both V and F obtained ISO 14001 certification in the years of 1998/9.[97] Hence, compliance mechanisms assure from then on a relatively effective implementation process with precise, obligatory, demanding, and comprehensive procedural rules and strict third-party monitoring and sanctioning mechanisms.[98] However, the level of standards the firms' policies entail is rather low – not only in comparison with M t3 and B, but also with V after 2006 and F from 2007/8.[99] In this respect a difference to M t3 and B featured in the previous analysis is that neither V nor F explicitly incorporates German, European, or US environmental regulation into their policies. Instead, the policies of both firms are mainly oriented towards legal compliance with South African law. In comparison with V after 2006 and F from 2007/8, the firms did not set any emissions or effluent standards during that time, did not run sophisticated waste management systems, and based production on excessive use of water and electricity – not unlike M at t1.

For example, while the firms' policies formulate the goal of waste management and reduction, the policy is not specified. Thus, waste management has not been designated as a goal towards which the firms' ISO 14001 certified environmental management processes are oriented. In case of F this had rather visible consequences: "littering and waste production is, as you have seen [I took a tour of the plant], quite a serious problem on our site," comments the environmental manager of F.[100] Also, F uses 600 percent more energy for manufacturing a car than a comparable plant in Europe, Asia, or the US, in addition to an excessive use of water. The findings for V are similar in this respect. Both firms also did not control their emissions output during that time,

---

[97] Interview with the Health and Safety Manager and the Environmental Controller for Manufacturing Planning of V South Africa, September 22, 2008, Uitenhage, the Occupational Health, Employee Wellness, and HIV Manager, September 25, 2007, Uitenhage; interview with the Quality and Environmental Systems Engineer of F, September 30, 2008, Silverton.

[98] Referring to *Indicators 2a–e*.   [99] Measuring *Indicators 1a–d*.

[100] See interview with the Quality and Environmental Systems Engineer of F, September 30, 2008, Silverton.

which was high for both firms, given that they operated coal ovens and old paint shops. Effluents, too, were neither measured nor systematically controlled – or limited by standards. Hence, F until 2007/8 and V until 2006 operated on rather lax environmental standards.

Cases 7 and 8: V since 2006 and F from 2007/8
At V this started to change in 2006, after the South African branch won a new bid from V Germany.[101] From then on V has had a sophisticated, obligatory, demanding, and encompassing waste management policy which includes waste separation, recycling, reuse, and waste minimization. To continuously improve the waste management system, V even participates in a local "waste club" with BMW, Mercedes, and other firms to benchmark processes and learn from best practices. The policy, in addition, is incorporated in the ISO 14001-certified processes at V and therefore fully implemented. The firm also increased the level of standards in other important impact areas. For example, it formulated strict and demanding energy and water reduction targets of about 10 percent per year. As the ISO 14001 management system is fully implemented, third-party audited, and certified, this increase in the level of standards also reflects the level of successfully implemented policy practices.

V has also started to conduct regular and comprehensive impact assessments regarding emissions, other industrial fallout, and effluents, and has recently begun to measure these aspects regularly. The firm is currently in the process of setting internal emissions limits and reduction goals, and of setting effluent limits to be fully implemented after the current trial phase in 2009. Hence, in comparison with V before 2006 and F before 2007/8, the firm operates since 2006 on a significantly higher level of environmental standards. At the same time, however, the firm does not transfer home standards abroad, and thus operates on clearly lower levels of environmental policies and practices as B and M t3.

A similar development has taken place at F since 2007/8.[102] F began in 2007 to reimplement its ISO 14001 management system in order to gain control over the plant's littering problem and to implement basic principles

---

[101] Interview with the Health and Safety Manager and the Environmental Controller for Manufacturing Planning of V South Africa, September 22, 2008, Uitenhage, the Occupational Health, Employee Wellness and HIV Manager, September 25, 2007, Uitenhage.
[102] Interview with the Quality and Environmental Systems Engineer of F, September 30, 2008, Silverton.

of reuse and recycling. In addition, global headquarters forced the branch to reduce the yearly consumption of energy and water by 18 to 20 percent in two consecutive years. It threatened to otherwise hold back the investment.[103] The firm thus raised its level of policies in the crucial impact areas of waste management, and energy and water consumption. F was at the time of the interview (2008) also in the process of measuring its impact in the area of effluents and emissions and of setting standards in these areas. In comparison with the time period before 2007/8 – and also with V before 2006 – the firm thus has been operating from 2007/8 on a significantly higher level of environmental standards. While thus scoring higher in this respect than the mentioned cases, the firm does not transfer home standards abroad and thus operates on clearly lower levels of environmental policies and practices as B and M t3.

Cases 9 and 10: N (before and after 2005/6)
Before 2005, the Japanese headquarters demanded a strict ISO 14001 environmental management implementation and began to formulate aggressive reduction targets in the areas of energy and water consumption of about 10 percent per year [104] The firm also began to measure its impact in the areas of effluents and emissions in 2004 and formulated limits and reduction targets for these areas as well as a recycling policy during 2005. Hence, the level of environmental policies was on the rise. However, since 2006 this policy has declined: the environmental manager of N concedes that the firm did not observe closely the ISO 14001 processes from then on any more, so that recertification became a challenge. The manager – as well as the corporate social responsibility manager of the firm – also said that the reduction targets concerning energy and water consumption have remained unobserved since then. The newly developed standards in the fields of emissions and effluents were never implemented in the end and the recycling policy is not strictly followed. The company still meets the minimum requirement set by South African law, but does not show any activities to protect the environment beyond these. Hence, the level of environmental policies has decreased between 2004 and 2006.

Table 5.6 summarizes the findings for the ten cases regarding the level of environmental standards on which the five firms operate over time.

[103] Ibid.
[104] Interviews with the CSR Manager, the Manager Integrated Systems and the Senior Manager in Corporate Affairs, N South Africa, February 14, 2007, Rosslyn.

Table 5.6 Summary of environmental policies of multinational car companies in South Africa

The dependent variable: environmental policies in the South African car industry across cases and over time

Indicators for policies detailing environmental process standards	Comparison 1: multinational carmakers — Producers of high-end cars				Comparison 1: multinational carmakers — Producers of mass cars					
	M (German high-end market producer)		B (German high-end market producer)		V (German mass-market producer)		F (US mass-market producer)		N (Japanese mass-market producer)	
	Case1: t1 (1996–2000/1)	Case 2: t2 (2000–2005/6)	Case 3: t3 (from 2006 on)	Case 4 (1998–2008)	Case 5 (before 2006)	Case 7 (from 2007 on)	Case 6 (before 2007/8)	Case 8: (from 2007/8 on)	Case 9: (before 2005/6)	Case 10: (from 2006 on)
Indicator 1: procedural norms — Impact assessment (yes or no); Management system implemented? Measured as strict, demanding and concise, and with respect to degree of implementation	Low scores. Impact assessment in areas of water and energy. However, not third-party audited. No impact assessment in areas of emissions and waste. Management system theoretically in place, but not implemented; no ISO 14001 certification	Medium scores. Third-party audited impact assessment in area of water and energy; no assessment in areas of emissions and waste. ISO 14001 certification (in 2003); however, weakly implemented only	High scores. Comprehensive, third-party audited impact assessment in all areas. Bi-annually, third party certified ISO 14001 and VDA 6.1 management system, complete implementation, strong emphasis on continuous improvement	High scores. Comprehensive, third-party audited impact assessment in all areas. Bi-annually, third party certified ISO 14001 and VDA 6.1 management system, complete implementation, strong emphasis on continuous improvement	Medium scores. Third-party audited impact assessment in area of water and energy; no assessment in areas of emissions and waste. ISO 14001 certification (in 1999)	Medium scores. Third-party audited impact assessment in area of water and energy; no assessment in areas of emissions and waste. Stricter implementation of ISO 14001 certification when compared to before 2006	Medium to low scores. Third-party audited impact assessment in area of water and energy; no assessment in areas of emissions and waste. ISO 14001 certification (in 1998/99); however, medium strong implementation only	Medium scores. Third-party audited impact assessment in area of water and energy; no assessment in areas of emissions and waste. ISO 14001 certification (in 1998/99); increase in strictness of implementation	Medium scores. Third-party audited impact assessment in area of water and energy; assessment in areas of emissions, effluents, and waste. ISO 14001 certification; strict implementation with emphasis on continuous improvement	Medium to low scores. Third-party audited impact assessment in area of water and energy; no assessment in areas of emissions, effluents and waste. ISO 14001 certification; rather lax implementation. Emphasis on continuous improvement is given up
Indicator 2: substantive rules — Level of standards of environmental protection: weak South African standards, above South African Standards or high standards from home country	Low level. South African local regulations non-systematically implemented. Where implemented, standards are lax and often even do not exist in important areas; e.g. no effluent standards, no emissions standards, no waste management directives etc.; high water and energy consumption)	Medium to low level. Third party audited legal compliance; i.e. standards are often lax or absent, but where standards exist M has implemented them.	High level. Highest level (EU and German standards implemented in South African plant, on a significantly higher level than the South African law). Water consumption has been reduced to almost zero, emissions equal those in German plants, no effluents, systematic recycling and reuse	High level. Highest level (EU and German standards implemented in South African plant, on a significantly higher level than the South African law). Water consumption has been reduced to almost zero, elimination of hazardous waste, emissions equal those in German plants, systematic recycling and reuse (for this end B has founded a waste club)	Medium to low level. Third party audited legal compliance; i.e. standards are often lax or absent, but where standards exist V has implemented them; high energy and water consumption, but less so than F before 2007/8	Medium level. High reduction targets (10% energy reduction per year) in area of energy consumption; also targets to reduce emissions and water usage and introduce recycling	Low to medium level. Third party audited legal compliance; i.e. standards are often lax or absent, but where standards exist F has implemented them; however, hardly any waste management system; high energy and water consumption	Medium level. High reduction targets (20% energy reduction, 18% water usage reduction per year) from F Global in areas of energy consumption and water usage; also targets to reduce emissions and introduce recycling	Medium level. High reduction targets in area of energy consumption; also targets to reduce emissions and water recycling were formulated	Medium to low level. No new reduction targets formulated since 2006; previous standards are no longer observed; however, plant operates quite resource-use efficient on account of the efforts made before 2006, and is ISO 14001 certified

Summary of the findings: asset specificity – resolving the puzzle?

The controlled, pair-wise comparisons suggest that, *ceteris paribus*, asset-specific investments from a strongly regulating home to a weakly regulating host country are an internal driver of standard diffusion. In the first comparison, the increase of asset-specific investments at the high-end carmaker M from the mid-1990s to 2008 (t1 to t3) resulted in an increase in the level of environmental standards each time. Potentially, this increase could just reflect a general trend in the industry and thus not be the result of asset-specific investments. However, the case of another high-end market carmaker, B, shows that the rising levels of environmental standards boil down to asset specificity and not a general trend. B has been operating on very high levels of asset specificity since the late 1990s and, accordingly, on exceptionally high levels of environmental standards in South Africa. The two high-end market firms M (at t3) and B also show that very high levels of asset specificity result not only in a spread of global environmental standards such as ISO 14001, but also in a transfer of high regulatory standards from the home market Germany to the weakly regulating host country South Africa.

The results of the second comparative analysis are additional confirming evidence for the theoretically stipulated relation between asset specificity and environmental standards. It features the mass-market carmakers V, F, and N. V and F's operations in South Africa were not particularly asset-specific for a long time – in the case of V until 2006 and in the case of F until 2007/8. In consequence, the level of environmental standards of both firms was rather low. However, when the firms decided to raise the level of long-term investments in South Africa, the level of environmental policies also increased.

This relation between asset-specific investments and environmental policies is also illustrated by the case of the Japanese mass-market producer, N. Before 2006, N planned to upgrade the South African plant from an assembly plant into an assembly plant with a production component – not unlike V in 2006 or F in 2007/8. To this end, the branch was expected to receive asset-specific investments – substantial investments with long durations before they pay off – such as in a paint shop and a new production line. Accordingly, the Japanese headquarters started to demand a strict ISO 14001 environmental management implementation and began to formulate aggressive reduction targets in the areas of energy and water consumption. However, in the end the envisioned investments were never made. N had to let go of employees in Japan, which caused a public outcry. In the context of these austerity measures, investments in South Africa could not be justified and were therefore scrapped altogether in 2005/6. The consequence of these developments is that the strict implementation of environmental management system ISO 14001 declined from then on, although the factory in South Africa is still certified. Also, the reduction targets of water and energy use and emissions output as well as recycling were not set by the Japanese headquarters any longer – and therefore also declined.

The two cases of N (cases 9 and 10, see Table 5.5) thus illustrate that the relation between asset specificity and environmental standards is valid in both ways: the first eight cases of M (t1, t2, t3), B, V (before and after 2006), and F (before and after 2007/8) over time show that increases in asset specificity lead to stricter environmental standards. The last two cases of N demonstrate that declining levels of asset specificity lead to a parallel decline in environmental policies.

These findings also resolve the puzzle of differential environmental policies in the South African automotive industry as demonstrated in Figure 5.1, which was discussed in the first part of this chapter. This discussion revealed that the known explanations in the literature for corporate social responsibility, voluntary standards, and diffusion, cannot explain the different levels of environmental standards in the South African car industry, which Figure 5.1 illustrates. Figure 5.2 below, however, shows that this puzzle is solved by asset specificity. An interesting aspect of the relation between asset specificity and environmental standards illustrated in Figure 5.2 is that this relation seems to be almost perfectly linear in as far as the measurement in the analysis above permits. Hence, the market orientation of firms (high-end vs. mass-market) does not seem to have any impact at all on the level of environmental standards on which multinational carmakers operate. This is remarkable. While the section "In search for an explanation: a literature review" (above) showed that company features such as the market orientation of firms cannot resolve the overall puzzle of differential environmental standards in the car industry in South Africa, we would nonetheless expect them to have some effect. This would be reflected in a slight deviation of the firm cases presented in Figure 5.2 from a perfectly linear relationship between asset specificity and

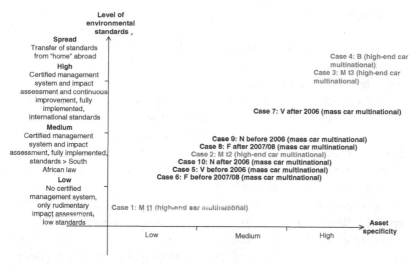

Figure 5.2 Mapping of environmental policies in relation to asset specificity

environmental standards. In Chapter 4, for example, firm size causes such a scattering of cases in Figure 4.2, which mapped the relation between asset-specific investments in employee skills and labor-related corporate social responsibility. We do not find any such scattering in Figure 5.2 below, which is an indication for asset specificity accounting for all of the variation of environmental standards in the car industry.

Tracing the diffusion process: technology vs. asset specificity

The analysis has demonstrated so far that, everything else being equal, variation of intra-organizational asset-specific investments in production units co-vary with the level of environmental standards. However, the inside-view approach in this book can do more than investigate correlations in that it can also trace the causal mechanism relating asset-specific investments in production technology to environmental policies (George and Bennett 2005: 205–10; Tilly 1997). By doing so, the analysis will consider an important, potentially alternative explanation to asset specificity: the "level of technology."

The "level of technology" is often included as a control variable in econometric studies of environmental business standards. It describes the level of technological advancement on which a firm operates (for example, Khanna *et al.* 2007). The argument behind the "level of

technology" is that new technology yields efficiency gains and will thus
have positive spin-offs for the resource use intensity of a firm. High-tech
firms will therefore have higher standards when compared to low-techs.
In addition, most technological innovations are developed in a highly
regulated market context, such as the EU, the US, or Japan. New technologies are developed to meet the high regulations in these markets.
When brought to weakly regulating countries, so the argument goes,
environmental standards diffuse with them. Different levels of technology may thus explain the different levels of environmental policies in the
South African car industry. So what is it that drives standard diffusion:
asset specificity or technology?

Asset-specific (foreign direct) investments almost always correlate
with the "level of technology"; they actually cause it in most cases. A
correlation-based comparative analysis would thus not lead to any
results regarding this question. Process tracing, however, will (George
and Bennett 2005: 217). The key question is: what are the observable
implications of the causal processes that can be deduced for the level of
technology and asset specificity, respectively, and where and how do
they differ?

Observable implications of the causal process
A first set of distinct observable implications concerns the sequence
of events leading from (foreign direct) investments to environmental
standards. The level of technology argument implies that high standards
emerge *after* the investment has been made, i.e. *with* new technology. By
contrast, according to the argument for asset specificity high standards
precede (foreign direct) investments and the advent of new technology:
before making asset-specific investments, management insists on the
adoption of high environmental standards to mitigate the risks inherent
in such investments.

A second set of such implications concerns the interpretative frames
of key actors. The processes unleashed by asset specificity provoke
different sets of interpretation in relation to environmental standards
within firms than those regarding the level of technology. In the context
of asset specificity, managers will interpret environmental standards
as means of risk mitigation for head offices. In the event that new
technology drives standards up, managers would be inclined to say
that the firm contributes to environmental protection through technological advancements.

A third set of distinguishable implications pertains to differential effects which the distinct mechanisms of the level of technology and of asset specificity have in the dependent variable: new technology improves environmental standards only in areas impacted by it. New technology may thus reduce energy and water consumption. Waste management, recycling, and other areas unrelated to technology will, however, remain unaffected; there is no direct causal link between the latter and technology. The mechanism triggered off by asset-specific investments, by contrast, relates to all areas, including waste management: potentially increasing future costs of waste are from this perspective as much an uncertainty associated with asset-specific investments as are energy or water costs and therefore have to be mitigated through environmental standards (Table 5.7).

Sequence of events

What do the empirical cases reveal concerning these observable implications? With respect to the sequence of events (Implication 1) the cases analyzed clearly indicate that it is asset specificity and not the level of technology that causes standard diffusion. In the cases of M, V, and F, increases in the level of environmental standards *precede* the advent of new technology and (foreign direct) investments. For example, M pushed for a higher level of environmental standards in its factory in East London six months *before* any new technology arrived.[105] Similarly, F South Africa has recently begun to implement stricter environmental standards in order to be able to qualify for new investments from head office in the US. Hence, it did so *before* the anticipated technological upgrade and investments and even before the upgrade was ascertained. The findings are analogous in the case of V.

However, what does the case of N reveal in this respect? According to the logic of the level of technology argument N's decline of environmental policies should follow a previous technological decline. However, the plant's level of technology remained the same while the policies went down. When N decided in 2006 to scrap the planned investments in its South African plant, this did not – at least not immediately – affect the level of technology on which the plant operated at all. It just means that the plant would not be upgraded in the future and that the level of

---

[105] Interview with the Manager: Quality Management and Integrated Management System of M South Africa, September 23, 2008, East London.

Table 5.7 *Tracing the process – observable implications*

| | | **What causes standard diffusion?** Asset specificity *vs.* level of technology | | |
| | | | Observable implications | |
	Mechanism	(1) Sequence of events	(2) Interpretation of events	(3) Consequences
Asset specificity	Management fears information asymmetries vis-à-vis production unit and vulnerability to changes in environment and therefore adopts standards	Standards *precede* FDI	Standards mitigate risks associated with investments	Higher standards and targets in all areas (energy, water, emissions, waste)
Level of technology	Enhanced resource-use efficiency of new technology	Standards *follow* FDI (increase *with* new technology)	Contribution to environmental protection through technological advancement	Higher standards in areas of energy, emissions and water, but NOT in waste

investments decreased. While it does not directly confirm asset specificity, these aspects are clearly disconfirming evidence for the "level of techno-logy" argument.[106]

Patterns of interpretation

Concerning dominant patterns of interpretation (Implication 2), I asked M and B in an interview why these firms would voluntarily implement the strict German environmental regulations in their plants in East London and Rosslyn, respectively. The leading production engineer of M in East London, who had been sent to South Africa from Germany for a period of three years to supervise the upgrade of the East London plant in 2006, responded that for "us in management in Germany this is a way of dealing with the tremendous risks inherent in the massive investments we are making here [in the South African plant]."[107] To ensure that "the house is in order," as he expressed it, and that resources were used efficiently, head office management demanded the implemen-tation of high levels of environmental policies from the South African branch prior to investing in South Africa; moreover, they insisted on seeing to it personally that these policies were in place and third-party verified.

This interpretation of events is clearly in line with the asset specificity argument. The production engineer and member of head office manage-ment of M in Germany emphasizes risk mitigation and pressure from head office. At the same time, he does not mention the development or implementation of environmentally friendly technology as a reason for or explanation of events. Hence, the interpretation of the production engineer indicates that the causal logic of the level of technology argu-ments does not apply in this case.

The management of B in Munich gives a similar account of events. The managers asserted that, in view of the long production and investment cycles of their firm, "due processes for the functioning of our business model are much more important than short-term cost aspects. With product cycles of six to nine years for cars – from the initial development

---

[106] The case of B does not allow for any inference regarding this implication, as B is a constant throughout the period of analysis as concerns FDI, asset specificity, high levels of technology, and environmental standards. The decision sequence we are interested in here lies beyond the time frame this chapter analyzes.

[107] Interview with the Manager: Quality Management and Integrated Management System of M South Africa, September 23, 2008, East London.

of a new car model to the last sold units of it – and with break-even times of three to four years, environmental standards help us to deal with the potential risks and unknowns we confront."[108]

Similarly, the manager of F in South Africa says that head office insists on "aggressive" energy and water reduction targets prior to the investment in order to assure that the plant in Sylverton makes efficient use of the entrusted resources.[109] Otherwise, such investments would appear too risky – a statement confirming the causal logic of the asset specificity argument. Managers of N, in turn, associate the decline in environmental standards in their factory with the idea that South Africa has lost its importance for head office management. This again fits in with the asset specificity argument, as a lower importance is related to and compatible with a reduced risk perception in head offices, yet it does not seem to relate to the level of technology argument.[110] In sum, the patterns of interpretation of events in relation to environmental standards in the firms reflect the distinct processes that asset-specific investments trigger. No trace for the processes unleashed by new technology was found.

Consequences: type of resulting environmental policies
Regarding the third implication, the observation is that the respective upgrades in environmental standards include aspects that are entirely unrelated to technology.[111] For example, the integrated systems manager of B describes recycling as a focus area of her activities. The environmental manager of the American mass-market producer F says that in preparation for a major investment in the South African production site, one of his current tasks is to gain control over the littering problem on the plant site and the generally chaotic situation concerning

---

[108] Interview with the Director of Corporate and International Affairs Management of B, August 2, 2007, Munich. Statements were made in German: my own translation.

[109] See interview with the Quality and Environmental Systems Engineer of F SA, September 30, 2008, Silverton.

[110] The manager of V said that the decision for high environmental standards was made before they took office, and so did not know. The manager of V was actually hired to improve the level of standards. The case is thus neither confirming nor disconfirming evidence for any of the two causal mechanisms.

[111] All firms gave evidence in this respect with the exception of N, which refused to specify the areas in which the firm has become weaker recently during the interview.

waste collection and recycling.[112] Waste management is also a core area of activity for M and V. Improvements in waste management, however, cannot be induced by or be otherwise directly related to new technology. Hence, the level of technology argument cannot explain them. Waste management, however, is an integral part of "bringing the house in order," which is the function of environmental standards according to the asset specificity argument.

In conclusion, there is clear evidence for the distinct processes that unfold on account of asset specificity. These processes causally link asset-specific (foreign direct) investments to environmental standards. At the same time, there is no indication for any processes that may trace back to the level of technology. However, quite a number of observations rule out that these processes are at work here. These findings effectively disconfirm the level of technology argument for this set of cases and validate the asset specificity one. Table 5.8 summarizes the results.

Table 5.8 *Process tracing: summary of the findings*

Managerial dilemmas cause the diffusion of environmental standards		
	Observable implications	
Explanation	(1) Sequence of events	(2) Interpretation of events	(3) Consequences
Asset specificity	Confirming evidence: M, V, F B does not allow for any inference	Confirming evidence: M, N, F (data for V and B unavailable)	Confirming evidence: M, N, F, V (data for N unavailable)
Level of technology	Disconfirming evidence: M, V, F, N B does not allow for any inference	No confirming evidence found	Disconfirming evidence: M, N, F, V (data for N unavailable)

[112] Interview with the Quality and Environmental Systems Engineer of F, South Africa, September 30, 2008, Silverton.

The *technological specialization dilemma*: textile firms in South Africa

The chapter has so far concentrated on analyzing the *foreign direct investment dilemma*, which is a special instance of the *technological specialization dilemma*. The insights of the analysis of the former thus also apply to the latter. However, what we cannot infer from the analysis up till now is whether asset specificity is a driver of environmental policies generally, or only in the context of foreign direct investments. To establish the applicability, plausibility, and validity of asset-specific investments in production technology as a driver of environmental programs beyond the *foreign direct investment dilemma*, the chapter will now conduct a third controlled pair-wise comparison inquiring into the *technological specialization dilemma* and the effects it has for two genuine South African firms.

More specifically, the analysis will consider two cases in the textile industry of South Africa. Apart from allowing us to assess the validity of internal driver 2 in this different industry sector, these cases do not involve foreign direct investments and are thus highly different from the automotive cases analyzed before. They feature, in addition, small firms, whereas the analyses of multinational carmakers before comprised very large corporations. The two firms also allow us to see if asset specificity as an internal driver for environmental standards is valid on a low investment level. The cases of the previous analysis of multinational carmakers involved asset-specific investments on an exceptionally high level. In contrast to that, the two textile cases featured in this third comparative analysis are firms that generally operate on low investment levels. Is internal driver 2 – asset-specific investments in production technology – also leading to the predicted effects with respect to environmental policies in these cases?

Textile firms and the technological specialization dilemma

The two textile firms the analysis features are Pa and Sy. Pa is a dyeing and finishing plant in Garankuwa, located 40 kilometers from Pretoria. The factory colors and finishes fabrics to garments and apparel for stores such as Mr Price, Edgars, Foschini, and other South African mass-market retailers. Alternatively, Pa supplies intermediate fabric-related products to clothing firms that cut, make, and trim (CMT) garments and apparel (t-shirts, polos, shirts, trousers).[113] Pa was founded in 1990, has a turnover of about ZAR30 million (2007), and employs 150 people. When the Rand was devalued in the period right after apartheid, the firm exported to Europe and the US. With the appreciation of the currency, the South African textile exports became generally uncompetitive so that Pa – as many other textile mills as well – had to cut down in size and change its focus to the domestic market.[114] Today, 100 per cent of Pa's sales go to the South African market.

Sy, the second textile company, was part of Van Dyck Carpets until 2004 – a formerly large South African carpet maker. In 2004/5 CC, a South African company mentioned in the previous chapter as a manufacturer of hotel carpets, bought 51 percent of the shares of Sy, while an institutional South African investor named Industrial Development Corporation, IDC, acquired the remaining 49 percent.[115] While CC supports Sy with know-how and expertise, IDC supplies the firm with fresh capital. Sy is located in Hammarsdale near Durban and specializes in yarns, dyeing, and weaving for the making of polypropylene carpets and rugs. The company employs 130 people and has an annual turnover of ZAR20 million to ZAR35 million.[116] The firm's main market is South Africa, where its rugs are sold in the same stores as Pa's products.

Analyzing asset specificity – internal driver 2 – we can assess the *asset* dimension by focusing on the amount of investments made in the production site in terms of absolute investment sums, with the revenues of Sy and Pa being very similar (about ZAR30 million).[117] Thus, the

---

[113] See interview with the Managing Director of Pa, September 13, 2007, Garankuwa; additional information drawn from the website of Pa (April 18, 2008).

[114] However, the domestic market is also going down as it is now much cheaper to import textiles from China, Bangladesh, or Vietnam to South Africa than to produce there.

[115] Interview with the Director of Human Resources, the Assistant to the Managing Director, the Chief Engineer, and Environmental Manager of CC, September 28, 2007, Durban; website of CC (January 17, 2009); additional information drawn from the website of Sy (March 1, 2009).

[116] Turnover used to be ZAR35 million–ZAR40 million. However, the annual report published by IDC in 2006 anticipates a ZAR16.5 million loss and shrinking business. Annual Report (2006), Industrial Development Corporation (IDC) of South Africa Limited.

[117] Hence the analysis measures here *Indicator 1* operationalized for the assessment of asset specificity above.

total annual investments made by management in the respective production units also indicate the resources the two firms dedicate to
production in relative terms. Pa is a remarkable case for the analysis
of the *technological specialization dilemma*. Except for some minor
maintenance, the firm has not invested in its production facilities at all
for decades. From the very beginnings of the company it produced with
old equipment and machinery, which had been previously bought by
the owners of Pa from a firm that went bankrupt. Since then management had not invested in any new machinery. The assertion is therefore
that investments in production facilities of any kind are entirely absent
in the case of Pa.

   Different from Pa, Sy experienced some major investments for the
technological upgrade of production since 2004/5, mainly financed
by the Industrial Development Corporation.[118] More specifically, the
management of Sy has borrowed ZAR5 million to ZAR6 million from
IDC for investments in new machinery, facilities, and technology
over a period of four years.[119] Average calculated return of investment
is two to three years.[120] Hence, Sy is a case in which management
confronts the *technological specialization dilemma*. Table 5.9 summarizes the analysis of the level of asset-specific investments for both
cases.

Firm characteristics and control variables

As in the previous analyses, this one implies controlled comparisons,
i.e. a selection of highly similar cases. The control variables which
establish this similarity are the same as in the analysis of multinational
carmakers above. Table 5.10 summarizes the two cases Pa and Sy in
this respect.

---

[118] Measuring *Indicator 1* for Sy. Annual Report (2006), Industrial Development
       Corporation (IDC) of South Africa Limited. Interview with the Director of
       Human Resources, and the Chief Engineer and Environmental Manager
       of CC Holding, September 28, 2007, Durban. See also email questionnaire filled
       in by Sy.
[119] Annual Report (2008), Industrial Development Corporation (IDC) of South
       Africa Limited. Email questionnaire filled in by the SHE Representative of CC
       Holdings, February 13, 2009.
[120] Assessing *Indicator 2*.

Table 5.9 *Cases illustrating (variance of) the* technological specialization dilemma

	The *technological specialization dilemma*: empirical cases – textile firms		
Indicators	**Case 11** Pa (dyeing and finishing of apparel)		**Case 12** Sy (rug maker)
Indicator 1 Amount of annual investments in production facilities, machines, and technology	No investments	No levels of asset specificity	€500,000 in 2004/5 10% of annual turnover
Indicator 2 Period before envisioned return of investment	No period before return of investment		2–3 years

(brace: Case 11 → No levels of asset specificity; Case 12 → Significant levels of asset specificity)

Environmental policies

Analyzing the level of environmental policies of the two firms, the analysis first considers policy formulation.[121] It then turns to the analysis of the implementation process.[122] Pa does not have an environmental policy, nor does it take implementation measures. It also does not show practices from which some form of environmental management could be inferred. Quite to the contrary, the Managing Director reports that municipality representatives once arrived at the factory and asked him to conduct an environmental impact assessment. "But I said to them: you guys, don't come with this now! And I sent them away."[123] Hence, effluents are released unchecked and unprocessed and waste production and electricity and water consumption is not minimized. "This makes me sound like I was a bad industrialist" says the Director of Pa.[124] However, according to him the economic situation simply

---

[121] That is, *Indicators 1a–d.*
[122] By applying a combination of *Indicators 1a-d* and *Indicators 2a–e.*
[123] Interview with the Managing Director of Pa, September 13, 2007. [124] Ibid.

Table 5.10 *Cases analyzed with respect to control variables*

Control variables: the *technological specialization dilemma*		
	Comparison 3: textile industry Apparel and rug manufacturers	
Control variables	**Case 11** Pa (dyeing and finishing of apparel)	**Case 12** Sy (rug maker)
CV 1 Firm size	Small (150 employees)	Small (130 employees)
CV 2 The *human resources* *dilemma*	Hardly any training	Hardly any training
CV 3 NGO pressure	No	No
CV 4 Association/PPP Initiative	No	No
CV 5 Problem pressure	Impact areas: waste, energy, water, effluents	Impact areas: waste, energy, water, effluents
CV 6 Supply chain regulation	No	No
CV 7 Brand name/target market	B2B and lower end	B2B and lower end
CV 8 Home country regulation	N/A – South African	N/A – South African
CV 9 "Shadow of hierarchy"	Absent	Absent

does not allow Pa to spend any money or time on environmental measures. To remain competitive, he sees no other choice but to exploit the possibility of a systematic externalization of the production costs onto the environment.

Different from Pa, Sy has an environmental policy.[125] It is oriented towards ISO 14000, the environmental management system standard. Unlike its sister company, the hotel carpet manufacturer CC, Sy's management system is not officially certified, however, mainly out of cost reasons: the relative costs for certification are higher for smaller firms than for bigger ones.[126] This implies that implementation is not strictly monitored and enforced. Also, Sy is not subjected to a third-party legal compliance audit. However, Sy has carried out an environmental impact assessment, defined its critical areas, and has detailed processes with escalation procedures to control and reduce pollution and mitigate risks. Hence, implementation is taking place, though to a lesser extent than in factories with official ISO 14000 certifications.

In content, the policy of Sy is oriented towards the legal standards, which are relatively weak in the impact areas of Sy – effluents, waste, and energy and water consumption – and imprecise, incomprehensive, and not very demanding in South Africa. For example, Sy maintains a policy on water and energy consumption reduction and also keeps track of achievements in this respect. But the reduction goals are loosely formulated without precise targets. In conclusion, the assertion is therefore that Sy has a fully established environmental policy implemented, albeit on a rather low level – yet in comparison with Pa still quite profound (Table 5.11).

Conclusion

This chapter has brought to light that:

- everything else being equal, asset-specific investments in production technology are a predictor for the level of environmental standards firms operate on;
- in the context of foreign direct investments, asset specificity is a driver of standard diffusion from highly regulating "home" to weakly regulating "host" countries;

---

[125] Interview with the Director of Human Resources, the Assistant to the Managing Director, the Chief Engineer and Environmental Manager of CC Holding, September 28, 2007, Durban.

[126] Interview with an Environmental Management Systems Certifier of the South African Bureau of Standards (SABS), September 12, 2007, Pretoria.

Table 5.11 *Summary of environmental policies of South African textile firm cases*

The dependent variable: environmental policies		
	Comparison 3: textile industry Apparel and rug manufacturers	
Indicators	Case 6 Pa (dyeing and finishing of apparel)	Case 7 Sy (rug maker)
Indicator 2: management system implemented	No	Firm has management system, but not certified or third-party audited; incomplete implementation
Indicator 3: level of standards of environmental protection (weak South African standards or high international standards)	No	Environmental standards meet South African legislation

- internal driver 2 is valid in different sector contexts, on different levels of intensity of asset specificity, and irrespective of firm size – and thus attains general validity;
- the causal processes unleashed by asset specificity consist of management inventing environmental programs in order to mitigate the risks inherent in long-term investments – as theorized in Chapter 2.

What are the wider implications of these findings? First, they confirm for environmental standards what the analysis of labor-related corporate social responsibility had concluded in Chapter 4: *intra*-organizational asset-specific investments are important for our understanding of the relationship between regulatory standards and firm behavior under conditions of economic globalization. Such investments explain which firms diffuse standards, and why, and which firms may not do so, but instead propel "race to the bottom" dynamics. Second, they also reconfirm what was asserted in Chapter 4 concerning the mechanisms that bring about industry regulation. Most of the analyses in the context of the "worlds of welfare capitalism" or "varieties of capitalism" literature explain such regulation by emphasizing the importance of social forces and movements. The analysis shows there is also a rationale for management-driven social and environmental policies.

Another implication of the findings in this chapter pertains to the *brand reputation dilemma*. Figure 5.2 above indicates an almost perfectly linear relationship between asset-specific investments in production technology and environmental programs. This is surprising as some of the firms featured are high-end market firms (M and B) whereas others sell to the mass market (V, F, and N). We would thus expect the high-end market firms to show a linear causal relation between asset specificity and environmental policies on a lower level than mass-market firms. Chapter 6 will now turn to a detailed interpretation of these findings, and systematically assess internal driver 4, asset-specific investments in marketing.

6 | *Internal driver 4: the* brand reputation dilemma

The previous analysis of multinational car companies producing in South Africa raised some doubts concerning the validity of internal driver 4. The *brand reputation dilemma* – asset-specific investments in marketing – is supposed to cause in-house and supply chain policies in general, i.e. in the areas of the environment and social standards. The cases of the German-originating large multinational car companies B and M over time (t1, t2, and t3), of V after 2006, and of the US firm F before 2007/8, and their respective environmental policies, illustrate the point (see Chapter 5). The six cases are highly similar with respect to basic company features and potential factors of corporate social responsibility.[1] They vary, however, with respect to the *foreign direct investment* and the *brand reputation dilemmas*. The analysis in Chapter 5 therefore conducted separate controlled pair-wise comparisons for the high-end market firms on the one hand, and the mass-market firms on the other, so as to ensure that we see the isolated effects of the *foreign direct investment dilemma* (i.e. of internal driver 3). Table 6.1 summarizes once again the findings of Chapter 5 in this respect for the six cases of M t1, M t2, and M t3, B, V after 2006, and F before 2007/8.

To assess the isolated effects of the *brand reputation dilemma*, the analysis needs to define now how we can know the *brand reputation dilemma* when we want to see it and establish the degree to which this dilemma is represented in the six cases. With regard to the measurement of the *brand reputation dilemma*, the analysis concentrates on the average "price level"/"revenue per sold unit" (*Indicator 1*) or "investments in

---

[1] See Table 5.3, Chapter 5. Similarity is established on the basis of the control variables firm size, NGO pressure, associations, public–private and private–private partnerships, problem pressure, exports, and the level of regulation in home country of headquarters.

Table 6.1 Foreign direct investment dilemma, *multinational car companies*

Cases	Indicator 1 asset specificity: annual investments/annual turnover (€) Indicator 2 asset specificity: duration before return of investment	Intensity of the *technological specialization dilemma*
M t1	I1: >10 m/160 bn I2: no duration/less than 1 year	low
F	I1: >10 m/100–120 bn I2: less than 1 year	low
M t2	I1: 20–25 m/160 bn I2: less than 1 year, 2–3 years	low-medium
V	I1: 35 m/100 bn I2: less than 1 year, 3–4 years	medium
M t3	I1: *c.*100 m/100 bn I2: 3–4 years	high
B	I1: *c.* 50–100 m/55 bn I2: 3–4 years	high

marketing" (*Indicator 2*), which we find by relating marketing expenses to the annual turnover.[2] A proxy indicator for "investments in marketing" is brand indexes (Table 6.2).

Establishing the six cases in detail with respect to the *brand reputation dilemma*, the analysis relates sales revenues to sales numbers in order to establish revenues per sold unit, which also indicate the price level on which the firms sell.[3] The findings imply strong differences between, on the one hand, V and F, and on the other hand, M and B: in 2007 V sold 6.23 million cars. Sales revenues were €99 billion.[4] Accordingly, average revenues per sold unit were €15,891. F sold 6.55 million cars in that same year. Revenues were $154.4 billion.[5]

---

[2] "Investments in marketing" thus refer to the annual marketing budget as a percentage of the annual turnover.
[3] Thus measuring *Indicator 1*.
[4] See Management Report of V (2007). Section: "Net Assets, Financial Position and Results of Operation."
[5] See Annual Report of F (2008). Section: "Progress and Priorities"/2007 Annual Report, released March 6, 2008.

Table 6.2 *Measurement of the* brand reputation dilemma

The *brand reputation dilemma*		
Concept: asset specificity	Indicators	Assessment
Dimension 1: **target market** High-end vs. mass-market **Dimension 2: brand value** Marketing	**Indicator 1:** "price level"/"revenue per sold unit" **Indicator 2:** investments in marketing (proxy: brand indexes)	High vs. low High High vs. low Low

Hence, F generated about €15,000–€18,500 in revenues per car.[6] In comparison, M's and B's revenues per sold unit are on a higher level. M sold 1.29 million cars in 2007. The sales revenues of the Car Group were €52.5 billion.[7] Revenues per unit are €40,310. Sales of B exceeded 1.5 million units in 2007; sales revenues amounted to €56 billion.[8] Accordingly, the revenues per car are €37,333. Hence, the average price for a car of V or F is half that of the price of a model of M or B. Thus, B and M target in comparative perspective a high-price market, while V and F are oriented towards a lower, mass-market price segment (see also Kirmani *et al.* 1999).[9]

A "brand parity study" provides for additional evidence.[10] The study concludes that both B and M have the highest brand values in the automotive industry, while the values for V and F are within the range of other mass-market producers such as Nissan, Fiat, General Motors, Mazda, or Citroen (see BBDO Consulting 2009). Table 6.3 groups the

---

[6] The exact amount, depending on the current exchange rate, is irrelevant as long as the finding clearly indicates that F's revenues per sold unit are lower than M's and B's.

[7] See Management Report of M (2007). Revenues of the Car Group do not include sales of trucks and commercial vehicles or the revenues generated by financial services and other industrial activities.

[8] See Annual Report of B (2007). Section: "Review of the Financial Year 2007."

[9] The finding is valid for the time before 2007 as well. The distinction between high-end market OEMs and mass-market OEMs thus also concerns M t1, M t2 and F, V, and B in the 1990s and between 2000–7.

[10] The results for *Indicator 2* are thus additional evidence in this respect.

Table 6.3 Foreign direct investment *and* brand reputation dilemmas

Production-specific assets	High-end market orientation	Mass-market orientation
Low	M t1	F
Low-medium	M t2	
Medium		V
High	M t3, B	

(Consumer market asset specificity)

six cases according to their features with respect to the *brand reputation dilemma* and the *foreign direct investment dilemma*.

What can we deduce from Table 6.2 with respect to the effects of the *brand reputation dilemma*? Do the empirical cases meet the theoretical expectation? First, according to the theoretical argument, the high-end market firm M should show stronger environmental policies at t1 than the producer of cars for the mass-market, F. Viewing the environmental policies of M at t1 and F, however, the empirical findings indicate just the opposite. The mass-market US car firm F attained ISO 14001 certification in the period of t1 in 1998/9. The standards that are being implemented by the environmental management system of F have been on the level of the legal standards of South Africa since then. The policy is therefore weak in comparison with B and M t3, which incorporate the highest European and German environmental laws. However, M only started ISO 14001 certification during t2 in 2003 – five years later than F. Before, M's policy was implemented less systematically than F's. Moreover, M's environmental policy was, as F's still is, oriented towards meeting the South African legal requirements and did not go beyond these before 2006 (i.e. throughout t2). Only after the decision had been made to increase the level of asset specificity in the South African operations was the environmental policy of M upgraded to the level of B. Thus, the finding contrasts with the theoretical expectation: M t1 does not show a stronger policy than F before 2007/8, but operates on a lower level of environmental standards.

Second, additional disconfirming evidence derives from a juxtaposition of M t2 with V (after 2006). According to the argument for the *brand reputation dilemma*, M t2 should be at least on par with the policy of V after 2006, considering that the asserted differences between the two cases with respect to the degree to which they embody the *foreign direct investment dilemma* are rather small.[11] However, the analyses conducted in Chapter 5 revealed that the ISO 14001 certified management system of V is based on demanding, concise, and encompassing goals and standards on a level above South African law, albeit below European or German regulatory standards.[12] Dissimilar to the prediction of the theoretical argument, the assessment therefore assigns higher values to the policy of the mass-market producer V after 2006 than of high-end market firm M t2, because M t2's is oriented towards meeting the legal requirements of South Africa only. Additional evidence for this assertion is that V obtained ISO 14001 certification in 1999 already, whereas M started the certification process only much later during t2 after a major asset-specific investment was made in the paint shop in 2002/3. To conclude, the evaluation of multinational car companies' environmental policies results in disconfirming evidence for internal driver 4.

However, what about the argument for the *brand reputation dilemma* with respect to supply chain policies? Do investments in marketing result in stricter supply chain regulation? In line with the theoretical expectation, the high-end market car companies B and M show stricter, more demanding, precise, and encompassing supply chain governance in the field of environment than the mass-market producers V and F.[13] More precisely, B and M require first-tier suppliers to be certified according to ISO 14001. As a result, today 90 percent of all first-tier suppliers of the firms have attained certification.[14] The remaining 10 percent are service providers, such as the canteen or health service firms, at which the requirement was never directed. Moreover, B and M demand from

---

[11] See Table 6.1. The analysis of the OEMs' in-house policies makes use of the same indicators as explicated in Chapter 5.

[12] See Table 5.6, Chapter 5.

[13] The general indicators laid out in Chapter 3 measure the policies of firms vis-à-vis suppliers. The analysis thus measures here *Indicators 1a–d*.

[14] Measuring *Indicator 2e* and *Indicator 3a–c*. Interview with the Project Leader VPS, Safety, Health and Environment (SHE) Representative, and the General Manager Corporate Planning of B South Africa, February 20, 2007, Midrand; with the Occupational Health Manager, February 14, 2007, Rosslyn; with the Manager: Quality Management and Integrated Management System of M South Africa, September 23, 2008, East London; with the Corporate Health Manager of M South Africa, February 26, 2007, East London.

key suppliers TS 16949 certification. TS 16949 is a standard specifically for the automotive industry that combines ISO 9001 quality management systems standards with ISO 14001 environmental management. A constitutive element of TS 16949 is that certified firms must require ISO 14001 certification from their key suppliers as well. By making TS 16949 a requirement, the two high-end market firms thus actively push the environmental management system ISO 14001 down the supply chain.

V, the firm which sells cars to the mass-market segment, by contrast, just "encourages" first-tier suppliers to achieve ISO 14001 certification, but says that generally the firm is "not too strict about it."[15] F, on the other hand, claims to strictly demand ISO 14001 certification from its suppliers.[16] However, suppliers of F disprove this claim by saying that F does not demand ISO 14001 of them. According to these suppliers, only B and – to a lesser extent – M require ISO 14001 certification strictly.[17] V and F, by contrast, are tolerant in this respect.

While these findings are in line with the theoretical prediction, an additional assessment of the cases from a longitudinal perspective uncovers facts that point in a different direction. M started to demand ISO 14001 and TS 16949 from suppliers only after 2006 (i.e. at t3). Before, the firm's policy was identical with V's and F's in that M did not require ISO 14001 or TS 16949 certification from suppliers. The implications are twofold: first, the cases of M t1 and M t2 disconfirm the argument that the *brand reputation dilemma* moves firms to adopt strong supply chain regulation. Between 1999 and 2006 (t1–t2) the supply chain policy of the high-end market firm M was on the same level with respect to environmental standards as the mass-market firms V's and F's.

---

[15] Interview with the Environmental Controller for Manufacturing Planning of V South Africa, September 22, 2008.

[16] Interview with the Quality and Environmental Systems Engineer of F South Africa, September 30, 2008, Silverton.

[17] Interview with the Human Resources Manager of AL, Interview, September 13, 2007, Rosslyn; with the SHE Manager of Fe, September 25, 2008, Durban; Interview with the Manager of Integrated Systems of Sä, September 22, 2008, Port Elizabeth; the Product Engineering and Corporate Quality Assurance Manager of Sh, September 22, 2008, Port Elizabeth; with the Quality and Human Resources Manager of FE, September 2008, 23, East London; with the Director of V, October 1, 2008, Rosslyn; with the Production Manager of CS, September 18, 2008, Cape Town.

Second, the *foreign direct investment/technological specialization dilemmas* may not only explain in-house policies, but also supply chain governance. The substantial increase of asset specificity generated in the case of M in 2006 did not only result in an upgrade of in-house environmental policies. It also made M adopt stricter environmental supply chain policies. The supply chain accounts for 60–70 percent of the value added to the products multinational car firms such as M sell. Production targets and costs, unforeseen events, and opportunism – bearing the potential of rendering an asset-specific investment in a production unit unprofitable – are consequently determined by outside factors to a great extent. To mitigate the risks inherent in this dependency on, and to reduce vulnerability to, such outside factors management may insist on the exercise of strict supply chain governance. Hence, by the same logic, in-house environmental policies *and* supply chain policies can be assumed to emerge as a consequence of the *technological specialization/foreign direct investment dilemma*. What we must take as a conclusion from these inductively arrived at considerations is, however, that the *brand reputation dilemma* must be rejected as an explanation for supply chain policies of the car companies. The findings with respect to the corporate social responsibility policies of the firms are more comprehensive, consistent, and plausibly explained by the incentives that the *technological specialization/foreign direct investment dilemma* gives management to engage in such policies.

In conclusion, the theoretical argument does not hold with respect to the *brand reputation dilemma* in the context of the South African automotive industry. With respect to in-house policies, the finding is that differences in the target market are not reflected in environmental policies. An analysis of the mass-market firms F and V as well as the high-end producer M between t1 and t3 does not reveal any significant differences between the firms' environmental engagements. Regarding supply chain policies, the finding is, however, that the high-end market firms M and B regulate the supply chain more strictly than the mass-market producers V and F. Yet, the high-end market firms' supply chain policies were identical to the mass-market ones until recently and changed only after investments in production increased drastically in 2006, resulting in the emergence of the *technological specialization dilemma*. While this is evidence that contradicts the argument for internal drivers with respect to the *brand reputation dilemma*, it is additional support for the explanatory power of the *technological specialization dilemma*. To conclude, the *brand reputation dilemma* is dismissed as an explanation for supply chain policies of multinational car companies.

The textile industry: luxury brand production in China

Additional, disconfirming evidence is the case of the luxury fashion brand C and its Chinese supplier CL. The case was mentioned in Chapter 1 as an example of a firm that produces in offshore locations for the purpose of facilitating human exploitation and exploitation of the environment; thus, as a firm driving the regulatory "race to the bottom." C is an important case for the analysis of the *brand reputation dilemma*: as a luxury goods firm it is a most likely case for observing the positive effects of investments in marketing.

C was founded in 1968. Soon after, the brand became widely known and expanded from a clothing firm to a brand that markets jeans, underwear, swimwear, accessories, hosiery, furniture, cosmetics, and eyewear. In 2002/3 C was sold to the PvH Group. PvH is the biggest shirt-maker on the American apparel market.[18] The Group owns several brands through which PvH targets all consumer market segments. PvH is managed from New York City where the global headquarters is located. In 2007 PvH had an annual turnover of $2.4 billion. CL, the supplier of C in China, was founded by a Taiwanese businessman in 1975.[19] In 1988, he moved production from Taiwan to mainland China. To be more precise, he relocated to a village on the outskirts of Tonglu, a small Chinese town in Zhejiang province, approximately 400–500 km south-west of Shanghai. CL employs about 2,000 people, most of them migrant workers from the provinces of Central China. The company specializes in leather garment products and leather furniture. CL also operates its own raw leather factory to secure high quality standards for its top-end market customers. Most importantly, however, CL consists of a number of factories in which leather garments and furniture are made for export to the US and Europe. The supplier is thus well integrated in production networks that deliver

---

[18] See www.pvh.com (February 15, 2009).
[19] Protocol, interview with the owner family of CL, and with a Manager of CL, April 24, 2008, Tonglu. Additional information drawn from the website of CL (15 February 2009).

to the West, where concerns for human rights and environmental standards are strong. The work processes in the factories include cutting, knitting, treatment with chemicals, and cleaning as well as coloring. Customers of CL are luxury fashion and furniture brands.

Establishing the *brand reputation dilemma* for the case, C sells garments in the price range between $250 and $10,000.[20] Hence, C sells at a high price level targeting the top 5 percent of the consumer market. In fact, PvH bought C in 2002/3 in order to enter the luxury and high-end segments of the apparel fashion market.[21] Brand ratings confirm these assertions.[22] Compared with low-price brands such as Chaps, Arrow, or Private Label (selling at an average price of $10 per unit) and middle-class or upper middle-class brands such as Tommy Hilfinger and Timberland, C scores significantly higher in an internal brand value ranking undertaken by PvH.[23] In fact, the relation between the two firms – C and its supplier CL – is an exemplary case for the presence of a strong *brand reputation dilemma*. According to the theoretical arguments for internal drivers, one would therefore expect CL to operate on relatively high corporate social responsibility standards. In addition, as a luxury fashion brand C should adopt a relatively strict corporate social responsibility supply chain policy vis-à-vis CL, which in turn is why CL should operate at relatively high standards.

However, the empirical findings are that the supplier of C, the Chinese leather factory CL, systematically violates the most basic international and Chinese labor standards. C is completely aware of the fact and acquiesces in it, which implies that in practice the fashion brand does not incorporate corporate social responsibility in its supply chain policies. For the assessment, I present the protocol of the factory visit at CL and an analysis of interviews with representatives of the firm.[24]

---

[20] The analysis thus turns now to a measurement of *Indicator 1*, "price level." Website of PvH: www.pvh.com/OurComp_CorpStrategy.html (February 15, 2009).

[21] *New York Times*, Sunday, December 18, 2002.

[22] Turning now to an evaluation of *Indicator 2*.

[23] Website of PvH: www.pvh.com/OurComp_CorpStrategy.html (February 15, 2009).

[24] I will evaluate the corporate social responsibility policies by looking at the policy practices of CL in the policy fields of labor relations and environment (thus, measuring *indicators 3a–c*), and the supply chain governance practices of C.

Protocol (part 1): Large leather sheets and other raw materials are delivered to CL's factory storeroom.[25] These materials are brought into the factory hall, where the quality of the sheets is assessed. Inspectors from the customers of CL closely monitor this assessment to ascertain that the materials used by CL for manufacturing meet the quality standards of the high-end market brands they represent.[26] The inspectors remain in the factory throughout the period of a production cycle – i.e. between 6 months and 1.5 years – to control the supplier and production processes on a daily basis. C has one quality inspector on-site at CL on a permanent basis. In addition, two inspectors who work for the local sourcing office in Shanghai regularly visit the factory to monitor CL's compliance with C's production standards.[27]

The workers that carry the sheets from the storeroom into the factory hall appear to be very young. Upon my inquiry, a Chinese manager estimates that they are between eight and ten years of age. He also remarks, "the company and also the customers do not care about their age or social concerns. They just care about quality and price."[28] According to the manager the minimum standard for employment at CL is therefore solely that "you are big enough to carry around some leather sheets and furniture." The impression that very young employees work at CL is repeatedly confirmed throughout the factory tour by the manager. For example, at a later stage he points to a group of very young-looking workers and says "I often feel sorry for the children when I see them working day and night."[29] Whenever intermediate products are brought from one production step to another, it seems that the factory uses children as carriers. The degree of automation is consequently rather low for a factory of this size.

Analysis: This first part of the protocol contains information about the degree to which the supplier of C, CL, shows corporate social

---

[25] The protocol summarizes the visual observation during the factory tour and the information provided by a manager of CL (who also guided the tour) and one representative of the owner-family of CL. Both interview partners were fluent in English. The protocol was written immediately after the factory visit and contains quotations. The factory visit took place April 24, 2008, Tonglu.

[26] During the factory tour I was also introduced to the quality manager of C, who apparently believed I represented one of CL's customers.

[27] These inspectors usually face harsh price pressure from the brands they represent. Even if they are supposed to supervise compliance with social standards, the incentivization system applied by the Western brands discourages this in practice.

[28] Protocol, remark by a manager of CL, April 24, 2008, Tonglu.   [29] Ibid.

responsibility practices in the policy field of labor relations. Designated areas of such practices are according to prevalent international institutions in the policy field and industry sector: "minimum age"; "minimum wage"; "over hours"; the "compensation of overtime work"; "freedom of association"; "health and safety"; and "forced labor."[30] We can assess the degree to which the practices of CL in these areas show signs of a corporate social responsibility policy in relation to international standard setting institutions, the Chinese labor law, and the official corporate social responsibility supply chain policy of the PvH Group.[31]

This first part of the protocol delineates the practices of CL with regard to the minimum age of employees. It reveals that CL has no policy implemented that would define a minimum age or prohibit child labor, because "the company ... does not care about [it]."[32] As a consequence the age of workers on the factory floor is non-compliant with international standards such as the International Labour Organization's (ILO) core labor standards, which strictly prohibit child labor, defined as employment under the age of fourteen.[33] The employment practices at CL are also infringing on Chinese labor law, which requires a minimum age of fourteen as well.[34] Aside from that, CL is violating the official supply chain policy of PvH by employing children at an age of eight to ten. The policy states in this respect that "employees of our vendors must be over the applicable minimum legal

[30] See, e.g. the ILO core labor standards: www.ilo.org/declaration/principles/abolitionofchildlabour/lang–en/index.htm; the Global Compact principles: www.unglobalcompact.org/AboutTheGC/TheTenPrinciples/index.html; the code of conduct of the Fair Labor Association (FLA): www.fairlabor.org/about_us_code_conduct_e1.html; of Worldwide Responsible Accredited Production (WRAP): www.wrapcompliance.org/wrap-12-principles-certification; and of the Business Social Compliance Initiative (BSCI): www.bsci-eu.org/index.php?id=2020 (October 25, 2009).

[31] The analysis assesses here the degree to which the policy is demanding and systematically pursued (*Indicators 3a* and *c*).

[32] Protocol, remark by a manager of CL, April 24, 2008, Tonglu.

[33] See the core labor standard "effective abolition of child labor": www.ilo.org/declaration/principles/abolitionofchildlabour/lang--en/index.htm (October 25, 2009).

[34] Interviews with the World Watch Institute, China Watch, March 4, 2008, Washington, DC; The Asia Foundation, April 15, 2008, Beijing; ILO Workplace Education Programme China, April 17, 2008, Beijing; The American Chamber of Commerce People's Republic of China (AmCham), April 15, 2008, Beijing.

age requirement or be at least 14 years old . . ."[35] Hence, the automotive cases and the case of the textile firm CL provide disconfirming evidence for the argument that the *brand reputation dilemma* motivates firms to engage in corporate social responsibility. By contrast, the high-end market factory CL has no standards in place with regard to minimum age at all, but instead appears to systematically employ child workers.

Beyond that, the first part of the protocol provides the analysis with information about the supply chain policy practices of C vis-à-vis CL. The statement that "the company and the customers do not care [about the age of employees]" implies that C does not include standards prohibiting child labor in the governance rules that address CL.[36] The reported evidence furthermore shows that C has – theoretically – the organizational capabilities for an implementation of corporate social responsibility supply chain standards. It operates a "subunit" with sufficient "personnel" and applies "compliance mechanisms" to guarantee that the production at CL meets high quality standards.[37] The lack of effective implementation of PvH's corporate social responsibility supply chain policies is therefore not a consequence of insufficient organizational resources. Instead, C seems reluctant to implement its own supply chain policy. Hence contrary to what Chapter 2 theoretically expected, the high-end brand name firm C neither shows an interest in corporate social responsibility supply chain policies, nor does it demonstrate any practices in this regard.

Protocol (part 2): Asked what "day and night" means in the quote above ("I often feel sorry for the children when I see them working day and night") the manager of CL replies that working times depend on the season. In high season work usually starts at 8am and stops "most of the time not later than 10pm."[38] Thus, depending on the order volume and whether a lunch break is granted, employees at CL work 12–14 hour shifts, six days per week. Only the skilled workers are offered compensation for over-time. Unskilled workers are compensated with a fixed RMB400 (*c.* €40–45) per month.[39]

---

[35] www.pvh.com/CorpResp_WorldAction.html (February 15, 2009).
[36] Protocol, remark by a manager of CL, April 24, 2008, Tonglu.
[37] Hence, it has the organizational and compliance mechanisms to enforce supply chain governance, as laid out by *Indicators 2a,b,e.*
[38] Ibid.
[39] Skilled workers earn on average RMB2,000, depending on their over-time premiums.

Analysis: This second part of the protocol contains information about the practices of CL in the areas "minimum wage," "over hours," and "compensation for overtime work." Regarding the paid "minimum wage," the policy of PvH claims, "we will only do business with vendors who pay employees at least the minimum wage required by local law ..."[40] The prescription is almost identical with the standards proposed by the Business Social Compliance Initiative (BSCI), Worldwide Responsible Accredited Production (WRAP), or the Fair Labor Association (FLA).[41] The legal minimum wage in this part of Zhejiang is RMB870.[42] CL, however, pays only RMB400. Hence the firm drastically undercuts any accepted standard defining minimum wage. Corporate social responsibility policies or policy practices with regard to minimum wage are thus absent.

Concerning "compensation for overtime work" the policy of PvH, in accordance with the aforementioned international standard setting institutions, demands that "employees shall be compensated for over-time hours at the rate established by law in the country of manufacture or, in those countries where such laws do not exist, at a rate at least equal to their regular hourly compensation rate."[43] As CL does not compensate unskilled employees for over-time, non-compliance is also asserted in this area.

Finally, CL also infringes on existing standards limiting "over hours." The policy of PvH prohibits business relations with vendors that force employees to work for more than 60 hours per week at peak times.[44] CL's employees work for more than 80 hours at peak times. Such working times are non-compliant with any international standard limiting "over hours." They are also non-compliant with Chinese labor law. This law allows firms to demand extra work time from employees only in exchange for compensation and under the condition that the average work time does not exceed 48 hours. In addition, the maximum work time must stay below 60 hours per week even in

[40] www.pvh.com/CorpResp_WorldAction.html (February 15, 2009).
[41] See fn 24.
[42] Protocol, interview with the CEO of the Polymax Group, April 22, 2008, Ningbo.
[43] www.pvh.com/CorpResp_WorldAction.html (February 15, 2009).
[44] Ibid. On this aspect the policy of PvH is in conflict with many established labor standards, such as the "Workplace Code of Conduct" of the Fair Labor Association, of which C is a member.

peak times.[45] Hence, with regard to minimum wage, compensation for overtime work, and over hours, the practices are non-compliant with accepted international standards, the Chinese labor law, or the supply chain policy of PvH.

Protocol (part 3): The production process begins following the quality inspection of the leather sheets, which are brought to a cutting machine as a first step. Again, it is the child workers who carry the merchandise there. The operators of the cutting machines are adults, however. According to the manager the leather is too valuable to be cut by child workers. The machine requires some basic skills and experience. Unskilled workers would damage the leather sheets while using the machine.

Further production steps are carried out on the upper factory floor, separated from the main factory hall. On this upper floor the leather is cleaned with solvents prior to being colored and treated with chemicals. Before we arrive at this upper floor, the manager mentions that he "would not like to work here because of the gases and chemicals. It is very unhealthy."[46] Entering the upper floor, my eyes, nose, and throat swell up. Dense dust and mist consisting of a mix of solvents, chemicals, and color dominate the hall; visibility is less than ten meters. Breathing hurts. Experienced older workers are treating the leather with chemicals and colors. Child workers carry the leather from one production step to the next one. None of the workers are wearing a mask or any other form of protection; there are no signs of a ventilation system or air filters. It is "dangerous to work here," says the manager, "these workers fall sick and are then sent away by the factory owners without further assistance or compensation."[47] When asked whether the workers have insurance, he replies that this is not the case, at least not for the majority of workers. In fact, most workers at CL are not even in possession of a formal contract. Only the skilled workers, whom the factory pays the legal minimum wage, insurances, taxes, and compensation for overtime, have official employment contracts. The rest are employed informally. The manager, however, points out that "even if you have

---

[45] Interviews with the World Watch Institute, China Watch, March 4, 2008, Washington, DC; The Asia Foundation, April 2008, Beijing; ILO Workplace Education Program China, April 17, 2008, Beijing; AmCham, April 15, 2008, Beijing; SAI (Social Accountability International) China Workplace Program, April 15, 2008, Beijing.

[46] Protocol, remark by a manager of CL, April 24, 2008, Tonglu.   [47] Ibid.

a contract, it does not mean a thing! We are in China. It is just a piece of paper to throw away. If your boss has good contacts contracts mean nothing."[48]

Analysis: This part of the protocol covers, first, the area "health and safety." The policy of PvH states in this respect – again in line with the mentioned international standard setters – that, "employers shall provide a safe and healthy work environment to prevent accident and injury to health. Vendors should make a responsible contribution to the health care needs of their employees." Contrary to that, it seems that the production practices at CL are entirely unaffected by concerns about the health and safety of the workers. In fact, costs for masks, air filter systems, and other measures that would improve the safety of employees are spared. The costs that the production process imposes on individual workers that suffer from work-related injuries, sickness, or invalidity are ruthlessly externalized given that no insurance or compensation for work-inflicted injury or disability is paid out. Hence, the finding is that CL does not show any corporate social responsibility practices in the area of health and safety whatsoever.

Second, the fact that minors work in the factory without a contract potentially implies that the firm takes advantage of "forced labor" as well. The abolition of forced labor, however, is a central aim of corporate social responsibility standards worldwide. Hence, also with respect to the areas of health and safety and, potentially, forced labor, the analysis asserts that no standards are applied.

Protocol (part 4): Back on the ground floor, the treated and dried leather is stuffed (for clothes and furniture alike) and sewed in a next production step. Young women, according to the manager between fourteen and twenty years of age, sew the cushions for the leather couches. Significantly older and more experienced workers sew the garments. The manager remarks on this division of labor that the stitching is on the back of the cushions and therefore invisible. Hence, the stitching is not highly relevant for the product quality. The factory therefore decides to save costs and employs cheaper, inexperienced workers for this job. In contrast to that, the stitching on garments is visible, which is why older, experienced workers are hired. Generally, the factory seems to employ experienced older workers for work processes directly related to the quality of a product and

[48] Ibid.

inexperienced younger and cheaper workers (among them children and adolescents) for the work that is not relevant to the quality of the final products.[49]

After the factory tour we inspect the rear of the factory and dormitories of the workers. A small river runs past the factory in which the effluents – mainly deriving from the chemical treatment of the leather on the upper factory floor – are released without any prior treatment or reprocessing. When asked about environmental standards and effluent processing, the manager laughs out loud and states that "no one cares about that."[50]

Analysis: The fourth part of the protocol scrutinizes potential environmental policies and policy practices at CL. The finding is that environmental policies or practices from which policies could be inferred are absent. In conclusion, the analysis of the production processes of the high-end market brand C at the factory of the Chinese supplier CL finds additional disconfirming evidence for the argument that the *brand reputation dilemma* leads to corporate social responsibility. First, CL does not have a corporate social responsibility policy implemented. In fact, the factory operates on the basis of no or hardly any standards in the policy fields of labor relations and environment. The exception is experienced workers, who are paid the minimum wage and to whom the Chinese labor law is applied – a finding which is additional support for the effects of the *human resources dilemma* (i.e. internal driver 1). Experienced workers are, according to a manager of CL, increasingly hard to find in this region of China. Hence, management has to invest into these skills to avoid high costs for headhunting. At least in comparison with the unskilled child laborers, this implies that there is some degree of dependency in the relation between management and the more experienced workers – which translates into the firm adhering to minimum labor standards in its behavior towards them.

[49] The manager describes the division of labor between older workers and child workers thus: "Some of our workers are very young; indeed, very young. But in many areas of our production we need experienced workers, because of quality. We only make products for the best brands! There we cannot employ children. However, for the work for which you do not need many skills, the company hires very young boys because they are cheaper." Protocol, remark by a manager of CL, April 24, 2008, Tonglu.

[50] Ibid.

Second, C does not engage in corporate social responsibility supply chain governance. It is particularly interesting in this respect that C has built up sufficient organizational capacities at CL for an effective implementation of standards. However, the only standards C wishes to implement are cost efficiency-related or concerned with quality. The brand is aware of the labor standard violations at CL, but apparently sees no need to act upon it – despite high investments in marketing.

Chapter 2 envisioned two causal arguments relating the brand reputation dilemma to corporate social responsibility. First, high product quality necessitates asset-specific investments in production. These investments give rise to a governance order entailing corporate social responsibility standards. The case of C and the Chinese supplier CL, however, shows that high quality production does not necessarily lead to asset-specific investments in production facilities. CL draws on child labor – a cheap and fluid, non-specific asset – and not on machinery to sustain the production line. Second, high-end market brands implement corporate social responsibility standards to mitigate reputational risks. The case implies that this argument does not hold empirically either. To conclude, the argument that the *brand reputation dilemma* – investments of management into marketing – is accompanied by corporate social responsibility policies does not gain any support when subjected to systematic empirical analysis. To test this finding, the empirical investigation will now adopt a different, more inductive approach in a second step. Why is the *brand reputation dilemma* in the aforementioned cases of multinational car companies and the luxury fashion brand C ineffective? Under which additional conditions does the dilemma yield the theorized effects?

Re-evaluating confirming evidence: textile production in South Africa

The empirical investigation will now specifically search for confirming evidence in support of the argument of the *brand reputation dilemma*. In comparison with the disconfirming evidence in the previous sections of this chapter, this may allow us to specify why and under which conditions the dilemma exerts the theorized effects. This procedure, however, implies a change in the approach from a "forward" to a more "backwards" looking analysis (Scharpf 1997). The inquiry features three cases which illuminate further the whereabouts of the relation between the *brand reputation dilemma* and corporate social responsibility. These three cases consist of the large South African retailers W, E, and MP, which resemble each other in certain important aspects (Héritier *et al.* 2009). For example, they originate in South Africa and therefore have a weakly regulating home country in common. Besides, they are similar in size. As employers of 15,000–20,000 people, the three retailers rank among the largest firms in the country. Associative structures are generally weak in the retailing sector; partnerships with government agencies or NGOs are usually avoided as well. W, E, and MP also have in common that they focus on the domestic market. Only a small proportion of their business is carried out in neighboring African countries. The retailers source 80–90 percent of their textile products from trading agencies that source from suppliers in the Far East (that is, China, India, and Vietnam). Some smaller proportions are sourced directly from domestic textile and clothing firms.

Assessing "consumer market asset specificity," the analysis finds that one of the three South African textile and clothing retailers, W, serves a particularly high price segment of the market. E sells to a relatively well-off market segment as well, but not as affluent as W's and in addition to that less focused on quality.[51] This is different in the case of the third retailer, MP, which focuses on a price-conscious consumer base. For example, a supplier comparing the retailers W and E with MP says: "W and E are at different levels of the market place ... MP is selling a t-shirt for ZAR39.99, the others are selling it for ZAR59.99."[52] Additionally, differences in target markets are reflected

[51] Measuring *Indicator 1* for the *brand reputation dilemma*. See Héritier *et al.* 2009 and the interview with a Corporate Social Investment Specialist of W South Africa, September 21, 2007, Cape Town; the Good Business Journey Manager of W South Africa, October 2, 2007, Cape Town; the Merchandise Logistics Executive of E South Africa, September 30, 2008, Johannesburg. Additionally the assessment of other large retailers and competitors of the three firms were taken into account, such as the interview with the Risk Manager, the Group Logistics Director, and the Senior HR Manager: CSI and Wellness of Fo South Africa, September 16, 2008, Cape Town; with the Group Corporate Affairs Executive of Mass South Africa, September 29, 2008, Johannesburg.

[52] Quote from interview with the Managing Director of Pa, September 13, 2007. Confirmed by other suppliers to the three firms: interview with Project Developing Manager of TP South Africa, April 2, 2007, Cape Town; the CEO of Mon South Africa, September 16, 2008, Cape Town; the Director Dyehouse Division of Mig South Africa, September 17, 2008, Cape Town; the Group Human Resources Director of Fr South Africa, October 1, 2007, Durban.

in W highlighting the high expectations of its consumer base regarding the quality of products and environmental protection. According to the argument that the *brand reputation dilemma* inclines firms to engage in corporate social responsibility W should exercise the strictest supply chain regulation, followed by E, while they do not anticipate strong supply chain policies in the case of MP.

The empirical evidence matches this expectation with respect to the retailer W, which targets a high-end market. For example, this retailer formulates demanding and compulsory environmental governance rules for its suppliers. W, for instance, regulates the usage of chemicals in the production process. A supplier highlighted that he "was required to change to water-based adhesives within two years" after having become a contractor of W.[53] Furthermore, these requirements are also monitored and enforced. For one of the textile manufacturers the requirements were too high: "This retailer does not want to approve me as a fabric manufacturer because I do not comply with their standards ... they came here ... and they had their checklist of what they wanted. And we failed."[54] Another textile firm reported that the retailer sends auditors who require suppliers to provide extensive data relevant for both environmental protection and quality assessments.

In the case of the retailer MP, which targets the low-end of the market, supply chain governance is, as expected, absent. This retailer neither formulates a policy nor does it engage in implementation. Besides, MP sources from a textile manufacturer, which failed to comply with standards of the high-end retailer W. The retailer that takes a middle position regarding the targeted end-consumer market, E, takes a middle position with respect to the strength of the supply chain policy, too. These findings therefore confirm the argument that the *brand reputation dilemma* motivates firms for corporate social responsibility. However, why does the theoretical argument with respect to the *brand reputation dilemma* hold in the context of the South African textile industry, whereas it has no validity in the context of the South African car industry and for a globally marketed luxury textile brand sourcing from China (the case of C)?

---

[53] Interview with the CEO of Mon South Africa, September 16, 2008, Cape Town.
[54] Interview with the Managing Director of Pa, September 13, 2007.

An inductive reconsideration of the three retailer cases points at the "possibility of an NGO scandal" as a potential explanation. A remarkable aspect in the analysis of the three South African retailers is that they feel that they are being watched by NGOs willing to expose their supply chain policies (Héritier *et al.* 2009). However, the firms appear to have differential incentives to mitigate the risk of an NGO campaign: W indicates that an NGO scandal would have strong negative consequences given its high-end market-oriented business model and socially aware customers. Conversely, the medium- and low-end market retailers E and MP say they would be less affected by a scandal, because the "customer base is either interested in low price products or in quality but not in socially responsible behavior."[55] Consequently, W engages in strong supply chain corporate social responsibility to preempt potential NGO scandals while E does so to a lesser extent only, and MP refrains entirely from risk mitigation in this respect.

The inference thereof is that the *brand reputation dilemma* is activated by the presence of NGOs in the strategic environment of firms and only in this context is it an internal driver for corporate social responsibility. For example, the car manufacturers M, B, V, and F analyzed before do not feel the presence of NGOs. Generally, large car firms such as the four featured in the analysis are under pressure from NGOs in South Africa, but only for the cars they produce or, to be more precise, for the emissions levels of their cars. Usually, they are not targeted for their production processes. This is confirmed by managers of various firms who say they do not feel under pressure from NGOs in terms of their production processes.[56] This view is reinforced by an NGO representative who says, "regarding their production processes, I fully trust the car firms. In this respect, they are way above anything in South Africa. So we do not target them in this area. We only have problems with their

---

[55] Interview with the Merchandise Logistics Executive of E South Africa, September 30, 2008.

[56] Interview with the Manager: Quality Management and Integrated Management System of M South Africa, September 23, 2008, East London; with the Senior Manager Corporate Social Responsibility of M Germany, August 6, 2007 (phone); with the Project Leader VPS and SHE Representative, and the General Manager, Corporate Planning of B South Africa, February 20, 2007, Midrand; with the Corporate and Intergovernmental Affairs Manager, the Department Manager Corporate Messages, the Manager of Group Publications, and the Manager of Sustainability and Corporate and Intergovernmental Affairs of B Germany, August 2, 2007, Munich.

products."[57] Accordingly, the analysis was unable to trace any effect of the *brand reputation dilemma* on their environmental policies.

Additional support for this inductively derived claim is also found in the sourcing practices of South African retailers – among them the three retailers W, E, and MP – outside of South Africa. Usually the retailers source from overseas through trade agencies and generally do not engage in demanding and strict supply chain governance. This is also true for the high-end market retailer W.[58] To be more specific, the respective contracts between retailers and trading agencies often include a mentioning of corporate social responsibility-related aspects. However, these provisions are neither specified nor verified or enforced by the retailers. The sourcing managers of the retailers therefore reckon that the sourcing practices of the trading agencies remain unaffected by the respective provisions.[59]

Hence, there is a striking discrepancy between the high-end market firm W's supply chain governance "at home," on the one hand, which is demanding and strict, and "abroad," on the other hand, which is weak and shallow. The context factor "possibility of an NGO scandal" can account for this finding. South African NGOs are only domestically oriented and active and do not have branches or interests overseas such as in the Far East, from where the retailers source the textile products. Hence, while sourcing from these areas the possibility that the sourcing practices are exposed is not taken into account by the retailers. Consequently no differential engagements in corporate social responsibility are found. The overseas sourcing practices of W "abroad" are as weak and shallow as of, for example, the firms targeting lower ends of the consumer market, such as MP and E.

---

[57] Interview with the Trade and Investment Advisor and Automotive Sector Specialist of the World Wide Fund for Nature (WWF) South Africa, September 29, 2008, Johannesburg.

[58] See interview with a Corporate Social Investment Specialist of W South Africa, September 21, 2007, Cape Town; the Good Business Journey Manager of W South Africa, October 2, 2007, Cape Town; the Merchandise Logistics Executive of E South Africa, September 30, 2008, Johannesburg. Additionally the assessment of other large retailers and competitors of the three firms were taken into account, such as the interview with the Risk Manager, the Group Logistics Director, and the Senior HR Manager: CSI and Wellness of Fo South Africa, September 16, 2008, Cape Town; with the Group Corporate Affairs Executive of Mass South Africa, September 29, 2008, Johannesburg.

[59] Ibid.

The case of C and its supplier CL is in line with these considerations as well. On the one hand, the status of the firm as a top-rated US brand certainly puts its sourcing practices on the agenda of watchdog NGOs.[60] On the other hand, in the particular context of China, where the supplier of C, CL, is located, the work of NGOs is extremely difficult. The government actively suppresses confrontational NGOs. As a consequence, these NGOs have withdrawn from China altogether, adopted a conformist approach, or formed alliances with small, informal, and often illegal networks of researchers that provide them with information.[61] Considering that China is a huge country with thousands of exporting firms in the textile industry alone and that informal networks of researchers are rather small, limited in scope and capacity, the "possibility of an NGO scandal" seems relatively small from the perspective of C. Hence, in the specific case of the relation of C with a Chinese supplier, the factor "possibility of an NGO-scandal" may simply be absent.

In conclusion, this additional analysis of the *brand reputation dilemma* finds that the argument for this dilemma lacks general validity. However, in the context of the additional factor of a perceived "possibility of an NGO scandal," the argument for the *brand reputation dilemma* regains explanatory power. More specifically, the factor NGO triggers a logic according to which high-end market brands engage in corporate social responsibility to mitigate the risk of reputational damages: the absence of the "possibility of an NGO scandal" explains why high-end market car firms such as M do not show stronger engagement in environmental programs than mass-market OEMs such as V or F, and why humiliating labor conditions and unconstrained environmental pollution were asserted in the supply chain of C – a luxury fashion brand with a global reach. Conversely, the presence of the factor "possibility of an NGO scandal" in the South African retail industry results in a variation of corporate social responsibility supply

---

[60] The Clean Clothes Campaign (CCC), for example, specifically targets luxury brands. Interview with CCC, February 15, 2008 (phone). See the website of the CCC: www.cleanclothes.org/urgent-actions/prada-the-real-price-of-luxury (October 20, 2009).

[61] Interviews with the World Watch Institute, China Watch, March 4, 2008, Washington, DC; The Asia Foundation, April 15, 2008, Beijing; CCC, February 15, 2008 (phone); Worker Rights Consortium (WRC), March 11, 2008, Washington, DC; National Labor Committee (NLC), March 4, 2008, New York City; China CSR Map/Danish Institute for Human Rights, January 30, 2008 (phone); World Wide Fund for Nature (WWF) China, February 4, 2008 (phone).

chain policies of W, E, and MP that reflect their respective asset-specific investments in the consumer market.

The *brand reputation dilemma* 2.0: the internal–external driver nexus

The analysis now turns to a systematic assessment of the argument that the *brand reputation dilemma* is a driver for corporate social responsibility under the condition of NGO pressure, and to this end switches back to a more "forward-looking" (Scharpf 1997) approach. More specifically, the analysis in this section varies the degree and intensity of the *brand reputation dilemma*, while holding constant the external factor strong and persistent NGO pressure. I expect that under these conditions the theoretical argument with respect to the *brand reputation dilemma* is valid. The comparison features the sportswear and apparel firm Nike, the apparel firm Gap, and the discounter Wal-Mart.[62]

Nike is one of the most valuable brands in the world. Founded in 1964 (under the name of Blue Ribbon Sports) the firm is the global market leader in the sportswear industry with revenues of about $18 billion in 2007.[63] Nike employs more than 30,000 people worldwide; the headquarters are in Beaverton, Oregon. As is very common for the sportswear and apparel industry, Nike has outsourced production.[64] According to its own estimation Nike drew on more than 700 suppliers in 52 countries in 2006, thereby indirectly employing 800,000 workers. As Nike, Gap Inc. is a well-established global brand. Doris and Don Fisher founded Gap in 1969 in San Francisco, where the firm's headquarters are still today.[65]

Gap operates more than 3,000 stores with an annual turnover of $15.8 billion in 2007.[66] The corporation controls three major brands:

---

[62] The data on which the analysis draws mainly derives from publications (e.g. media articles, NGO publications), interviews with NGOs, experts, trading agencies, and suppliers. The original brand names of these firms can therefore be used in the analysis without violating an agreement of confidentiality with an interviewee. Of the three firms, only representatives of Nike were interviewed. These interviews are authorized.

[63] www.nikebiz.com/company_overview/facts.html (February 16, 2009).

[64] The firm is a design, distribution, logistic, sourcing, and marketing organization.

[65] www.gapinc.com/public/About/abt_milestones.shtml (February 15, 2009).

[66] www.gapinc.com/public/About/abt_fact_sheet.shtml (February 15, 2009).

GAP, Old Navy, and Banana Republic. Sales peaked at $16.6 billion in 2004, but since then revenues have decreased every year. As Nike, Gap outsources production to contractor factories worldwide. Wal-Mart is the biggest discounter in the world and, with 1.4 million employees, also one of the biggest single employers in the US.[67] In 2007 sales reached almost $375 billion.

The story of Wal-Mart begins in 1962 when Sam Walton opened the company's first discount store in Rogers. Five years later twenty-four Wal-Mart stores existed in Arkansas, ringing up $12.6 million in sales. Today, Wal-Mart operates roughly 7,300 stores worldwide. The company outsources production to more than 61,000 suppliers around the globe. Wal-Mart is a wholesale retailer, i.e. it sells everything its customers could possibly want to buy.

The three firms are in many respects comparable. They are at the center of the campaigns of many NGOs. Ever since the early 1990s, NGOs in the US have accused Nike, Gap, and Wal-Mart of child labor, humiliating working conditions, and exploitation of workers in supplier factories. The pressure may have weakened slightly over time, but the possibility of an NGO scandal is still a dominating feature in the strategic environment of the three firms, as campaign websites such as "Nike-Watch" or "Wal-Mart Watch" indicate.[68] Besides exposure to persistent NGO pressure, the firms have in common that they originate in the US and source globally. In addition, with a turnover of $18.6 billion and $15.8 billion respectively, Nike and Gap resemble each other in terms of sales. Wal-Mart is, of course, the much bigger company. However, of the $370 billion annual sales revenues, apparel sales account for 10–15 percent (hence, $30 billion–$40 billion).[69] Therefore, as a textile firm, Wal-Mart compares to Nike and Gap. As purchasers of finished textile products the production chains of the three firms are also similar. This also pertains to the intensity of areas in which negative externalities are created. The human dimension refers to a potential exploitation of workers, child labor, and not paying minimum wages.

---

[67] http://walmartstores.com/FactsNews/FactSheets (February 16, 2009).
[68] www.oxfam.org.au/campaigns/labour-rights/nikewatch/; http://walmartwatch.com/ (February 17, 2009).
[69] See "Wal-Mart Apparel Executive Resigns," July 21, 2007, *Los Angeles Times*; "Top Wal-Mart Apparel Merchant Resigns," July 20, 2007, *USA Today*.

Environmental impact areas of textile production concern effluents, waste, and energy and water consumption. Nike collaborates with the Fair Labor Association (FLA) and Gap with Social Accountability International (SAI). Wal-Mart is associated with Worldwide Responsible Accredited Production (WRAP). Thus, should the firms decide to implement corporate social responsibility in the supply chain, they can draw on managerial support.[70]

Assessing the *brand reputation dilemma* for the three cases the analysis concentrates on "investments in marketing."[71] Nike spent on average $2 billion per year on marketing and advertising between 2003 and 2008.[72] Hence, the firm invested 11–13 percent of its total sales revenue in its brand reputation.[73] Accordingly, Nike is rated one of the top fifty brands in the world.[74] In the light of such outstandingly high marketing expenses, Nike is a case that represents a particularly strong *brand reputation dilemma.* Gap has spent $520 million on average on advertisements and marketing in the past three years.[75] Given total sales revenues of about $15.8 billion in 2007, Gap invests about 3 percent of its annual turnover in marketing and advertising. In comparison with other firms, these are remarkable numbers. When compared with Nike, however, the investments are on a lower level. Wal-Mart invested on average $1.6 billion $ in advertising and marketing between 2005 and 2008.[76] When put in relation to the annual turnover, the "marketing

---

[70] The FLA and SAI are business consultancies offering managerial support to firms that want to implement corporate social responsibility policies. WRAP is a business association that sponsors a corporate social responsibility standard against which suppliers can be audited. Hence, the association does not set out to solve collective action problems on the level of buyers such as Wal-Mart, but on the level of suppliers. The cooperation of Wal-Mart with WRAP is consequently limited to the announcement of the discounter that suppliers with WRAP certification will be accepted by Wal-Mart.

[71] I thus focus here on the measurement of *Indicator 2* of the *brand reputation dilemma.*

[72] In 2009 the firm has earmarked almost $500 million for athlete endorsement alone.

[73] "Nike, Inc. Annual Report on Form 10-K": http://sec.gov/Archives/edgar/data/320187/000119312508159004/d10k.htm (February 17, 2009).

[74] Corporate Social Responsibility Report of Nike, 2005–6, 11.

[75] "Annual Report of Gap Inc. on Form 10-K": www.gapinc.com/public/Investors/inv_fin_annual_reports_and_proxy.htm (February 17, 2009); Gap Inc. 2005–6 Social Responsibility Report.

[76] Annual Report of Wal-Mart, 2007: http://walmartstores.com/Media/Investors/2007_annual_report.pdf (February 17, 2009).

expenses" of the discounter indicate significantly lower degrees of the *brand reputation dilemma* than Nike's and Gap's: about 0.5 percent is invested in marketing and advertising at Wal-Mart.

In conclusion, Nike's investments of 10–13 percent of sales revenue in marketing are the most extensive. Gap invests about 3 percent in its brand name, which is still remarkable, but less than Nike's. The marketing expenses of Wal-Mart are one-sixth of those of Gap and therefore by far the lowest. According to the revised argument with respect to the *brand reputation dilemma,* that the dilemma motivates firms to engage in corporate social responsibility under the condition of NGO pressure, Nike should apply the strictest supply chain policies vis-à-vis suppliers, followed by Gap, whereas Wal-Mart should demonstrate the least effort in regulating suppliers.

The findings support the theoretical argument. While each of the three firms has a supply chain policy oriented towards the ILO core labor standards, there is a certain variation in the strictness and level of standards between three firms.[77] For example, Nike's minimum age of employment in supplier factories is sixteen, Gap's fifteen, and Wal-Mart's fourteen. Also, while Nike and Gap set specific goals to be achieved within a certain time-frame, such as supplier training on corporate social responsibility, Wal-Mart's policy is rather vague in this respect.

Turning to the analysis of the compliance mechanisms the firms apply towards suppliers in order to implement these policies, stark differences between the firms become apparent. At Wal-Mart, "200 ethical standards associates" work in Wal-Mart's "social responsibility team."[78] The supply chain of the discounter is vast, including more than 61,000 factories from industry sectors as diverse as textile, food, electronics, toys, kitchenware, and hosiery.[79] The textile business accounts

---

[77] The analysis measures here *Indicators 1a–d* of corporate social responsibility policies. There is a certain variation in the strictness and level of standards between the three firms. For example, Nike's Code of Conduct: www.nikeresponsibility.com/tools/Nike_Code_of_Conduct.pdf (February 24, 2009); GAP Inc.'s Code Of Vendor Conduct: www.gapinc.com/public/documents/code_vendor_conduct.pdf (March 6, 2009); Report On Ethical Sourcing of Wal-Mart, 2006.

[78] Report On Ethical Sourcing of Wal-Mart, 2006.

[79] http://walmartstores.com/FactsNews/FactSheets (February 16, 2009).

for approximately 10–15 percent of Wal-Mart's total sales, number of suppliers, and personnel dedicated to the task of supply chain regulation. Hence, twenty to thirty persons implement the policy in the textile supply chain. Nike employs ninety persons at the headquarters for the task of monitoring overseas factory conditions.[80] Similarly, Gap states that it "employs a team of more than ninety people around the world who are dedicated to improving the lives of garment workers."[81] In addition to that, the two firms employ about the same number of persons for the implementation of the code of conduct in the local sourcing offices.

For example, the staff of a sourcing bureau in Cape Town consists of six full-time Nike employees who supervise, monitor, and develop two suppliers in the region.[82] Of the six full-time employees, two are employed exclusively for the task of implementing the corporate social responsibility policy. Suppliers of Gap report a similar personnel-intensive supervision.[83] In contrast to that, the implementation of Wal-Mart's supply chain policy is centrally organized from the American headquarters and does not involve local sourcing offices. In summary, Nike and Gap employ between 150–200 persons for the task of implementing their codes of conduct in their respective supply chains, which consist of approximately 700 suppliers. Wal-Mart's 20–30 personnel for this task is smaller, while the number of suppliers is much higher. Hence, the resources applied to regulate suppliers are much higher in the cases of Nike and Gap than in the case of Wal-Mart.

Assessing the compliance mechanisms that the three firms employ, the analysis finds a comprehensive mix of regulatory approaches in the cases of Nike and Gap.[84] The two firms set positive incentives, provide for extensive managerial support, and engage in monitoring and enforcement to facilitate compliance of suppliers with their

---

[80] Corporate Social Responsibility Report of Nike, 2005/6: 130.
[81] Corporate Social Responsibility Report of Gap Inc., 2005/6: 25.
[82] Interview with the Commercialization Manager of Nike South Africa, October 2, 2008, Cape Town; with the Corporate Responsibility Specialist of Nike South Africa, October 1, 2008, Midrand.
[83] Interview with the Project Developing Manager and the Training Coordinator of TP, April 2, 2007, Cape Town.
[84] I thus turn now the analysis of *Indicator 2e* of corporate social responsibility policies.

codes of conduct. Suppliers report, for example, that in the period before they became approved suppliers, teams of managers from the brands assisted them in their effort to implement the required standards.[85] In one case Nike supported a factory for more than two years before it was granted the status of an accredited supplier, which is a precondition for becoming a business partner of the sportswear brand.[86]

Managerial support aside, the brands create positive incentives for suppliers to implement standards. More specifically, in exchange for compliance Nike and Gap offer suppliers long-term contracts and purchasing quotas.[87] This mix of compliance mechanisms is complemented by monitoring and sanctioning devices. Nike and Gap audit suppliers regularly in addition to conducting unannounced investigations of production sites.[88] This is confirmed by suppliers who report, for instance, that representatives of the brands attend their factories almost every day to ensure that suggested measures of improvement are taken and to verify that the factories operate on the level of standards prescribed.[89] Moreover, the firms publish supplier lists that allow NGOs and other stakeholders to specifically investigate their supplier factories; this, in turn, enhances transparency and facilitates independent third party monitoring.[90]

---

[85] Interview with the CEO of Jo, September 20, 2007, Cape Town; with the Project Developing Manager, the HIV/AIDS and Occupational Health Manager, and the Training Coordinator of TP, April 2, 2007, Cape Town.

[86] Interview with the Production Executive and the Sales Executive of Mon, September 16, 2008, Cape Town.

[87] Ibid. and interview with the Commercialization Manager of Nike South Africa, October 2, 2008, Cape Town; with the Corporate Responsibility Specialist of Nike South Africa, October 1, 2008, Midrand.

[88] Corporate Social Responsibility Report of Nike, 2005/6: 30; interview with the Commersialisation Manager of Nike, October 2, 2008, Cape Town.

[89] Interviews with the Human Resources Manager, the Production Executive and the Sales Executive of Mon, September 16, 2008, Cape Town; with the CEO of Jo, September 20, 2007, Cape Town; with the Project Developing Manager, the HIV/AIDS and Occupational Health Manager, and the Training Coordinator of TP, April 2, 2007, Cape Town. In addition to that, complaint hotlines enable workers in contractor factories as well as local NGOs to anonymously report on labor standard infringements and environmental pollution.

[90] This is particularly noteworthy, as it refers to NGO demands and is only done by very few companies. In the textile industry, supplier lists are regarded as firms' most valuable asset and therefore kept secret.

With regard to sanctioning mechanisms, the first step following non-compliant behavior is to make recommendations for improvement. If a supplier does not improve accordingly, accreditation is withheld or withdrawn: "The last time Nike did a major audit," reports a supplier, "three aspects did not adhere to their standards. They highlighted those three issues and asked us to address them. Since they did that, we have been addressing those issues and report back our progress in this respect. They will nonetheless come out at one point in January or February – we do not know when – and check that those three aspects are now sorted and completed so they can re-approve us."[91] This report of a supplier of Nike shows, first, that the monitoring mechanisms of Nike are effective. Non-compliance was detected. Second, upon detection the supplier's accreditation was put on hold, which means that during this period the factory could not supply Nike. Hence, sanctioning mechanisms are applied. Third, the sanctioning mechanisms are adequate. The supplier felt obliged to implement changes according to Nike's policy. Hence, the compliance mechanisms applied by Nike are effective. The findings concerning Gap are similar in this respect.[92]

Considering the "compliance mechanisms" of Wal-Mart, the discounter conducts monitoring through an audit scheme.[93] Usually, the audit takes place once, with a potential re-audit after 120 days. Aside from that, the firm does not engage with suppliers on matters related to corporate social responsibility. No punishment or sanction for detected non-compliance is applied.[94] Hence, the finding is that compliance mechanisms exist only rudimentarily. The effectiveness of these mechanisms is, as confirmed by a self-assessment of Wal-Mart, rather low. The firm finds it impossible to "identify in the auditing process when workers have been coached by factory

[91] Interview with the Production Executive of Mon, September 16, 2008, Cape Town.
[92] Interview with the Project Developing Manager and the Training Coordinator of TP, April 2, 2007, Cape Town.
[93] Report On Ethical Sourcing of Wal-Mart, 2006: 21–4.
[94] As confirmed by suppliers of Wal-Mart. Protocol of the factory visit and the interview with the owner and the Assistant Director of Fu, April 10, 2008, Hencu; protocol of the factory visit and the interview the Foreign Trader Manager of Da Garments, April 5–6, 2008, Tonglu.

management."[95] According to NGOs and experts social audits often have – especially when conducted preannounced as in the case of Wal-Mart – a reverse effect, provoking opportunism in terms of giving false information rather than compliance on the side of suppliers.[96] In response to such criticism, the discounter plans to offer some of its main suppliers extra managerial support to facilitate the implementation of its policy, as Nike and Gap do. So far, however, the firm has not executed such plans. Hence, Wal-Mart's compliance mechanisms are, apart from being rudimentary, relatively ineffective.

In summary, Nike and Gap apply strict, demanding, and comprehensive policies and compliance mechanisms vis-à-vis suppliers, with Nike being slightly stricter and more demanding than Gap. These mechanisms are according to suppliers to both firms highly effective: they invest time, know-how, and personnel to offer managerial support, set positive incentives for compliance, conduct unannounced monitoring of sites, and sanction those factories that are unwilling to comply with their codes of conduct. Wal-Mart, by contrast, only conducts (usually announced) audits, which are, according to the self-assessment of the discounter, not achieving the intended effects. The analysis therefore asserts that the implementation measures taken by Nike and Gap are much more profound than those in the case of Wal-Mart.[97]

Some textile cases that are part of the sample analyzed for this book confirm and illustrate these findings.[98] For example, when asked about the level of standards Nike enforces a current South African supplier

[95] Report On Ethical Sourcing of Wal-Mart, 2006: 7. Asked about working conditions, workers of non-compliant suppliers give false information in the auditing process for the achievement of a positive audit result.

[96] Often suppliers operate on such low levels that the standards of the respective supply chain policies seem unattainable. Devoid managerial support and positive incentives, as argued by independent observers, NGOs, business representatives, and experts in the field, these firms lack know-how and motivation to upgrade. According to the same commentators, these suppliers often just learn what they have to say to pass an audit successfully. Interview with the World Watch Institute, China Watch, March 4, 2008, Washington, DC; The Asia Foundation, April 17, 2008, Beijing; the ILO Workplace Education Program China, April 17, 2008, Beijing; Social Accountability International (SAI) China Workplace Program, April 15, 2008, Beijing.

[97] Nike and Gap thus score significantly higher on *Indicators 2a–e* than Wal-Mart.

[98] The analysis turns now to an assessment of policy practices as measured by *Indicator 3*.

says, "it is very high. Nike demands a world standard, which is a challenge to meet no matter where you are."[99] Compared with the supply chain policies applied by other international textile brands and retailers, another South African supplier remarks that, "Nike operates on the highest standard in the industry."[100] Moreover, these standards are also above the legal standards in South Africa. For example "the legal minimum age for a person to work is sixteen. Nike's age is eighteen years, so we had to change our policy."[101] Hence, in practice Nike implements its policy as prescribed. Since the policy is highly demanding, the practices are demanding as well.

Gap also shows policy practices on a very high level. The sample of cases evaluated for this study includes one former supplier of Gap and one factory that failed to become a supplier of Gap. The firm Da Garments is a sewing and knitting factory with about 100 employees located in Tonglu, China. The firm tried to become a supplier of Gap recently, but was rejected. According to the Foreign Trade Manager of Da Garments who was responsible for managing the accreditation process with Gap, the main reason for the rejection was that the level of labor, health, and safety standards in the factory were too low.[102] For instance, the company employs girls who are between 12 and 14 years of age; most of the workers do not have contracts or insurance; there are no clear regulations at Da Garments that clarify how overtime work is compensated. On grounds of these infringements a representative of Gap who visited the factory refused to accredit Da Garments as a supplier. In fact, the manager of Da Garments reports that the factory was not even invited to participate in Gap's factory development program for future suppliers. The standards on which Da Garments operates were considered as being too low. It is remarkable that international brands such as Quicksilver, Eli Tahari, and H&M have approved Da Garments as a supplier, despite the described

---

[99] Interview with the Directors of Mig, September 17, 2008, Cape Town.
[100] Interview with the Human Resources Manager, the Production Executive, and the Sales Executive of Mon, September 16, 2008, Cape Town. This assertion is confirmed by a former supplier of Nike who lost business with the sportswear brand two years ago. Interview with the CEO of Jo, September 20, 2007, Cape Town.
[101] Ibid.
[102] Interview with the Foreign Trader Manager of Da Garments, April 5/6, 2008, Tonglu. Protocol of further interviews with the Foreign Trader Manager of Da Garments and of a factory visit, April 5/6, 2008, Tonglu.

infringements on basic labor standards. Hence, the standards these brands apply are less demanding than Gap's.

The assertion of demanding policy practices is also confirmed by a representative of the former South African supplier of Gap, which is TP, a dyeing and finishing textile mill on the outskirts of Cape Town. When asked if Gap demanded higher environmental standards than other customers, a manager of TP replied "yes, there were higher requirements." He added that "to meet the requirements of Gap, we even had to get an environmental committee together to get ISO 14001 certification."[103] Hence, the standards of Gap were on such a high level that TP decided to adopt a systematic environmental management system according to the ISO system to meet them. ISO 14001 certification is rare in the textile industry in South Africa, which illustrates that the requirements of Gap are on a higher level than those of other brands or retailers.[104]

While these cases illustrate the effectiveness and strictness of the supply chain regulation of Nike and Gap with respect to corporate social responsibility, other cases demonstrate how Wal-Mart does not reach the same level. Two recent Chinese suppliers of Wal-Mart have been analyzed in the context of this study. The sewing and knitting factory Fu with – depending on the season – 50–700 employees, passed the Wal-Mart audit despite non-compliance with most provisions stipulated by the code of conduct of the discounter. For example, when asked about the regular work time at Fu, the Assistant Director replied: "in the low season, the shift is 8 hours, 6 days per week. When the factory is busy, the shifts are as long as 14 hours a day or more, 7 days per week."[105]

These comments show that the firm does not regulate work time and over-time according to Wal-Mart's policy – and, in addition, infringes

[103] Interview with the Project Developing Manager of TP, April 2, 2007, Cape Town.
[104] Before TP attained the ISO 14001 certificate, however, Gap relocated production from South Africa and stopped engaging with TP. The appreciation of the Rand made South African textile exports uncompetitive. Accordingly, TP terminated the certification process just as the environmental management program. The environmental manager of TP said that in contrast to the period when the factory was a supplier of Gap, today the firm has such a negative impact on the environment with its "dye water" of which "most ... now just ends up in the sea" that "we kill all our whales" (ibid.).
[105] Protocol of a factory visit and of the interview with the owner and the Assistant Director of Fu, April 10, 2008, Hencun. The owner was under the impression that I was a buyer for a Western brand or a trade agency.

on Chinese labor law. Pointing at young looking workers he remarked jokingly: "you do not have to know how young they are."[106] In response to the question whether Fu has a policy regulating the minimum age, minimum wage and over-time he said, "No, we do not. But write us an email with what you need. We can confirm that we have one."[107] Hence, this factory is in many respects non-compliant with Wal-Mart's supply chain policy. Nonetheless, it passed the Wal-Mart audit and was given the status of an accredited supplier. The case therefore illustrates, first, the asserted ineffectiveness of the social audits conducted by Wal-Mart. As a consequence, it exemplifies, second, that Wal-Mart's implementation measures are in practice lax and shallow.

Da Garments is the second supplier of Wal-Mart analyzed for this study. While the factory was not accepted by Gap as a supplier for its infringements on basic labor standards, it passed the audit of Wal-Mart successfully. The case of this supplier therefore provides for additional evidence supporting the assertions of ineffective monitoring conducted by Wal-Mart and lax and shallow implementation of standards in practice. Moreover, the case illustrates that in a comparative perspective, Wal-Mart's state of implementation of the code of conduct is on a much lower level than Gap's. While Nike and Gap show demanding policy practices, Wal-Mart's are rather shallow.

To conclude, Nike shows the strongest engagement in implementing corporate social responsibility in the supply chain.[108] The sportswear

---

[106] Ibid.   [107] Ibid.

[108] The assertions made with respect to the policy practices of Nike are confirmed by sources not related to Nike as well. For example, a trade agent who sources for Asics, a competitor of Nike, remarked in regard to Nike's supplier factories: "I have been to them. They are model factories, all of them. Even in China they have got these incredibly high health standards. In China they regularly work a 15.5 hour day. In the Nike factory they are only allowed to work 8 hours, so the factory stops after eight hours and all the people go and work for another factory, a second factory the same day apart from their Nike employment . . . but Nike is doing what is right." Interview with the Managing Director of Jordan Footwear, September 20, 2007, Cape Town. Similar comments about Nike factories were made by the President of LP apparel, Inc. and LP apparel Group, April 11, 2008, Hangzhou; and the Social Accountability International (SAI) China Workplace Program Manager, April 2008, Beijing. NGOs usually see Nike more critically. However, when asked what they would regard as the "best practice" in the industry, spokespersons and activists would regularly point at Nike as well. Interview with the Senior Program Officer of The Asia Foundation, April 15, 2008, Beijing; and with the National Labor Committee (NLC), March 4, 2008, New York City.

and apparel brand's policy is highly demanding – requiring a minimum age for employees of 16 and 18, respectively – specified for implementation, obligatory and comprehensive.[109] In addition, Nike has dedicated a substantial amount of personnel to the task of implementation of the policy, applying a complex mix of compliance mechanisms – managerial support offered to suppliers, positive incentives, and strict monitoring and sanctioning.[110] Accordingly, the policy practices of Nike are the most demanding and comprehensive. They cover almost 100 percent of the supplier base according to a Nike report.[111] In line with this, an externally verified report lists 810 unannounced audits in 2006 in the 653 contracted factories of Nike.[112]

The results for Gap are similar, even though the policy of Gap is slightly weaker. Also, the percentage of the suppliers covered by Gap's implementation measures is lower than that in the case of Nike.[113] According to the firm itself, the supply chain policy is applied to about 80 percent of suppliers while Nike covers nearly 100 percent.[114] Wal-Mart reveals the weakest supply chain policy.[115]

---

[109] As concerns *Indicators 1a–d* of corporate social responsibility policies.

[110] Measuring *Indicator 2b* and *Indicator 2e*.

[111] Corporate Social Responsibility Report of Nike, 2005/6; interview with the Commersialisation Manager of Nike South Africa, October 2, 2008, Cape Town. Confirmed by suppliers of Nike, Interview with the Production Executive of Mon, September 16, 2008, Cape Town; with the CEO of Jo, September 20, 2007, Cape Town.

[112] Corporate Social Responsibility Report of Nike, 2005/6: 30.

[113] The assertions made with respect to the policy practices of Gap are confirmed by sources not related to Gap as well. For example, a trade agent who sources for discounters and another trade agent sourcing for European retailers both called Gap factories "model factories" in regard to their social, health, and environmental standards. Protocol of the interview with a Consultant Sourcing and Production for Lloyd Textile Trading Limited, April 11, 2008, Hangzhou; with the CEO of Wonderful Earth (Far East) Ltd., April 8, 2008, Shanghai. Similar comments about Gap were made by the President of LP apparel, Inc. and LP apparel Group, April 11, 2008, Hangzhou; and the SAI China Workplace Program Manager, April 15, 2008, Beijing. NGOs see Gap – as Nike – usually rather critically. However, when asked about "best practices" in the industry, spokespersons and activists would regularly refer to Nike and Gap. Interview with the Senior Program Officer of The Asia Foundation, April 2008, Beijing; and with the NLC, March 4, 2008, New York City.

[114] Measuring *Indicator 3c* of corporate social responsibility policies. Corporate Social Responsibility Report of Gap Inc., 2005/6: 25.

[115] The assertions made with respect to the policy practices of Wal-Mart are confirmed by sources not related to Wal-Mart. For example, a trade agent who sources for discounters thinks that Wal-Mart has no interest in seriously

These findings demonstrate that the *brand reputation dilemma* can motivate firms to adopt corporate social responsibility programs – in-house and in the supply chain. However, the effect of this factor is contingent on strong and persistent NGO pressure. Hence, we are confronted here with an internal–external factor nexus. I shall call this the *brand reputation dilemma 2.0*. The firm cases are summarized in this respect in Table 6.4.

Conclusion

This chapter finds that:

- Internal driver 4 – asset-specific investments in marketing – and the *brand reputation dilemma* it gives rise to, is not a full driver of corporate social responsibility in the sense of a sufficient condition. Everything else being equal, variation of this internal driver does not in all cases lead to a concern for the wellbeing of employees and the environment on the part of firms;
- however, the *brand reputation dilemma* gains explanatory power in the context of the external pressure factor "possibility of an NGO scandal";
- while the factor "possibility of an NGO scandal" is thus a necessary condition for the effects of the *brand reputation dilemma*, the dilemma is in turn also a necessary condition for this external pressure factor; hence, there is an internal–external driver nexus here: combined, the *brand reputation dilemma* and "possibility of an NGO scandal" are sufficient cause for corporate social responsibility.

What are the wider implications of these findings? They, first, show that the perspective in this book on internal drivers may be different and new, but is in no way competing – or mutually exclusive – with the one in literature on external drivers. Second, even though they contain disconfirming evidence for internal driver 4, the findings in this chapter actually point to the importance of considering internal drivers in

applying the supply chain policy. Protocol of the interview with a Consultant Sourcing and Production for Lloyd Textile Trading Limited, April 11, 2008, Hangzhou. An NGO activist who has campaigned against Wal-Mart since the 1990s remarks that "it is just a game for them. They play hide and seek with us and the public." Interview with the Director of the NLC, March 4, 2008, New York City.

Table 6.4 *Empirical cases, analyzed with respect to control variables, the brand reputation dilemma 2.0 and corporate social responsibility*

Comparison/ industry sector	Firm cases			Control variables/firm features			Internal–external driver nexus *brand reputation dilemma 2.0*		Corporate social responsibility	
							The NGO pressure/brand reputation-nexus			
		Firm size	Level of home country regulation	Association, PPP and initiatives	Problem pressure/impact areas	Level of human resources dilemma/ technological specialization dilemma	External driver: NGO pressure (perceived)	Internal driver: brand reputation dilemma	Corporate social responsibility, in-house	Corporate social responsibility, supply chain
Automotive, large multinational car companies	M t0	Large	High	Many, but the same as B, V, and F	Medium/waste, energy, water, effluents, CO₂ fallout	Low	Low (OEM not targeted for production processes)	High (high-end market firm)	Weak environmental program (for an OEM)	Weak environmental policies (for an OEM)
	M t1	Large	High	Many, but the same as B, V, and F	Medium/waste, energy, water, effluents, CO₂ fallout	Low–medium	Low (OEM not targeted for production processes)	High (high-end market firm)	Weak to medium environmental program (for an OEM)	Weak environmental policies (for an OEM)
	M t2	Large	High	Many, but the same as B, V, and F	Medium/waste, energy, water, effluents, CO₂ fallout	High	Low (OEM not targeted for production processes)	High	Strong environmental program	Strong environmental policies
	B	Large	High	Many, but the same as M, V, and F	Medium/waste, energy, water, effluents, CO₂ fallout	High	Low (OEM not targeted for production processes)	High	Strong environmental program	Strong environmental policies
	V	Large	High	Many, but the same as B, M, and F	Medium/waste, energy, water, effluents, CO₂ fallout	Medium–low	Low (OEM not targeted for production processes)	Low	Medium to strong environmental program (for an OEM)	Weak environmental policies (for an OEM)
	F	Large	High	Many, but the same as B, V, and M	Medium/waste, energy, water, effluents, CO₂ fallout	Low	Low (OEM not targeted for production processes)	Low	Medium environmental program (for an OEM)	Weak environmental policies (for an OEM)
Textile brand	C – CL	Large	High	Fair Labor Association	High/ILO-core labor standards	N/A	Low (OEM not targeted for production processes)	Very high	N/A	No CSR

Table 6.4 (*cont.*)

Comparison/industry sector	Firm cases	Firm size	Level of home country regulation	Association, PPP and initiatives	Problem pressure/impact areas	Level of human resources dilemma / technological specialization dilemma	External driver: NGO pressure (perceived)	Internal driver: brand reputation dilemma	Corporate social responsibility, in-house	Corporate social responsibility, supply chain
				Control variables/firm features			**Internal–external driver nexus *brand reputation dilemma 2.0***		**Corporate social responsibility**	
Large South African retailers	W	Large	Low	Associations weak in retail sector; general reluctance to engage with NGOs and in PPP	In South Africa: medium/ effluents, water and energy consumption / In China: high/ILO-core labor standards	N/A	In South Africa: **high** / In China: **low**	**High**	N/A	**In South Africa: strong CSR / In China: no CSR**
	E	Large	Low	Associations weak in retail sector; general reluctance to engage with NGOs and in PPP	In South Africa: medium/ effluents, water and energy consumption / In China: high/ILO-core labor standards	N/A	In South Africa: **high** / In China: **low**	**Medium to high**	N/A	**In South Africa: medium to strong CSR / In China: no CSR**
	MP	Large	Low	Associations weak in retail sector; general reluctance to engage with NGOs and in PPP	In South Africa: medium/ effluents, water and energy consumption / In China: high/ILO-core labor standards	N/A	In South Africa: **high** / In China: **low**	**Low**	N/A	**In South Africa: No CSR / In China: no CSR**
Large global textile sellers	Nike	Large	High	Fair Labor Association	High/ILO-core labor standards	N/A	**Very high**	**Very high**	N/A	**Very strong CSR**
	Gap	Large	High	Social Accountability International	High/ILO-core labor standards	N/A	**Very high**	**High**	N/A	**Strong CSR, but weaker than Nike**
	Wal-Mart	Large	High	Worldwide Responsible Accredited Production (WRAP)	High/ILO-core labor standards	N/A	**Very high**	**Low**	N/A	**Weak CSR**

The NGO pressure/brand reputation-nexus

research on corporate social responsibility in general. NGO and consumer-induced "California-effects" are the most common and acknowledged set of factors in regard to standard diffusion and corporate social responsibility in the literature, and also in public discourse. The findings in here, however, suggest that we cannot simply assume that firms, which originate from countries where NGOs and consumers are concerned about human rights and the environment, will behave in accordance with international standards. The analysis shows that it takes exceptional circumstances for this logic to unfold: the firm has to be exceptionally dependent on its brand value on account of massive investments in marketing; and NGOs have to put recurrent pressure on the firm over long periods of time.

In contrast to that, internal drivers 1, 2, and 3 – the *human resources dilemma*, the *technological specialization dilemma*, and the *foreign direct investment dilemma* – are valid predictors of corporate social responsibility, irrespective of context conditions. This raises the question whether cases of corporate social responsibility and the spread of global standards, that have hitherto been attributed to be the outcome of external pressure factors, are in reality not caused by the internal drivers suggested in this book.

7 | Conclusion: internal drivers, corporate social responsibility, and the spread of global standards

This study assumed a context of regulatory void typical for production conditions in emerging markets. Its leading question was: why do some firms care about the wellbeing of their workers and the natural environment while others remain indifferent and are even complicit in social and environmental exploitation? In areas of regulatory void, the state lacks the capacity – or the willingness – to set or enforce legal standards effectively. A credible threat on the part of the state to regulate industry is thus absent. This means that the main factor scholars underline in regard to self-regulation by business, the "shadow of hierarchy," simply does not exist. This being the way it is, how then can corporate social responsibility be at all possible?

Skeptics believe that it is indeed not possible; they point to examples of corporations relocating to emerging markets precisely to evade strict regulation. According to them, firms force states into a regulatory "race to the bottom" – competitive regulatory downsizing to avail of comparative cost advantages (Bohle 2008; Chan 2003; Singh and Zammit 2004). However, empirically oriented analyses of firm behavior in areas of regulatory void show that examples of corporate social responsibility abound, which is contrary to what has been hitherto assumed under the "race to the bottom" argument (Deitelhoff and Wolf 2010; Flohr *et al.* 2010; Thauer and Börzel 2013). In some instances firms even drive a regulatory "race to the top." The literature suggests some intriguing explanations for these findings. Most authors focus on external drivers as "functional equivalents" (Börzel and Risse 2010) to the "shadow of hierarchy": NGO activism, self-regulation in the context of business associations, consumer pressure, and public–private partnerships are external *pressure* factors that, when acting upon firms, can bring about corporate social responsibility – even in the regulatory void.

However, while these approaches have improved our understanding of corporate social responsibility, they have also limited it. Perspectives on empirical phenomena have a "denotation and a connotation" (Krasner 1991: 361). The denotation (explicit logic, ibid.) of the mentioned literature is that voluntary standards and firms' interest in profit-maximization are generally incompatible. Not only is the "race to the bottom" argument based on this assumption, but also external driver oriented analyses, as they point to the importance of putting pressure on firms so as to make them behave more in line with social expectations. The connotation (implicit logic), in turn, is that in most cases the internal logic of economic organization, i.e. *intra*-organizational dynamics, management, and decision-making, can be ignored in the analysis of corporate social responsibility.[1] But can it really?

This book and the research it presents were spurred by the conviction that they should not be ignored and that the assumption of a general incompatibility of firm interests and high standards is not helpful. It therefore suggested a new, different perspective on corporate social responsibility, one that focuses on internal drivers in order to investigate varying preferences of firms towards corporate social responsibility.

This difference in perspective is also reflected in the organization of the research: external pressure factor-oriented analyses usually vary factors in the strategic environment of firms (NGO pressure, consumer activism, associational structures, to name a few) in order to explain their different levels of corporate social responsibility. They hereby presume that firm preferences are a constant – in fact, constantly hostile, that is. In contrast, the research design for this study varies the preferences of firms in order to investigate their behavioral effects with respect to corporate social responsibility. It does so while keeping external pressure factors constant. But how, why, and under which conditions do the preferences of firms towards social and environmental standards differ?

Explaining corporate social responsibility differently: internal drivers

This book argued that managerial dilemmas, which emerge on account of *intra*-organizational asset-specific investments, motivate managers in

---

[1] The connotation of research programs "suggests which questions are most important, what kind of evidence should be gathered, and, often tacitly, which issues should be ignored" (Krasner 1991: 361).

firms to engage in corporate social responsibility. There are all in all four such dilemmas and thus four internal drivers which define the interest of firms towards social and environmental standards:

(1) The *human resources dilemma*: investments in rare employee skills. The dependency such investments create between management and employees motivates managers to adopt labor-related corporate social responsibility with the aim of keeping employees healthy and productive, reduce staff turnover, and deal with developments in society which could potentially negatively affect the workforce (such as HIV/AIDS in South Africa).

(2) The *technological specialization dilemma*: asset-specific investments in a production site. Such investments motivate management to adopt strict environmental standards in order to reduce the emerging information deficits of management vis-à-vis the production unit and to ensure the profitability of the investment irrespective of future (potentially higher) costs for basic resources and raw materials (energy, water, waste, air).

(3) The *foreign direct investment dilemma*: a *technological specialization dilemma* which involves a transnational element and diverging regulatory contexts; management is located in a highly regulating country, production in a weakly regulating country. A management that, on account of high levels of asset-specific investments, confronts the managerial dilemma with gravity will impose the highest attainable environmental standards on the production unit and thus transfer high standards from "home" to operations "abroad."

(4) The *brand reputation dilemma*: investments in marketing to support alternative means of product differentiation to the price mechanism. In order to mitigate the risk of an investment's devaluation on account of quality problems or bad image, managers adopt strict in-house and supply chain corporate social responsibility as proscribed by international institutions.

The preferences of firms towards high social and environmental standards vary with the intensity of the dilemma situation, i.e. with different levels of asset-specific investments. However, do different preferences in relation to corporate social responsibility also lead to corresponding differences in firm policies? In other words: are the theorized dilemmas really driving corporate social responsibility policies empirically?

Relating internal drivers to outcomes: key findings

The *human resources dilemma* and the *technological specialization dilemma* are valid predictors – i.e. full and forceful independent variables – for corporate social responsibility. The *human resources dilemma* causes firms to adopt HIV/AIDS workplace programs in South Africa. The *technological specialization dilemma* makes firms adopt high environmental standards. The relation between the two dilemmas and corporate social responsibility holds across highly different industry sector contexts (automotive and textile), on different levels of intensity of asset-specific investments, and when taking into account firms of different sizes (small, medium, and large firms). In addition, they are valid irrespective of specific constellations of external pressure factors: the analysis showed that these two internal drivers gain explanatory power even in the absence of NGO pressure, consumer demands, self-regulation by business associations or public–private partnerships. They also explain corporate social responsibility irrespective of the respective firm's origins – i.e. whether it originates from a highly regulating country or not or is based on foreign direct investment or domestic business. These internal drivers are thus valid predictors and explanations of corporate social responsibility.

The *foreign direct investment dilemma* is a specific instance of the *technological specialization dilemma*. As such, its applicability is, when working with the theoretical argument for this dilemma, naturally limited to firms in the regulatory void, running on foreign direct investment from a highly regulating country. Within these scope conditions, however, the *foreign direct investment dilemma* is also a full independent variable, explaining the transfer of regulatory standards from highly regulating "home" countries to weakly regulating "host" ones.

In contrast to that, the *brand reputation dilemma* does not have the same causal status as the three other dilemmas. When tested as an independent variable, this internal driver failed to predict corporate social responsibility: some firms with high investments in marketing adopt stronger social and environmental standards than firms that do not invest a lot in marketing. However, others do not show any such differences in their behavior. An inductive inquiry into the variation of effects indicates that this internal driver is a valid predictor of corporate social responsibility only in combination with the external driver "NGO pressure." The investigation also revealed that "NGO pressure" by itself is also not a sufficient condition for corporate social responsibility. It depends on the *brand reputation dilemma*.

Hence, whereas the *human resources dilemma*, the *technological specialization dilemma* and the *foreign direct investment dilemma* are sufficient (though unnecessary) conditions for corporate social responsibility, the *brand reputation dilemma* does not have this strong causal effect. Instead, the *brand reputation dilemma*, in conjunction with "NGO pressure," forms an internal–external nexus driver: each is a necessary condition for the other to exert effects; together, they form a sufficient (unnecessary) condition for corporate social responsibility. Disassociated from each other, neither has much causal force.

Beyond this specification of necessary and sufficient conditions, the analysis also found the logic of the theorized causal arguments relating internal drivers to corporate social responsibility, to be valid. This is important as explanatory factors correlating with corporate social responsibility may do so for reasons other than theoretically assumed. For example, this study argued that the *human resources dilemma* causes labor-related corporate social responsibility as a consequence of management's concerns with the wellbeing and productivity of employees. Alternatively, investments in rare skills of employees may empower unions' and workers' demands and based on this bring about social policies (see Chapter 4). Applying process tracing methods, however, the analysis showed that the labor-related workplace programs that emerge as a consequence of asset-specific investments are, as theorized, inspired by management and not by unions or worker demands.

We can also conceive of an alternative explanation for the effects of the *technological specialization/foreign direct investment dilemmas*. The argument in this study has been that environmental policies emerge as a result of management's attempt to stay in control *intra-organizationally* after having made asset-specific investments and to reduce the uncertainty with respect to the firm's dependence on externally determined cost factors (of energy, water, waste management etc.). Alternatively, asset-specific investments in production sites may be associated with high standards on account of an increase in technological advancement brought about by the investments. However, process tracing also in this case revealed that – as theoretically argued – it is management that imposes high standards on the firm in order to mitigate the risks inherent in asset-specific investments – and that it is not new technology that makes asset specificity a driver of environmental policies. Hence, not only their predictions, but also the causal arguments for internal drivers themselves are valid accounts of what happens when firms make asset-specific investments and why they opt for corporate social responsibility.

Finally, the analysis showed that internal drivers are not only valid predictors of corporate social responsibility – with the exception of the *brand reputation dilemma* being a driver only when connected with NGO pressure. Internal drivers can also solve important empirical puzzles. In South Africa, HIV/AIDS workplace programs encompass many firms – even small and medium sized ones. This diffusion of corporate social responsibility is important in various aspects. These firms fill a governance gap in the country as the state has proven itself incapable and unwilling to adequately respond to the HIV/AIDS pandemic. So, everything else being equal, industrialized areas in which large parts of the population are employed by firms will experience a higher level of health care services on account of this diffusion than areas with no firms and high unemployment (Hönke and Thauer 2013). Hence, the phenomenon of firms fighting HIV/AIDS in the workplace contributes to the debate about governance and common goods provision in areas of limited statehood in a crucial way (Risse 2011; Krasner and Risse 2014).

Besides, these findings concerning firms fighting the disease are also relevant in the context of the debate about the relation between business standards and global trade. Most of the firms that engage in the fight against HIV/AIDS are parts of global production networks. Their activities are thus (potential) instances of so-called trade-based diffusion. Taking the example of nine automotive and textile firms, the analysis found that the argument pointing to external pressure factors in the literature fails to explain the (variation of the) nine firms' HIV/AIDS workplace programs. The firms were under pressure neither from NGOs, nor from consumers or self-regulatory initiatives by business associations when they decided to fight the disease. The *human resources dilemma*, however, *can* explain the emergence and variation of HIV/AIDS programs among the nine firms. Asset-specific investments in employee skills prompt the firms to take action against the disease.

Another important puzzle concerns multinational car firms with production sites in South Africa. These firms operate on strikingly different levels of environmental standards over time (see Chapter 5). The analysis found that this variation does not make sense should one follow any of the explanatory factors of corporate social responsibility and diffusion suggested in literature. Instead, it is the *foreign direct investment dilemma* that explains it. This finding is important not only in the context of the literature on the diffusion of business standards: it is also important for a reevaluation of the regulatory "race to the bottom" argument, which assumes that levels of foreign direct investments are associated with decreasing levels of social and environmental standards. The findings point to the opposite direction: the greater the foreign direct investment (in terms of asset specificity), the higher the standards on which firms operate.

A third empirical puzzle is solved by the analysis of the *brand reputation dilemma*. It is a common argument in literature that firms with a brand name behave more responsibly than firms without one. At the same time, media and NGO reports on corporate misconduct in areas of regulatory void – such as when firms make use of child labor or ruthlessly pollute the environment – usually feature brand name firms, too. The analysis may resolve this puzzle. A brand name alone is not a sufficient incentive for corporate social responsibility. Only in combination with NGO pressure do brand name firms behave differently from other firms and assume responsibilities for their workers and the environment. What is the potential then for generalizing these findings?

How far do the findings travel? The potential for generalization

While the analysis was inevitably limited in scope, this study has developed certain indications for the general applicability of the arguments for internal drivers. The first observation in this respect concerns the applicability of the *human resources dilemma* to a country context other than South Africa and a labor-related issue area different from HIV/AIDS. It pertains to the case of the Chinese supplier CL (a supplier to the high-end fashion brand C) analyzed in Chapter 6. This firm makes a significant distinction between workers who are spontaneously hired to carry out tasks that require no specific skills and those who have received training from CL for specific work processes at the leather firm. While the relation of management to the spontaneously hired workers is characterized by absent asset specificity, the relation to the trained ones is asset-specific. The former workers can be hired and fired at any point in time. They are easily substituted from the labor market. The latter, however, cannot be easily substituted. Smooth production processes in the firm depend a lot on the skills they acquire during training.[2]

CL treats the two types of workers very differently. Employees with specific skills are only a minority. Their employment is based on formal contracts. They are given full insurance, a wage beyond the legally required minimum, and they are exempt from working excessively without compensation for overtime. Hence, in relation to this group of workers CL shows corporate social responsibility. The majority of workers who have not attained such skills, however, are ruthlessly exploited. Child labor, wages below the legally required minimum, excessive and unpaid overtime, dangerous, health-threatening work conditions, and lack of contracts and of basic insurances feature in relation to this group of workers. This distinction in CL's treatment of workers on account of the level of asset-specific investments shows that the *human resources dilemma* also explains firm behavior in the context of China and labor standards.

An additional observation regarding the applicability of this internal driver beyond the issue area of HIV/AIDS concerns the German producer of apparel and underwear F. The firm was not included in the analyses of this book as many of its features were too diverse to those of other cases.[3] F invests in the skills of its employees; the case thus represents some levels of asset specificity in the relationship between management and employees. The resulting labor-related activities regarding corporate social responsibility, however, are not intensely related to the fight against HIV/AIDS, but to problems of drug addiction.[4] Based in Cape Town, the firm says that HIV/AIDS prevalence is a problem among workers, but regarded as less pressing than the

---

[2] Protocol, interview with the owner family of CL and with a Manager of CL, April 24, 2008, Tonglu. Additional information drawn from the website of CL (February 15, 2009).

[3] The empirical part consisted exclusively of controlled, pair-wise comparisons (see Chapter 3, methodological considerations). Hence, only cases were compared that resembled each other in all potentially important aspects except for the managerial dilemma they represent in order to assess the effects of the dilemma on the respective firms' corporate social responsibility policies. Therefore, only a small proportion of cases I researched are featured in this book.

[4] Interviews with the Production Manager of F, September 1, 2007, Cape Town and the Human Resources and Occupational Health Manager, September 21, 2007, Cape Town.

problems caused by the abuse of "crystal meth" – a drug causing rapid deterioration among its users. Given its limited resources, the firm decided to run only a rudimentary HIV/AIDS program and to focus its full attention on the drug problem instead. This case shows that the logic underlying the *human resources dilemma* is not confined to the issue areas of HIV/AIDS, but indeed pertains to labor-related corporate social responsibility in general.

With regard to the *technological specialization dilemma* the analysis in Chapter 6 shows that this internal driver explains more than just in-house environmental corporate social responsibility. The dilemma turned out to also account for the supply chain policies. Cases in point are the large multinational car firms B, F, M, and V. At first sight, the asserted differences in supply chain policies among these firms appeared to be caused by their differences with respect to asset-specific investments in marketing (i.e. the different levels of the *brand reputation dilemma* they represent): the high-end market car companies B and M were found to show stricter, more demanding, precise, and encompassing supply chain governance in the field of environment than the mass-market producers V and F. The high-end market firms M and B require suppliers to attain, for example, ISO 14001 certification. In addition, they push environmental management certification schemes down their supply chains by expecting their suppliers to have their suppliers, in turn, certified as well. In contrast, V and F, the firms that sell cars to the mass-market segment, do not make such demands.

An additional analysis of the cases from a longitudinal perspective, however, uncovered facts that disconfirm the supposition that it is the *brand reputation dilemma* accounting for the differences in supply chain policies. The high-end market firm M started to demand ISO 14001 environmental management systems from suppliers only after 2006. Beforehand, the firm's policy was identical to those of the mass-market firms V and F in that M did not require ISO 14001 certification from suppliers. The implications, as argued in Chapters 5 and 6, are twofold: first, the case of M disconfirms the argument that the *brand reputation dilemma* inclines firms to engage in strong supply chain regulation with respect to corporate social responsibility. Prior to 2006, the supply chain policy of the high-end market firm M was on the same level with respect to environmental standards as the mass-market firms V and F.

Second, the *technological specialization dilemma* does not only explain in-house policies, but also supply chain governance. A substantial increase of investments with a long duration before returns are generated, as in the case of M in 2006, was accompanied by an upgrade of in-house environmental policies – but also of environmental supply chain policies. The supply chain accounts for 60–70 percent of the value added to the products of large multinational corporations such as M, B, V, and F sell. Production targets and costs, unforeseen events, and opportunism are consequently determined by the supply chain to a great extent. To mitigate the risks inherent in this dependency on suppliers, management insisted on the exercise of strict supply chain governance.

Beyond the analyses in this book, recent studies on business and governance in areas of limited statehood provide additional evidence for the general relevance of internal drivers (Börzel and Thauer 2013). These studies find that asset specificity does not only explain firms' in-house and supply chain corporate social responsibility policies, but any firm activity contributing to governance in general: attempts to foster the regulatory capacities of state agencies, lobbying for stricter regulation, and cooperation with civil society for the end of public services. For example, firms in South Africa that have invested in rare skills of employees have – apart from running sophisticated HIV/AIDS workplace programs – lobbied the government for a more effective response to the disease (Thauer 2013a). Other firms having made investments in production capacities with long pay-off periods support the local government in setting stricter environmental standards in their localities (Thauer 2013b).

In summary, the arguments for internal drivers travel to other political contexts (such as China), issue areas (as labor standards and drug abuse), and beyond corporate social responsibility. While thus generally relevant, what are the findings of this book for debate beyond corporate social responsibility?

Internal drivers and the diffusion of business standards

This study has some important implications for the debate about the diffusion of social and environmental business standards. Studies inspired by diffusion theory show that such standards proliferate with foreign direct investment and through global production networks. More precisely, foreign direct investment in a weakly regulating "host" country originating from a highly regulating "home" country is associated with a spread of global standards. Similarly, production networks in areas of regulatory void, which are oriented towards "Western" consumer markets where concerns for social and environmental standards are strong, facilitate a diffusion of standards.

The underlying explanatory model of these claims usually assumes an NGO and consumer pressure-induced international "California effect" (Vogel 1995): NGOs and consumers in countries with strict regulation and a strong emphasis on environmental, labor, and human rights (i.e. in the "Western" world) put pressure on firms to comply across all of their business practices – including in offshore production locations and supply chains – with basic human rights, labor, and environmental standards. On account of this pressure, firms make sure that their branches in weakly regulating countries operate on high social and environmental standards (Prakash and Potoski 2006, 2007). In addition, importing firms in "Western" countries preferably source from exporting, offshore production locations and firms with a good human rights and environmental standards record. This preference among importing firms, in turn, makes exporting firms in emerging markets contexts adopt high labor and environmental standards (Cao *et al.* 2013; Greenhill Mosley and Prakash 2009).

The analysis in this study reveals that there are nonetheless important questions that remain unanswered by this external factor-based approach to diffusion. Consider the example of multinational car companies operating in South Africa, mentioned in Chapter 1 and analyzed in detail in Chapter 5 (see Figure 5.1). Each of these firms is based on foreign direct investments originating from a highly regulating country (from Germany, the US, and Japan). Yet they do not spread global and "home" market regulations to the same extent. While some transfer standards from "home" to South Africa, others do not. Rather, they operate on weak environmental standards. What explains this difference? Under which conditions will a cross-country diffusion of standards take place within a firm and what motivates this? Which multinational firms in a given industry sector will be more or less affected by diffusion dynamics at distinct points in time?

Internal driver 2, the *foreign direct investment dilemma*, is the answer. The implication of these findings is that it is not only important where foreign direct investment comes from, as pointed out by the literature. A highly regulating "home" country does not always and necessarily result in the spread of high standards to the "host" country market. It is the quality of the foreign direct investment that is pertinent: asset-specific foreign direct investments cause the spread of high standards.

The argument concerning production network-based diffusion of business standards in literature is similarly underspecified. The nine cases of South African firms in Chapter 4 running HIV/AIDS workplace programs on different levels illustrate this. Some of these firms run highly sophisticated programs offering employees comprehensive medical services in relation to the disease, including anti-retroviral therapy. Others, however, do not show any inclination to fight the disease at the workplace at all. All of the featured firms are fully integrated into global production networks of goods that are sold to consumers in the "Western" world, where concerns for labor and environmental standards are strong. While the overall sample of the nine cases indicates the emergence and spread of HIV/AIDS workplace programs in South Africa, what explains the striking differences among these firms?

The *human resources dilemma* – internal driver 1 – is the answer. The implication of this finding is that there is an alternative explanation to the one in the literature, which focuses on external pressure from NGOs and consumers for trade-based diffusion of standards from highly regulating countries to weakly regulating ones. Trade relations involving a skills gap between highly regulating countries and weakly regulating ones often cannot be compensated by the local labor market. Thus, skills have to be created in-house by businesses in weakly regulating countries. This, in turn, is associated with the emergence of labor standards in the weakly regulating country. In particular, as the analysis of the nine firm cases did not find any indication of NGO and consumer pressure-induced "California" effects – none of the importing trade partners ever mentioned the issue of HIV/AIDS in their dealings with the nine firms – this explanation seems highly plausible.

Internal drivers and (the emergence of) varieties of capitalism

The findings in this study are also relevant in the context of a recent debate in comparative political economy between the so-called "varieties of capitalism" and the "worlds of welfare capitalism" approaches to the emergence of social welfare state policies. Asset specificity is at the center of this debate. In *An Introduction to Varieties of Capitalism*, Hall and Soskice (2001) propose an "employer-centered" (Korpi 2006) explanation for welfare state policies. A main competitive advantage of firms in coordinated market economies (CMEs) vis-à-vis firms in liberal market economies (LMEs) is that they can make complex products (Busemeyer and Trampusch 2011; Hall and Soskice 2001; Mares 2001). This advantage, however, is tantamount to the willingness of employees to make asset-specific investments in skills specialization. In CMEs, social policies provide for strong incentives in this respect. They protect employees with specific skills from having to accept job offers that do not correspond to their qualifications. In consequence, firms that depend on specialized skills, as in the dominant industries in CMEs, emerge as the main supporters of strong social welfare state policies.

While theoretically plausible, this "employer-centered" explanation of social policies has provoked fierce criticism. Authors who study welfare state development historically – as Esping-Anderson in *The Three Worlds of Welfare Capitalism* (1990) – argue that welfare state policies are the result of class conflict. They emerge when strong working class organizations in coalition with left-wing parties succeed in pressing for social reforms *against* capitalist interests, rather than on behalf of them. In a counter-reaction to this criticism, the "varieties of capitalism" approach abandoned the idea of an "employer-centered" mechanism and adopted the idea of an "employee-centered" one instead (Iversen 2005; Iversen and Soskice 2001, 2009): "individuals who have made risky investments in skills will demand insurance against the possible future loss of income from those investments" and therefore "have strong incentives to support social policies" (Iversen and Soskice 2001: 875) – whereas employees who have not made such asset-specific investments have no such incentives.

We can thus identify three distinct mechanisms that may bring about social policies, of which two are based on asset specificity. Asset specificity may motivate and empower employees to push for social policies (Iversen 2005; Iversen and Soskice 2001, 2009); asset specificity may, alternatively, motivate managers to invent such policies to protect their investments (Hall and Soskice 2001). Finally, employees may press successfully for social policies for reasons entirely unrelated to asset specificity (Esping-Anderson 1990; Korpi 2006). The process tracing conducted in Chapter 4 tested the logic of these arguments empirically. This test clearly supports the second mechanism: it is managers who drive HIV/AIDS workplace programs on account of asset specificity, not unions or the demands of workers.

Additional evidence for these findings derives from recent studies of businesses' contributions to governance, going beyond corporate social responsibility. They show that managers, on account of asset specificity, also lobby the government to develop more effective health programs and coordinate a collective response to the disease with civic and other business actors on the local level (Börzel *et al.* 2012; Thauer 2013a). In addition, the analysis of the *technological specialization dilemma* in this book showed that "employer-based mechanisms" also bring about environmental policies – rather than social movements or NGOs. These are remarkable findings. They illustrate empirically the original "employer-centered" mechanism as suggested by Hall and Soskice (2001) in *Varieties of Capitalism*. The implication is that this mechanism should not be too easily dismissed as ahistorical.

At the same time, however, it should be emphasized that these findings in no way rule out the other two mechanisms for welfare state policies. Let us recall that the *human resources dilemma* and the *technological specialization dilemma* are sufficient but unnecessary conditions for corporate social responsibility. A case in point for a different mechanism leading to social policies, which is more in line with the one suggested by the historically oriented *Worlds of Welfare Capitalism* approach, is the mining industry in South Africa.

Mining is generally not very skills specific. Nonetheless, mining firms often run strong HIV/AIDS workplace programs (Hönke and Thauer 2013). In this case it is thus not asset specificity – and also not managers who press for these programs – but union activism combined with NGO pressure which account for this finding (Börzel *et al.* 2013; Hönke 2013). The industry's system of migrant labor and the sex industry that comes with it has been identified as the main cause for the high prevalence rates of HIV/AIDS in sub-Saharan Africa – not least among the mining workers. The unions, in collaboration with the NGO "Treatment Action Campaign," therefore decided to put recurrent and fierce pressure on mining firms to become active in the fight against the disease. As some large mining firms have a strong concern for their brand reputation, this pressure led to the firms' adoption of HIV/AIDS workplace programs and, beyond that, to collaborations with state institutions for a better public response to the disease (ibid.). Hence, empirically it seems that different mechanisms can bring social policies to the fore.

Finally, the inference we can make on the basis of the analyses in this book with respect to the emergence of *Varieties of Capitalism* and welfare state policies is limited. The study shows that "employer-based" mechanisms for social welfare policies exist in South Africa – for example in the area of HIV/AIDS. However, it does not allow us to say anything about the effectiveness of these mechanisms as concerns the creation of, for example, public health care programs in the country. For such an assessment, the state has to be brought into the equation. South Africa lacks, on the one hand, the capacities to improve its public health care system. On the other hand, HIV/AIDS is still a contested issue in the country so that there is also a lack of strong political will to improve the situation. In combination with high corruption levels and a lack of administrative coordination and competence, it may very well be that the pressure firms exert on the government to create stronger health policies will turn out to be not very effective. Hence, one may not too easily jump to hasty conclusions such as that South Africa is now, on account of business attempts to press for social welfare policies, on its way to developing an adequate public health response to the disease.

Internal drivers and governance in areas of regulatory void

Finally, the findings in this book have important implications for the study of governance in the regulatory void. The conventional political science approach to governance is that common good and public service provision are the direct outcomes of the effectiveness of state institutions; in other words that the level of governance is a function of state capacities. Recent studies, however, show that this is the case only under conditions of strong, consolidated statehood (Krasner and Risse 2014; Risse 2011). In areas of limited statehood, the level of governance is largely decoupled from the level of state capacities and the effectiveness of state institutions. It is as yet unclear which actors – and under which conditions – account for these varying levels of governance, given that it is not the state.

Governance contributions coming from business – as in the context of corporate social responsibility – is one potential explanation. The findings in this book show that firms adopt corporate social responsibility policies more frequently and for a greater variety of reasons (i.e. on account of internal drivers) than previously assumed, thereby contributing to governance. In addition, where these contributions are driven by internal drivers, they seem particularly powerful.

For example, Mercedes Benz is a firm that has accepted the necessity to counter HIV/AIDS in East London (South Africa) on account of its strong dependence on highly specialized skills (Thauer 2013a). In the context of the workplace and supply chain HIV/AIDS programs of Mercedes, which also include the families of employees, about 60,000 persons have gained access to free health care services so far (Lorentzen 2006).[5] The firm itself has only 3,800 employees. The other multinationals in the car industry in South Africa have similar programs. The implication is that, everything else being equal, the level of health governance provided in those areas of limited statehood in which firms cluster and make attempts to contribute to service provision on account of internal drivers will be higher than in areas without firms – or where firms do not make such attempts. Hence, firms may be among those actors that account for the mentioned decoupling of state capacities and levels of governance in areas of limited statehood.

If so, however, this raises some important additional questions: why should firms make high investments in specific skills of employees or in the production site in the first place if that means they will have to extensively provide for governance?

At a time of economic stagnation in the old triad of Europe, the US and Japan, emerging markets – such as the BRICS and other G20 states (see Armijo 2007) – have become the main engine of growth for many industries. An example is the car industry. The investment strategy of this industry in emerging markets is long-term oriented, aiming at an increase in sales and market shares. The rising consumer markets and the promise of continuing growth is the main incentive for these firms' investments. To them, the benefits of making asset-specific investments, for example in South Africa, therefore easily outweigh the additional costs of governance contributions, which such investments incur.

However, if firms are now really taking over governance, does this imply that the state as the basic ordering principle and main provider of governance is becoming redundant? It does not: this book showed that preferences of businesses towards corporate social responsibility vary. This variation boils down to internal drivers. On the one hand, there are industries and firms marked by high levels of investments and asset specificity, and on the other, those characterized by low levels of

---

[5] Mercedes Benz 2011. "HIV/AIDS Policy." Available online at https://members. weforum.org/pdf/Initiatives/GHI_HIV_CaseStudy_DCSA.pdf (December 6, 2012).

investment and fluid assets. Firms and industry sectors based on low levels of investments and fluid assets often drive regulatory "race to the bottom" dynamics. They relocate production to wherever social, environmental, and health standards are lowest in order to avoid regulation and contributing to governance. In all likelihood these firms will not regulate themselves effectively or contribute to governance in the future either.

A case in point is the firm CL in China, which was analyzed in Chapter 6. The leather firm ruthlessly exploits workers and the environment. As the analysis showed, NGO activism and reputational concerns of firms alone will in all likelihood not be able to make firms such as CL disappear: only under the exceptional circumstances of strong reputational concerns of companies and recurrent and fierce NGO pressure will international brands such as C, the luxury goods firm that imports the products of CL, have sufficient incentives to impress high standards on suppliers. Purely voluntary modes of governance will thus remain largely ineffective in these cases (see for this point also Vogel 2010). No actor other than the state can systematically discourage such business practices.

The situation is, of course, a different one when we look at firms and industry sectors that are characterized by high levels of investments and asset specificity. However, even here governance by business alone cannot substitute functioning state institutions. When firms contribute to governance, they still follow their own profit-maximizing interests. Hence, governance by business will often result in an unequal distribution of governance services, which may even turn out to be club goods rather than common goods (Börzel *et al.* 2012; Hönke and Thauer 2013). To illustrate this point, in South African townships located far away from industrial centers, the consequences of the HIV/AIDS pandemic are often felt most strongly. However, if the social situation in these townships is not negatively affecting firms' business procedures, governance by business is unlikely to emerge. In other words: in terms of social justice, business is ill-equipped to organize governance. By contrast, functioning state institutions apply, ideally, a needs-based approach to the provision of governance services such as HIV/AIDS-related health programs. Governance by business is therefore also limited in its problem-solving capacity: as long as the health situation in the mentioned townships is not improved, these communities will remain a breeding ground for the HIV/AIDS pandemic with inevitable negative spillovers on society (and business) as a whole. A needs-based approach, as promised by functioning state institutions, is therefore not only more legitimate but also likely to be more effective than governance by business.

However, the fact remains that in large parts of the world functioning state institutions are simply not available – and will not be in the foreseeable future. As an ideal, functioning state institutions remain uncontested. In practice, governance by business is often all that is available with the alternative being that no governance is provided at all. To those benefiting from it – and there are quite a few of them – it certainly makes a difference.

References

Abbott, K. W., R. O. Keohane, A. Moravcsik, A.-M. Slaughter, and D. Snidal (2000). "The Concept of Legalization." *International Organization*, 54 (3): 401–19.

Abbott, K. W. and D. Snidal (2009). "The Governance Triangle. Regulatory Standards Institutions and the Shadow of the State." In *The Politics of Regulation*, W. Mattli and N. Woods (eds.). Princeton University Press, 44–89.

Alfaro, L. (2003). "Foreign Direct Investment and Growth: Does the Sector Matter?" Unpublished, Boston, MA: Harvard Business School, http://gwww.grips.ac.jp/teacher/oono/hp/docu01/paper14.pdf (accessed November 20, 2012).

Alchian, A. A. and H. Demsetz (1972). "Production, Information Costs, and Economic Organization." *American Economic Review*, 62: 777–95.

Ammenberg, J. and O. Hjelm (2003). "Tracing Business and Environmental Effects of Environmental Management Systems – a Study of Networking Small and Medium-sized Enterprises using a Joint Environmental Management System." *Business Strategy and the Environment*, 12 (3): 163–74.

Anton, W. R. Q., G. Deltas, and M. Khanna (2004). "Incentives for Environmental Self-regulation and Implications for Environmental Performance." *Journal of Environmental Economics and Management*, 48 (1): 632–54.

Armijo, L. E. (2007). "Special Edition: the BRICs Countries (Brazil, Russia, India, and China) in the Global System." *Asian Perspective*, 31 (4).

Auld, G., S. Bernstein, and B. Cashore (2008). "The New Corporate Social Responsibility." *Annual Review of Environment and Resources*, 33: 413–35.

Axelrod, R. (1981). "The Emergence of Cooperation among Egoists." *American Political Science Review*, 75: 306–18.

Aykut, D. and S. Sayek (2007). "The Role of the Sectoral Composition of Foreign Direct Investment on Growth." In *Do Multinationals Feed Local Development and Growth?*, L. Piscitello and G. D. Santangelo (eds.). Amsterdam: Elsevier, 35–62.

Baldwin, R. and M. Cave (1999). *Understanding Regulation. Theory, Strategy, and Practice*. Oxford University Press.

Bansal, P. (2005). "Evolving Sustainability: A Longitudinal Study of Corporate Sustainable Development." *Strategic Management Journal*, 26 (3): 197–218.

Barnes, J. and A. Black (2003). "Motor Industry Developing Program." *Review Report*. Durban and Cape Town.

Barney, J. B. and W. Hesterly (2006). "Organizational Economics: Understanding the Relationship between Organizations and Economic Analysis." In *The SAGE Handbook of Organization Studies*, S. R. Clegg, C. Hardy, T. B. Lawrence, and W. R. Nord (eds.). London: Sage, 111–49.

Barry, C. M., K. C. Clay, and M. E. Flynn (2012). "Avoiding the Spotlight: Human Rights, Shaming and Foreign Direct Investment." *International Studies Quarterly*, http://onlinelibrary.wiley.com/doi/10.1111/isqu.12039/ full (accessed February 1, 2013).

BBDO Consulting GmbH (2009). *Brand Parity Study 2009*. Düsseldorf: BBDO, February.

Ben-Porath, Y. (1980). "The F-Connection: Families, Friends, and Firms and the Organization of Exchange." *Population and Development Review*, 6: 1–30.

Besley, T. (2006). *Principled Agents. The Political Economy of Good Government*. Oxford University Press.

Black, A. (2001). "Globalization and Restructuring in the South African Automotive Industry." *Journal of International Development*, 13: 779–96.

Black, A. and S. Mitchell (2002). "Policy in the South African Motor Industry: Goals, Incentives, and Outcomes." *South African Journal of Economics*, 70 (8): 1273–97.

Black, D. (1999). "The Long and Winding Road: International Norms and Domestic Political Change in South Africa." In *The Power of Human Rights. International Norms and Domestic Change*, T. Risse, S. C. Ropp, and K. Sikkink (eds.). Cambridge University Press, 78–109.

Blanton, S. L. and R. G. Blanton (2007). "What Attracts Foreign Investors? An Examination of Human Rights and Foreign Direct Investment." *Journal of Politics*, 69 (1): 143–55.

(2009). "A Sectoral Analysis of Human Rights and FDI: Does Industry Type Matter?" *International Studies Quarterly*, 53: 469–93.

Bohle, D. (2008). "Race to the Bottom? Transnational Companies and Reinforced Competition in the Enlarged European Union." In *Neoliberal European Governance and Beyond – The Contradictions and Limits of a Political Project*, B. Van Apeldoorn, J. Drahokoupil, and L. Horn (eds.). London: Palgrave, 163–86.

Börzel, T. A. and T. Risse (2010). "Governance without a State – Can It Work?" *Regulation and Governance*, 4 (2): 1–22.

Börzel, T. A., A. Héritier, N. Kranz, and C. R. Thauer (2011). "A Race to the Top? Firms Regulatory Competition in Areas of Limited Statehood." In *Governing without a State? Policies and Politics in Areas of Limited Statehood*, T. Risse (ed.). New York: Columbia University Press, 122–46.

Börzel, T. A., J. Hönke, and C. R. Thauer (2012). "Does it Really Take the State? Limited Statehood, Multinational Corporations, and Corporate Responsibility in South Africa." *Business and Politics*, 14 (3): 1–34.

(2013). "Conclusion: A Race to the Top?" In *Business and Governance in South Africa. Racing to the Top?*, T. A. Börzel and C. R. Thauer (eds.). Houndmills: Palgrave Macmillan, 215–47.

Börzel, T. A. and C. R. Thauer (eds.) (2013). *Business and Governance in South Africa. Racing to the Top?*. Houndmills: Palgrave.

Brady, H. F. and D. Collier (eds.) (2010). *Rethinking Social Inquiry: Diverse Tools, Shared Standards*, 2nd edn. Lanham, MD: Rowman and Littlefield.

Bray, Z. and C. R. Thauer (2014). "Utopian Spaces, Dystopian Places? Corporate Social Responsibility and Globalization: A Local Community-based Perspective." Paper under review.

Brousseau, E. and M. Fares (2000). "Incomplete Contracts and Governance Structures: Are Incomplete Contract Theory and New Institutional Economics Substitutes or Complements?" In *Institutions, Contracts and Organizations: Perspectives from New Institutional Economics*, C. Ménard (ed.). Cheltenham: Edward Elgar, 399–422.

Busemeyer, M. R. (2009). "Asset Specificity, Institutional Complementarities and the Variety of Skill Regimes in Coordinated Market Economies." *Socio-Economic Review*, 7: 375–406.

Busemeyer, M. R. and C. Trampusch (eds.) (2011). *The Comparative Political Economy of Collective Skill Systems*. Oxford University Press.

Cao, X., B. Greenhill, and A. Prakash (2013). "Where is the Tipping Point? Bilateral Trade and the Diffusion of Human Rights, 1982–2004." *British Journal of Political Science*, 43 (1): 133–56.

Carroll, A. B. (1991). "The Pyramid of Corporate Social Responsibility." *Business Horizons*, 34 (4): 39–48.

(1999). "Corporate Social Responsibility. Evolution of a Definitional Construct." *Business and Society*, 38 (3): 268–95.

Carroll, A. B. and A. K. Buchholtz (2000). *Business and Society: Ethics and Stakeholder Management*, 4th edn. Cincinnati: Thomson Learning.

Chakraborty, C. and P. Nunnenkamp (2008). "Economic Reforms, FDI, and Economic Growth in India: A Sector Level Analysis." *World Development*, 36: 1192–212.

Chan, A. (2003). "A Race to the Bottom." *China Perspectives*, 46: 41–9.

(2005). "Recent Trends in Chinese Labor Issues – Signs of Change." *China Perspectives*, 57, http://chinaperspectives.revues.org/1115#quotation (last accessed April 1, 2014).

Chan, A. and R. J. Ross (2003). "Racing to the Bottom. Industrial Trade without a Social Clause." *Third World Quarterly*, 24 (6): 1011–28.

Chan, G., P. K. Lee, and L. H. Chan (2008). "China's Environmental Governance: The Domestic–International Nexus." *Third World Quarterly*, 29 (2): 291–314.

Chatham House (2007). *Civil Society and Environmental Governance in China*. Beijing: Workshop Report.

Cherry, M. A. and J. F. Sneirson (2011). "Beyond Profit: Rethinking Corporate Social Responsibility and Greenwashing after the BP Oil Disaster." *Tulane Law Review*, 85 (4): 983–1033.

Chick, M. (2011). "Network Utilities." In *The Oxford Handbook of Business and Government*, G. Wilson, W. Grant, and D. Coen (eds.). Oxford University Press, 684–702.

Coase, R. (1937). "The Nature of the Firm." *Economica*, 4 (16): 386–405.

Coen, D., W. Grant, and G. Wilson (2010): "Political Science: Perspectives on Business and Government." In *The Oxford Handbook of Business and Government*, G. Wilson, W. Grant, and D. Coen (eds.). Oxford University Press, 9–34.

Cohen, Stephen (2007). *Multinational Corporations and Foreign Direct Investment*. Oxford University Press.

Collinsworth, T. J., W. Goold, and P. J. Harvey (1994). "Labor and Free Trade." *Foreign Affairs*, 77 (1): 8–13.

Cottier, Thomas (2002). "Trade and Human Rights." *Journal of International Economic Law*, 5: 111–32.

Crawford, S. E. S. and E. Ostrom (1995). "A Grammar of Institutions." *American Political Science Review*, 89 (3): 582–601.

Cutler, C., V. Haufler, and T. Porter (1999). *Private Authority and International Affairs*. New York: State University of New York Press.

Dashwood, H. S. (2012). *The Rise of Global Corporate Social Responsibility: Mining and the Spread of Global Norms*. Cambridge University Press.

DEAT (2000). "State of the Environment Report South Africa," www.ngo.grida.no/soesa/nsoer/index.htm (accessed January 2, 2008).

Deitelhoff, N. and K.-D. Wolf (eds.) (2010). *Corporate Security Responsibility? Corporate Governance Contributions to Peace and Security in Zones of Conflict*. Houndmills: Palgrave.

Demsetz, H. (1991). "The Theory of the Firm Revisited." In *The Nature of the Firm. Origins, Evolution, and Development*, O. E. Williamson and S. G. Winter (eds.). Oxford, New York: Oxford University Press, 159–79.

Denzin, N. (2006). *Sociological Methods: A Sourcebook*. New Brunswick, NJ: Transaction Publishers.

Department of Health (2000). "HIV/AIDS/STD Strategic Plan for South Africa, 2000–2005," www.doh.gov.za/docs/index.html (accessed June 10, 2006).

    (2003). "Operational Plan for Comprehensive HIV and AIDS Care, Management and Treatment for South Africa," www.doh.gov.za/docs/index.html (accessed June 10, 2006).

Dickinson, D. (2004). "Fronts or Front-Lines? HIV/AIDS and Big Business in South Africa." *Transformation: Critical Perspectives on Southern Africa*, 55: 28–54.

Dickinson, D. and M. Stevens (2005). "Understanding the Response of Large South African Companies to HIV/AIDS." *Journal of Social Aspects of HIV/AIDS*, 2 (2): 286–95.

DiMaggio, P. and W. M. Powell (1991). *The New Institutionalism in Organizational Analysis*. University of Chicago Press.

Dossani, R. (2012). "A Decade After Y2K: Has Indian IT Emerged?" In *Re-examining the Service Revolution*, D. Breznitz and J. Zysman (eds.). New Haven, CT: Yale University Press, 156–78.

Dow, G. K. (1985). "Internal Bargaining and Strategic Innovation in the Theory of the Firm." *Journal of Economic Behavior and Organization*, 6: 301–20.

Draude, A., T. Risse, and C. Schmelzle (2012). "Grundbegriffe der Governanceforschung. Ein Beitrag aus dem Teilprojekt A1." SFB 700 Working Paper, No. 36. Berlin: Freie Universität Berlin.

Eberhardt, M. and J. Thoburn (2007). "China, the World Trade Organization and the End of the Agreement on Textiles and Clothing: Impacts on Workers." In *Marginalization in China. Perspectives on Transition and Globalization*, H. Xiaoquan, B. W. Zhang, and R. Sanders (eds.). Aldershot: Ashgate, 176–95.

Eccks, R. G. (1985). *The Transfer Pricing Problem*. Lexington, MA: Lexington Books.

Epstein, M. J. (2008). *Making Sustainability Work. Best Practices in Managing and Measuring Corporate Social, Environmental and Economic Impacts*. Sheffield: Greenleaf Publishing.

Esping-Anderson, G. (1990). *The Three Worlds of Welfare Capitalism*. Princeton University Press.

Farrell, D., R. Jain, and B. Pietracci (2007). "Assessing Brazil's Offshoring Prospects." *McKinsey Quarterly*, Special Edition.

Flohr, A., L. Rieth, S. Schwindenhammer, and K. D. Wolf (2010). *The Role of Business in Global Governance. Corporations as Norm-Entrepreneurs*. Houndmills: Palgrave Macmillan.

Frederick, W. C. (2006). *Corporation, Be Good! The Story of Corporate Social Responsibility*. Indianapolis: Dog Ear Publishing.

Freeman, J. and C. Kolstad (2007). *Moving to Markets in Environmental Regulation: Lessons from Twenty Years of Experience*. New York: Oxford University Press.

Freeman, R. E., S. R. Velamuri, and B. Moriarty (2006). *Company Stakeholder Responsibility: A New Approach to CSR*. Charlottesville, VA: Business Roundtable Institute for Corporate Ethics.

Ganghof, F. (2005). "Kausale Perspektiven in der Politikwissenschaft: X-zentrierte und Y-zentrierte Forschungsdesigns." In *Vergleichen in der Politikwissenschaft*, S. Kropp and M. Minkenberg (eds.). Wiesbaden: VS Verlag für Sozialwissenschaften, 76–96.

Garcia-Johnson, R. (2000). *Exporting Environmentalism: US Multinational Chemical Corporations in Brazil and Mexico*. Cambridge, MA: MIT Press.

George, A. and A. Bennett (2005). *Case Studies and Theory Development in the Social Sciences*. Cambridge MA: MIT Press.

Gereffi, G. and O. Memedovic (2003). "The Global Apparel Value Chain: What Prospects for Upgrading by Developing Countries?" United Nations Industrial Development Organization (UNIDO), Working Paper.

Gill, S. (1995). "Globalisation, Market Civilization and Discliplinary Neoliberalism." *Millenium*, 24: 399–423.

Greenhill, B., L. Mosley, and A. Prakash (2009). "Trade-based Diffusion of Labor Rights: A Panel Study, 1986–2002." *American Political Science Review*, 103 (4): 669–90.

(2010). "Contingent Convergence (or Divergence): Unpacking the Linkages between Labor Rights and Foreign Direct Investment." Paper presented at the annual conference of the International Studies Association, New Orleans (February 17–20, 2010).

Greenstein, S. and V. Stango (eds.) (2007). *Standards and Public Policy*. Cambridge University Press.

Groenewald, Y. (2005). "Shootout at the Coalface." *Mail and Guardian*, March 14, 2005.

Gunningham, N., R. Kagan, and D. Thornton (2003). *Shades of Green. Business, Regulation, and Environment*. Stanford University Press.

Guthrie, D. (2006). *China and Globalization*. New York: Routledge.

Hafner-Burton, E. M. (2005). "Trading Human Rights: How Preferential Trade Agreements Influence Government Repression." *International Organization*, 59: 593–629.

Halfteck, G. (2008). "Legislative Threats." *Stanford Law Review*, 61 (available at SSRN: http://ssrn.com/abstract=1113173).

Hall, P. and D. Soskice (2001). "An Introduction to Varieties of Capitalism." In *Varieties of Capitalism. The Institutional Foundations of Comparative Advantage*, P. Hall and D. Soskice (eds.). Oxford University Press, 1–68.

Hall, R. B., and T. J. Bierstecker (eds.) (2002). *The Emergence of Private Authority in Global Governance.* Cambridge University Press.

Hancké, B. (2010). "Varieties of Capitalism and Business." In *The Oxford Handbook of Business and Government*, G. Wilson, W. Grant, and D. Coen (eds.). Oxford University Press, www.oxfordhandbooks.com/view/10.1093/oxfordhb/9780199214273.001.0001/oxfordhb-9780199214273-e-6 (accessed April 2, 2014).

Hargreaves Heap, S. and M. Hollis (1998). *A Theory of Choice. A Critical Guide.* Oxford, Cambridge, MA: Blackwell.

Harrington, W., R. D. Morgenstern, and T. Sterner (2004). *Choosing Environmental Policy: Comparing Instruments and Outcomes in the United States and Europe.* Washington, DC: RFT Press.

Hart, D. M. (2010). "The Political Theory of the Firm." *The Oxford Handbook of Business and Government*, G. Wilson, W. Grant, and D. Coen (eds.). Oxford University Press, 173–91.

Haufler, V. (2001). *A Public Role for the Private Sector: Industry Self-regulation in a Global Economy.* Washington, DC: Carnegie Endowment for International Peace.

Hendry, J. R. (2006). "Taking Aim at Business. What Factors Lead Environmental Non-Governmental Organizations to Target Particular Firms?" *Business and Society*, 45 (1): 47–86.

Héritier, A. and D. Lehmkuhl (eds.) (2008). "The Shadow of Hierarchy and New Modes of Governance." *Journal of Public Policy*, special issue, 28 (1).

Héritier, A., A. K. Müller-Debus, and C. R. Thauer. (2009). "The Firm as an Inspector: Private Ordering and Political Rules." *Business and Politics*, 11 (4): Art. 2.

Hickey, A. (2002). "Governance and HIV/AIDS: Issues of Public Policy and Administration." In *HIV/AIDS, Economics and Governance in South Africa: Key Issues in Understanding Response*, K. Kelly, W. Parker, and S. Gelb (eds). Johannesburg: USAID (Cadre), 37–53.

Hickey, A., N. Ndlovu, and T. Guthrie (2003). *Budgeting for HIV/AIDS in South Africa: Report on Intergovernmental Funding Flows for an Integrated Response in the Social Sector.* Cape Town: IDASA.

Hoffmann, A. (2001). *From Heresy to Dogma: An Institutional History of Corporate Environmentalism.* Palo Alto, CA: Stanford University Press.

Hönke, J. (2013). "Between Cause and Cure: The Mining Industry and HIV/AIDS Governance in South Africa." In *Business and Governance in South Africa. Racing to the Top?*, T. A. Börzel and C. R. Thauer (eds.). Houndmills: Palgrave, 67–88.

Hönke, J. and N. Kranz (2013). "Cleaning up their Act, or More? Mining Companies and Environmental Protection in South Africa." In *A Race to the Top? Business and Governance in South Africa*, T. A. Börzel and C. R. Thauer (eds.). Houndmills: Palgrave Macmillan.

Hönke, J., N. Kranz, A. Héritier, and T. A. Börzel (2008). "Fostering Environmental Regulation? Corporate Social Responsibility in Countries with Weak Regulatory Capacities. The Case of South Africa." SFB-Governance Working Paper, No. 9, February 2009, Research Center "Governance in Areas of Limited Statehood," Berlin.

Hönke, J. and C. R. Thauer (2014). "Multinational Corporations and Service Provision in Sub-Saharan Africa: Legitimacy and Institutionalization Matter." *Governance*, in press.

Hopmann, P. T. (1996). *The Negotiation Process and the Resolution of International Conflict.* Columbia: University of South Carolina Press.

Howard-Grenville, J. (2007). *Corporate Culture and Environmental Practice. Making Change at a High-tech Manufacturer.* Cheltenham: Edward Elgar.

Hiß, S. (2009). "From Implicit to Explicit Corporate Social Responsibility: Institutional Change as a Fight for Myths." *Business Ethics Quarterly*, 3: 433–51.

Iklé, F. C. (1964). *How Nations Negotiate.* New York: Praeger.

Iversen, T. (2005). *Capitalism, Democracy, and Welfare.* New York: Cambridge University Press.

Iversen, T. and D. Soskice (2001). "An Asset Theory of Social Preferences." *American Political Science Review*, 95 (4): 875–93.

(2009). "Distribution and Redistribution: The Shadow of the Nineteenth Century." *World Politics*, 61: 438–86.

Jackson, G. and A. Apostolakou (2010). "Corporate Social Responsibility in Western Europe: An Institutional Mirror or Substitute?" *Journal of Business Ethics*, 94 (3): 371–94.

Jackson G. and R. Deeg (2006). "How Many Varieties of Capitalism? Comparing the Comparative Institutional Analyses of Capitalist Diversity." MPIfG Discussion Paper, 06/2, Max Planck Institute for the Study of Societies, Cologne.

Jai-Ok, O., M. Traore, and C. Warfield (2006). *The Textile and Apparel Industry in Developing Countries.* Abington: Woodhead Publishing.

Jönsson, C. (2002). "Diplomacy, Bargaining and Negotiation." In *Handbook of International Relations*, W. Carlsnaes, T. Risse, and B. A. Simmons (eds.). London, Thousand Oaks, New Dehli: Sage Publications, 212–35.

Joskow, P. L. (1988). "Asset Specificity and the Structure of Vertical Relationships: Empirical Test of Transaction Cost Analysis." *Journal of Law, Economics and Organization*, 4: 121–39.

Keck, M. E. and K. Sikkink (1998). *Activists Beyond Borders. Advocacy Networks in International Politics.* Ithaca, NY: Cornell University Press.

Kell, G. and J. G. Ruggie (1999). *Global Markets and Social Legitimacy: The Case of the "Global Compact." Governing the Public Domain beyond the Era of the Washington Consensus? Redrawing the Line between the State and the Market.* York University, Toronto: UN Global Compact.

Khanna, M., P. Koss, C. Jones, and D. Ervin (2007). "Motivations for Voluntary Environmental Management." *Policy Studies Journal*, 35 (4): 751–72.

King, G., R. O. Keohane, and S. Verba (1994). *Designing Social Inquiry: Scientific Inference in Qualitative Research.* Princeton University Press.

Kirmani, A., S. Sood, and S. Bridges (1999). "The Ownership Effect in Consumer Responses to Brand Line Stretches." *Journal of Marketing*, 63 (1): 88–101.

Kirton, J. J. and M. J. Trebilcock (2004). *Hard Choices, Soft Law: Voluntary Standards in Global Trade, Environment, and Social Governance.* Aldershot: Brookfield.

Klein, B. (1988). "Vertical Integration as Organizational Ownership: The Fisher Body – General Motors Relationship Revisited." *Journal of Law, Economics and Organization*, 4: 199–213.

Koremenos, B., C. Lipson, and D. Snidal (2001). "The Rational Design of International Institutions." *International Organization*, 55 (4): 761–99.

Korpi, W. (1978). *The Working Class in Welfare Capitalism.* London: Routledge and Kegan Paul.

(2006). "Power Resources and Employer-Centered Approaches in Explanations of Welfare States and Varieties of Capitalism: Protagonists, Consenters, and Antagonists." *World Politics*, 58: 167–206.

Krasner, S. (1991). "Global Communications and National Power: Life on the Pareto Frontier." *World Politics*, 43 (3): 336–66.

Krasner, S. D. and T. Risse (2014). "External Actors, State-building, and Service Provision in Areas of Limited Statehood: Introduction." *Governance*: in press.

Ladwig, B. and B. Rudolf (2011). "International Legal and Moral Standards of Good Governance in Fragile States." In *Governance without a State? Policies and Politics in Areas of Limited Statehood*, T. Risse (ed.). New York: Columbia University Press.

Lake, D. A. and R. Powell (1999). "International Relations: A Strategic-Choice Approach." In *Strategic Choice and International Relations*, D. A. Lake and R. Powell (eds.). Princeton University Press, 3–39.

Levi, M. (1997). "A Model, a Method, and a Map: Rational Choice in Comparative and Historical Analysis." *Comparative Politics: Rationality, Culture and Structure*, M. I. Lichbach and A. S. Zuckerman (eds.). New York: Cambridge University Press, 19–42.

Levy, D. L. and R. Kaplan (2008). "CSR and Theories of Global Governance: Strategic Contestation in Global Issue Arenas." In *The Oxford Handbook of Corporate Social Responsibility*, A. Crane, M. Abagail, D. Matten, J. Moon, and D. S. Siegel (eds.). Oxford, New York: Oxford University Press, 432–52.

Locke, R. M., F. Qin, and A. Brause (2007). "Does Monitoring Improve Labor Standards – Lessons from Nike." *Industrial and Labor Relations Review*, 61 (1): 1–31.

Lorentzen, J. (2006). "Multinationals on the Periphery. DaimlerChrysler South Africa, Human Capital Upgrading and Regional Economic Development." Occasional Papers of the Human Research Council South Africa, 2.

Lorentzen, J. and J. Barnes (2004). "Learning, Upgrading, and Innovation in the South African Automotive Industry." *European Journal of Development Research*, 16 (3): 465–98.

Lorentzen, J., G. Robbins and J. Barnes (2004). "The Durban Auto Cluster: Global Competition, Collective Efficiency, and Local Development." Working Paper No. 41, School of Development Studies, University of KwaZulu-Natal.

Luce, R. D. and H. Raiffa (1957). *Games and Decisions*. New York: Wiley.

Lund-Thomsen, P. (2005). "Corporate Social Responsibility in South Africa: The Role of Community Mobilizing in Environmental Governance." *International Affairs*, 81 (3): 619–33.

Madsen, Peter M. (2009). "Does Corporate Investment Drive a 'Race to the Bottom' in Environmental Protection? A Reexamination of the Effect of Environmental Regulation on Investment." *Academy of Management Journal*, 52 (6): 1297–318.

Mahtaney, P. (2007). *India, China and Globalization. The Emerging Superpowers and the Future of Economic Development*. Basingstoke: Palgrave Macmillan.

Malone, T. W., K. R. Grant, F. A. Turbak, S. A. Brobst, and M. D. Cohen (1987). "Intelligent Information-Sharing Systems." *Communications of the ACM*, 30: 390–402.

Manheim, F. T. (2009). *The Conflict Over Environmental Regulation in the United States. Origins, Outcomes, and Comparisons with the EU and Other Regions*. New York: Springer.

Mani, M. and D. Wheeler (1998). "In Search of Pollution Havens?" *Journal of Environment and Development*, 7 (3): 215–47.

March, J. G. (1962). "The Business Firm as a Political Coalition." *Journal of Politics*, 24: 662–78.

Mares, I. (2001). "Firms and the Welfare State: When, Why and How Does Social Policy Matter to Employers?" In *Varieties of Capitalism: The Institutional Foundations of Comparative Advantage*, P. Hall and D. Soskice (eds.). Oxford, New York: Oxford University Press, 184–212.

Marquis, C. and M. W. Toffel (2012). "When Do Firms Greenwash? Corporate Visibility, Civil Society Scrutiny, and Environmental Disclosure." Working Paper No. 11–115, Harvard Business School Organizational Behavior Unit.

Matten, D. and J. Moon (2008). "'Implicit' and 'Explicit' CSR: A Conceptual Framework for a Comparative Understanding of Corporate Social Responsibility." *Academy of Management Review*, 2: 404–24.

Marx, A. (2008). "Limits to non-state market regulation: A Qualitative Comparative Analysis of the International Sport Footwear Industry and the Fair Labor Association." *Regulation and Governance*, 2: 253–73.

McGuinness, T. (1994). "Markets and Managerial Hierarchies." In *Markets, Hierarchies and Networks*. G. Thompson, J. Frances, and J. C. Mitchell (eds.). London: Sage, 66–81.

Meyn, M. (2004). "The Export Performance of the South African Automotive Industry. New Stimuli by the EU–South Africa Free Trade Agreements?" Berichte aus dem Weltwirtschaftlichen Colloquium der Universität Bremen, 89.

Mihalache-O'keef, A. and Q. Li (2011). "Modernization vs. Dependency Revisited: Effects of Foreign Direct Investment on Food Security in Less Developed Countries." *International Studies Quarterly*, 55: 71–93.

Milgrom P. and J. Roberts (1988). "An Economic Approach to Influence Activities in Organizations." *American Journal of Sociology*, 94 (Supplement): 8154–79.

Miller, G. J. (1992). *Managerial Dilemmas. The Political Economy of Hierarchy*. Cambridge, New York: Cambridge University Press.

(2005). "The Political Evolution of Principal-Agent Models." *Annual Review of Political Science*, 8: 203–25.

Mol, A. P. J. (2001). *Globalization and Environmental Reforms: The Ecological Modernization of the Global Economy*. Cambridge, MA: MIT Press.

Moran, T., E. M. Graham, and M. Blomstrom (eds.) (2005). *Does Foreign Direct Investment Promote Development?* Washington, DC: Institute for International Economics.

Müller-Debus, A. K., C. R. Thauer, and T. A. Börzel. (2009a). "Governing HIV/AIDS in South Africa: The Role of Firms." SFB-Governance Working Paper, No. 20, June 2009, Research Center "Governance in Areas of Limited Statehood," Berlin.

(2009b). "Firms, Associations and the Governance of HIV/AIDS in South Africa." *Zeitschrift für Menschenrechte*, 3 (2): 157–89.

National Association of Automobile Manufacturers of South Africa (NAAMSA) (2006). "Industry Vehicle Sales, Export and Import Data 1995–2007," www.naamsa.co.za/papers/20060124/export_import_1995_2007.htm (accessed September 11, 2006).

Nattrass, N. (2007). *Mortal Combat: AIDS Denialism and the Struggle for Antiretrovirals in South Africa*. Scottsville: University of KwaZulu-Natal Press.

Nordas, H. K. (2004). "The Global Textile and Clothing Industry post the Agreement on Textiles and Clothing." Working Paper VII-2004, World Trade Organization (WTO), Geneva.

North, D. C. (1990). *Institutions, Institutional Change and Economic Performance*. Cambridge University Press.

OECD (2007). *OECD Environmental Performance Reviews: China*. Paris: OECD.

Ostrom, E. (1990). *Governing the Commons. The Evolution of Institutions for Collective Action*. Cambridge, New York, Melbourne: Cambridge University Press.

(1999). "Institutional Rational Choice: An Assessment of the Institutional Analysis Framework." In *Theories of the Policy Process*, P. A. Sabatier (ed.). Boulder, CO: Westview Press, 35–73.

Parker, C. (2002). *The Open Corporation: Effective Self-regulation and Democracy*. Cambridge University Press.

Prakash, A. (2000). *Greening the Firm. The Politics of Corporate Environmentalism*. Cambridge University Press.

Prakash, A. and Potoski, M. (2006). *The Voluntary Environmentalists. Green Clubs, ISO 14001, and Voluntary Environmental Regulations*. Cambridge University Press.

(2007). "Investing Up: FDI and the Cross-Country Diffusion of ISO 14001 Management Systems." *International Studies Quarterly*, 51: 723–44.

Ramos, C. A., and I. Montiel (2005). "When Are Corporate Environmental Policies a Form of Greenwashing?" *Business and Society*, 44: 377–414.

Richards, D. L., R. D. Gelleny, and D. H. Sacko (2001). "Money with a Mean Streak? Foreign Economic Penetration and Government Respect for Human Rights in Developing Countries." *International Studies Quarterly*, 45: 219–39.

Risse, T. (ed.) (2011). *Governance without a State? Policies and Politics in Areas of Limited Statehood*. New York: Columbia University Press.

Rodrik, D. (2008). "Understanding South Africa's economic puzzles." *Economics of Transition*, 16: 769–97.

Ronit, K. and V. Schneider (2000). *Private Organizations in Global Politics.* New York: Routledge.

Rosenbrock, R. (1998). "Politics Behind AIDS Policies: Appropriate Approaches, Fostering and Impeding Factors." In *Politics Behind AIDS Policies. Case Studies from India, Russia and South Africa,* R. Rosenbrock (ed.). Berlin: Wissenschaftszentrum Berlin für Sozialforschung, 6–13.

Sappington, D. E. M. (1991). "Incentives in Principal–Agent Relationships." *Journal of Economic Perspectives,* 5 (2): 45–66.

Scharpf, F. W. (1997). *Games Real Actors Play. Actor-Centered Institutionalism in Policy Research.* Boulder, CO: Westview.

Schepers, D. H. (2006). "The impact of NGO network conflict on the corporate social responsibility strategies of multinational corporations." *Business and Society,* 45 (3): 282–99.

Sethi, P. and B. Elango (1999). "The Influence of 'Country of Origin' on Multinational Corporation Strategy: A Conceptual Framework." *Journal of International Management,* 5 (4): 285–98.

Siedman, G. (2007). *Beyond the Boycott.* New York: Russell Sage Foundation.

Shipan, C. R. and C. Volden (2008). "The Mechanisms of Policy Diffusion." *American Journal of Political Science,* 52: 840–57.

Schmitter, P. C. and G. Lehmbruch (1979). *Trends Towards Corporatist Mediation.* Beverly Hills: Sage.

Simmons, B. A., F. Dobbin, and G. Garrett (2006). "Introduction: International Diffusion of Liberalism." *International Organization,* 60: 781–810.

Simon, D. F. and C. Cong (2008). "China's Emerging Science and Technology Talent Pool: A Quantitative and Qualitative Assessment." In *Greater China's Quest for Innovation,* H. S. Rowen, M. G. Hancock, and W. F. Miller (eds.). Stanford, CA: Walter H. Shorenstein Asia-Pacific Research Center, 181–97.

Simon, H. A. (1961). *Administrative Behavior.* New York: Oxford University Press.

Singh, A. and A. Zammit (2004). "Labour Standards and the 'Race to the Bottom': Rethinking Globalization and Workers' Rights from Developmental and Solidaristic Perspectives." *Oxford Review of Economic Policy,* 20 (1): 85–104.

Skjaerseth, J. B. and T. Skodvin (2003). *Climate Change and the Oil Industry: Common Problems, Varying Strategies.* Manchester University Press.

Skyrms, B. (2004). *The Stag Hunt and the Evolution of Social Structure.* Cambridge, New York: Cambridge University Press.

Smith, C. N. (2008). "Consumers as Drivers of Corporate Social Responsibility." In *The Oxford Handbook of Corporate Social Responsibility,* A. Crane, M. Abagail, D. Matten, J. Moon, and D. S. Siegel (eds.). Oxford, New York: Oxford University Press, 303–23.

Snidal, D. (1986). "The Game Theory of International Politics." In *Cooperation under Anarchy*, K. A. Oye (ed.). Princeton University Press, 25–57.

Spar, D. L. and L. T. La Mure (2003). "The Power of Activism: Assessing the Impact of NGOs on Global Business." *California Management Review*, 45: 78–101.

Stein, A. A. (1983). "Coordination and Collaboration: Regimes in an Anarchic World." In *International Regimes*, S. D. Krasner (ed.). Ithaca, NY: Cornell University Press, 115–40.

Sternfeld, E. (2006). "Umweltsituation und Umweltpolitik in China." *Aus Politik und Zeitgeschichte*, 49: 27–35.

Strang, D. (1991). "Adding Social Structure to Diffusion Models: an Event-history Framework." *Sociological Methods and Research*, 19: 324–53.

Streeck, W. and K. Yamamura (2001). *The Origins of Nonliberal Capitalism: Germany and Japan in Comparison*. Ithaca, NY: Cornell University Press.

Szablowski, D. (2007). *Transnational Law and Local Struggles: Mining, Communities, and the World Bank*. Portland, OR: Hart.

Task Force on Environmental Governance (2006). "Environmental Governance in China." Unpublished document evaluating the system of environmental governance in China. Beijing, December 11.

Thauer, C. R. (2013a). "Coping with Uncertainty. The Automotive Industry and the Governance of HIV/AIDS in South Africa." In *Business and Governance in South Africa. Racing to the Top?*, T. A. Börzel and C. R. Thauer (eds.). Houndmills: Palgrave, 45–67.

(2013b). "Upgrading the Periphery? Car Companies and Environmental Governance in South Africa." In *Business and Governance in South Africa. Racing to the Top?*, T. A. Börzel and C. R. Thauer (eds.). Houndmills: Palgrave, 128–52.

(2014). "Goodness Comes from Within. Intra-organizational Dynamics of Corporate Social Responsibility." *Business and Society*, April: 1–34.

Thelen, K. (2004). *How Institutions Evolve: The Political Economy of Skills in Germany, Britain, the United States and Japan*. Cambridge University Press.

Tilly, C. (1997). "Means and Ends of Comparison in Macrosociology." *Comparative Social Research*, 16: 43–53.

Trullen, J. and W. B. Stevenson (2006). "Strategy and Legitimacy: Pharmaceutical Companies' Reaction to the HIV Crisis." *Business and Society*, 45 (2): 178–210.

Udayasankar, K. (2008). "Corporate Social Responsibility and Firm Size." *Journal of Business Ethics*, 83 (2): 167–75.

United Nations Industrial Development Organization (UNIDO) (2002). *Corporate Social Responsibility: Implications for Small and Medium Enterprises in Developing Countries*. UNIDO.

UNAIDS (2005). "Access to Treatment in the Private-sector Workplace: The Provision of Antiretroviral Therapy by Three Companies in South Africa," (UNAIDS 05/11E): http://books.google.de/books?id=IKkRTYV CSK4C&printsec=frontcover&hl=de&source=gbs_ge_summary_r&cad=0#v=onepage&q&f=false (accessed January 2, 2013).

US Department of Commerce (2005). "South African Market for Automotive Components and Parts." CS Market Research. Country and Sub-sector Industry, http://strategis.ic.gc.ca/epic/internet/inimr-ri2.nsf/en/gr-01995e.html (accessed September 17, 2006).

Van Tulder, R. and A. Kolk (2001). "Multinationality and Corporate Ethics." *Journal of International Business Studies*, 32 (2): 267–83.

Vlok, E. (2006). "The Textile and Clothing Industry in South Africa." In *The Future of the Textile and Clothing Industry in Sub-Saharan Africa*, H. Jauch and R. Traub-Merz (eds.). Bonn: Friedrich-Ebert-Stiftung, 227–46.

Vogel, D. (1995). *Trading Up: Consumer and Environmental Regulation in a Global Economy*. Cambridge, MA: Harvard University Press.

(2005). *The Market for Virtue. The Potential and Limits of Corporate Social Responsibility*. Washington, DC: The Brookings Institution.

(2010). "Taming Globalization?" In *The Oxford Handbook of Business and Government*, D. Coen, W. Grant and G. Wilson (eds.). Oxford University Press, 472–94.

Vogel, D. and R. Kagan (2004). *Dynamics of Regulatory Change: How Globalization Affects National Regulatory Policies*. Berkeley, Los Angeles: University of California Press.

von Soest, C. and M. Weinel (2006). *The Treatment Controversy – Global Health Governance and South Africa's HIV/AIDS Policy*. Hamburg: German Institute of Global and Area Studies.

Waltz, K. N. (1954). *Man, the State and War. A Theoretical Analysis*. New York: Columbia University Press.

Wang, H. (2011). *China's National Talent Plan: Key Measures and Objectives*, http://ssrn.com/abstract=1828162.

Whiteside, A. and C. Sunter (2000). *AIDS: the Challenge for South Africa*. Cape Town: Tafelberg.

Wick, I. (2007). *Aldi's Clothing Bargains – Discount Buys Discounting Standards? Working Conditions in Aldi's Suppliers in China and Indonesia*. Siegburg: SÜDWIND Institut für Ökonomie und Ökumene.

Williams, O. F. (2004). "A Lesson from the Sullivan Principles. The Rewards for Being Pro-active." In *Hard Choices, Soft Law: Voluntary Standards in Global Trade, Environment, and Social Governance*, J. J. Kirton and M. J. Trebilcock (eds.). Aldershot: Ashgate, 57–82.

Williamson, O. E. (1975). *Markets and Hierarchies: Analysis and Antitrust Implications. A Study in the Economics of Internal Organization.* New York: Free Press/Macmillan Publishing.

(1985). *The Economic Institutions of Capitalism. Firms, Markets, Relational Contracting.* New York: Free Press.

(1996). *The Mechanisms of Governance.* New York: Oxford University Press.

(2000). "Strategy Research: Competence and Governance Perspectives." In *Competence, Governance, and Entrepreneurship: Advances in Economic Strategy Research,* N. Foss and V. Mahnke (eds.). New York: Oxford University Press, 21–54.

(2002). "The Lens of Contract: Private Ordering." *American Economic Review,* 92 (2): 438–43.

Xing, Y. and C. Kolstad (2002). "Do Lax Environmental Regulations Attract Foreign Investment?" *Environmental and Resource Economics,* 21 (1): 1–22.

Zaheer, A. and N. Venkatraman (1994). "Determinants of Electronic Integration in the Insurance Industry: An Empirical Test." *Management Science,* 40: 549–66.

Zartman, I. W. (1977). "Negotiation as a Joint Decision-Making Process." *Journal of Conflict Resolution,* 21 (4): 619–38.

Zeng, K. and J. Eastin (2007). "International Economic Integration and Environmental Protection: The Case of China." *International Studies Quarterly,* 51 (4): 971–95.

Zürn, M. (1992). *Interessen und Institutionen in der internationalen Politik. Grundlegung und Anwendung des situationsstrukturellen Ansatzes.* Opladen: Leske and Budrich.

Interviews

Organization name	Organization type	Function/position	Time and place	Form	Documentation
Accurate Limited – Hitting The Mark in China Business	Company: textile consulting and sourcing for Western brands and retailers in China	Managing Partner	April 11, 2008, Hangzhou	In person	Notes
Adidas	Company: textile industry, sports brand	HR Manager	September 20, 2007, Cape Town	In person	Recording, transcription
African Institute of Corporate Citizenship (AICC)	NGO	CEO	February 15, 2007 and September 19, 2008, Johannesburg	In person	Recording, transcription
AHK, DIHK (Delegation of German Industry and Commerce Shanghai)	Associations of German industry in China	Deputy General Manager	April 2, 2008, Shanghai	In person	Recording, notes
AIDS Relief Fund for China	NGO	Grants Program Co-ordinator	March 27, 2008, San Francisco	In person	Notes
American Chamber of Commerce (AmCham), People's Republic of China	Association of US American industry in China	Governor	April 15, 2008, Beijing	In person	Recording, notes
American Chamber of Commerce (AmCham), People's Republic of China	Association of US American industry in China: CSR subcommittee	Corporate Social Responsibility Manager	April 15, 2008, Beijing	In person	Recording, notes
Andritz AG	Customized plants systems and services	Installation and Commissioning Manager	April 8, 2008, Shanghai	In person	Notes

Organization name	Organization type	Function/position	Time and place	Form	Documentation
The Asia Foundation	NGO	Program Assistant, Activist	April 15, 2008, Beijing	In person	Recording, notes
The Asia Foundation	NGO	Senior Program Officer	April 15, 2008, Beijing	In person	Recording, notes
August Laepple South Africa	Company: 1st tier supplier, automotive	Human Resources Manager	September 13, 2007, Rosslyn, South Africa	In person	Recording, transcription
August Laepple South Africa	Company: 1st tier supplier, automotive	Environmental and Safety Manager, Quality Systems Department	September 13, 2007, Rosslyn, South Africa	In person	Recording, transcription
Automotive Industry Development Centre (AIDC), Gauteng	Government Agency: policy fields HIV and industrial development	Manager: Socioeconomic Programs, HIV Workplace Programs	February 12, 2007, Rosslyn, South Africa	In person	Recording, notes
Automotive Industry Development Centre (AIDC), Gauteng	Government Agency: policy fields HIV and industrial development	Chief Operations Officer	Feb 12, 2007, Rosslyn, South Africa	In person	Recording, notes
B&M Analysts	Consultancy, expert	Chairman	October 1, 2007, Durban	In person	Recording, transcription
BDI (Federation of German Industries): CSR Germany	Association of German industries: CSR	Director International Affairs and Manager CSR Germany	April 26, 2007, Berlin	In person	Notes, recording
Beier Albany	Company: automotive and textile supplier	CEO	September 28, 2007, Durban	In person	Recording, transcription

Organization	Description	Role	Date, Location	Mode	Documentation
Beier Albany	Company: automotive supplier and textiles	Industrial Health Nurse, HIV Nurse	September 28, 2007, Durban	In person	Recording, transcription
Billabong South Africa	Company: textile manufacturing and sportswear and fashion brand	Managing Director	September 25, 2007, Port Elizabeth	In person	Recording, transcription
Billabong South Africa	Company: textile manufacturing and sportswear and fashion brand	Human Resources	September 25, 2007, Port Elizabeth	In person	Recording, transcription
BMW Group, Germany	Company: automotive, OEM	Director Corporate and Intergovernmental Affairs, Department Manager Corporate Sustainability	August 2, 2007, Munich	In person	Recording, transcription
BMW Group, Germany	Company: automotive, OEM	Manager Corporate Messages, Group Publications	August 2, 2007, Munich	In person	Recording, transcription
BMW South Africa	Company: automotive, OEM	Environmental Manager	February 20, 2007, Rosslyn, South Africa	In person	Recording, transcription
BMW South Africa	Company: automotive, OEM	General Manager, Corporate Planning	February 20, 2007, Midrand, South Africa	In person	Recording, transcription
BMW South Africa	Company: automotive, OEM	Occupational Health and HIV/AIDS Program Manager	February 14, 2007, Midrand, South Africa, and February 19, 2008, Cape Town	In person	Recording

Organization name	Organization type	Function/position	Time and place	Form	Documentation
BMW South Africa	Company: automotive, OEM	Project Leader VPS and Security, Health, and Environment (SHE) Representative	February 20, 2007, Rosslyn, South Africa	In person	Recording, transcription
Border Kai Chamber of Commerce (BKCC)/ Daimler Chrysler Health Trust, "Siapkana"	Public–private partnership: HIV/AIDS workplace program facilitation	Managing Director of public–private partnership	September 27, 2008, East London, South Africa	In person	Recording, transcription
Bundesvereinigung der Deutschen Arbeitgeber-verbaende (BDA): CSR Germany	Association of German employers: CSR	European Union and International Social Policy Manager, Manager CSR Germany	April 26, 2007, Berlin	In person	Notes, recording
Business Social Compliance Initiative (BSCI)	Association: labor standards and CSR in the textile and apparel industry/NGO	Managing Director	February 19, 2008	Phone	Recording
Cape Town Fashion Council (CTFC)	Public–private partnership, association: textile industry	Manager	September 18, 2008, Cape Town	In person	Recording, transcription
Capewell Springs	Company: 2nd and 3rd tier automotive supplier, textile supplier	Production Manager	September 18, 2008, Cape Town	In person	Recording, transcription

Organization	Type	Role	Date	Method	Record
China CSR Map, Danish Institute for Human Rights, Nordic Institute of Asian Studies	University, NGO	NGO Activist, Researcher	January 30, 2008	Phone	Notes
China Environment and Sustainable Development Reference and Research Center (CESDRRC)	Government Agency, part of SEPA (Ministry of the Environment, China)	Manager Reference and Research Centre	February 1, 2008	Phone	Notes
China–Europe Textile Alliance (CETA)	Association, public–private partnership: textile industry, CSR and industrial development	Director	April 2008, Shanghai	In person	Recording, notes
Chinese Government (Ministry of the Environment, SEPA), national and province of Zhejiang	Government Agency	Technical Advisor	April 11, 2008, Hangzhou	In person	Recording, notes
Chinese Government (Ministry of the Environment), national and province of Zhejiang; and Environment-oriented Enterprise Consultancy (EECZ), Chinese Government and German Technical Development Agency (GTZ)	Government Agency (environment), public–private partnership (Chinese Government and GTZ – German Technical Development Agency)	Program Manager	April 11, 2008, Hangzhou	In person	Recording, notes

Organization name	Organization type	Function/position	Time and place	Form	Documentation
Clean Clothes Campaign (CCC)	NGO	Office Manager and Campaigner	February 15, 2008	Phone	Recording, notes
Clothing Bargaining Council Cape Town, Advisor to Government	Union (SACTWU) and Employers	Chairperson Health	March 27, 2007, Cape Town	In person	Recording, transcription
Clothing Export Council, Clotrade	Association: textile industry	Executive Director	March 27, 2007, Cape Town	In person	Recording, transcription
Cosieleather Garments (Hua Tong Group)	Company: textile	Manager	April 24, 2008, Hencun	In person	Notes, protocol, visual inspection
Cosieleather Garments (Hua Tong Group)	Company: textile	Owner family	April 24, 2008, Hencun	In person	Notes, protocol, visual inspection
Crossley Carpets and Safyr	Companies: textile, industrial carpets, supplier to hotels and crusaders (Crossley Carpets) and rug maker (Safyr)	Director Human Resources	September 28, 2007, Durban	In person	Recording, transcription
Crossley Carpets and Safyr	Company (textile, industrial carpets, supplier to top hotels and crusaders)	Chief Engineer and Environmental Manager	September 28, 2007, Durban, South Africa	In person	Recording, transcription

Organization	Type	Position	Date, Location	Mode	Documentation
Crossley Carpets and Safyr	Companies: textile, industrial carpets, supplier to hotels and crusaders (Crossley Carpets) and rug maker (Safyr)	Assistant Director Human Resources	September 28, 2007, Durban	In person	Recording, transcription
Daimler AG, China	Company: automotive, OEM	Manager Human Resources	April 17, 2008, Beijing	In person	Recording
Daimler AG, External Affairs and Public Policy	Company: automotive, OEM	Senior Manager Corporate Social Responsibility	August 6, 2007	Phone	Recording, transcription
Daimler AG, South Africa	Company: automotive, OEM	Manager Corporate Health Services, HIV/AIDS Program	February 26, 2007 East London	In person	Recording, transcription
Daimler AG, South Africa	Company: automotive, OEM	Manager: Quality Management and Integrated Management System	September 23, 2008, East London	In person	Recording, transcription
DB Apparel (Playtex, Wonderbra), South Africa	Company: textile industry	Manager Human Resources	September 25, 2008, Durban	In person	Notes, recording
DB Apparel (Playtex, Wonderbra), South Africa	Company: textile industry	Manager Logistics, Sourcing and Production Design	September 25, 2008, Durban	In person	Notes, recording
DB Apparel (Playtex, Wonderbra), South Africa	Company: textile industry	Director of Manufacturing	September 25, 2008, Durban	In person	Notes, recording
DE International (Delegation of German Industry and Commerce, Beijing)	Association	Project Manager Industry and Technology	April 17, 2008, Beijing	In person	Notes

Organization name	Organization type	Function/position	Time and place	Form	Documentation
Democratic Nursing Organisation of South Africa (DENOSA) and South African NGO Coalition (SANGOCO)	NGO	Activist, Occupational Health Nurse and Program Advisor HIV/AIDS	February 13, 2007, Johannesburg	In person	Notes
Department of Economic Development and Tourism of the Western Cape	Government agency	Director Sector Development	September 18, 2008, Cape Town	In person	Recording, transcription
Department of Economic Development and Tourism of the Western Cape	Government agency	Sector Specialist: Marine Manufacturing Industries	September 18, 2008, Cape Town	In person	Recording, transcription
Department of Environmental Affairs and Development Planning of the Western Cape and Cape Town	Government agency	Assistant Director, Manager Integrated Environmental Management	September 15, 2008, Cape Town	In person	Recording, transcription
Department of Environmental Affairs and Development Planning of the Western Cape and Cape Town	Government agency	Principal Environmental Officer	September 15, 2008, Cape Town	In person	Recording, transcription

Organization	Type	Position	Date, Location	Mode	Documentation
Department of Environmental Affairs and Development Planning of the Western Cape and Cape Town	Government agency	Principal Environmental Officer	September 15, 2008, Cape Town	In person	Recording, transcription
Department of Trade and Industry (DTI) South Africa	Government agency	Automotive sector desk	February 19, 2007, Pretoria	In person	Recording
Deutscher Entwicklungsdienst (DED; German Development Service)	Development agency	Regional Co-ordinator Southern and Eastern Africa, Public–Private Partnerships (PPP)	February 20, 2007, Pretoria	In person	Recording, transcription
Deutsche Investitions- und Entwicklungsgesellschaft (DEG)	Development agency	Prokurist Programmfinanzen, Director Public Private Partnerships (PPP)	April 12, 2007, Colone	In person	Notes
Die Zeit	German newspaper	Journalist covering China, Wirtschafts-redaktion	June 1, 2008, at EUI in Florence	In person	Notes
DLA Piper China	International law firm	CSR Manager	January 23, 2008 and April 19, 2008, Beijing	Phone and in person	Notes
Dragon Up Holdings Limited	Company: textile and textile-related export and production facilitation	Director	On many occasions in April 2008, Hangzhou	In person	Protocol

Organization name	Organization type	Function/position	Time and place	Form	Documentation
Durban Chamber of Commerce and Industry, Durban Chamber Foundation	Association, NGO	Foundation Director	September 25, 2008, Durban	In person	Recording, transcription
ECONSENSE (Forum for Sustainable Development of German Business)	Association: German industry, CSR	Head of Office	April 27, 2007, Berlin	In person	Recording, notes
Edcon	Company: retailer, textile industry	Merchandise Logistics Executive	September 30, 2008, Johannesburg	In person	Recording, transcription
Edcon	Company: retailer, textile industry	Employee Wellness and Occupational Health Unit	September 30, 2008, Johannesburg	In person	Recording, transcription
European Union Chamber of Commerce in China (EUCCC)	Association	Business Manager	April 16, 2008, Beijing	In person	Recording, notes
The Fair Labor Association (FLA)	NGO, association, consultancy	NGO and Trade Union Coordinator	March 8, 2008, New York City	In person	Notes, protocol
Falke South Africa	Company: textile, underwear, and sportswear	Human Resources Manager, Occupational Health Manager	September 21, 2007, Cape Town	In person	Recording, transcription
Falke South Africa	Company: textile, underwear and sportswear	Production Manager	September 1, 2007, Cape Town	In person	Recording, transcription

Feltex Automotive	Company: automotive, 1st tier supplier	Procurement Manager	September 25, 2008, Durban	In person	Recording, transcription
Feltex Automotive	Company: automotive, 1st tier supplier	Security, Health and Environment (SHE) Manager	September 25, 2008, Durban	In person	Recording, transcription
Firstpro Engineering	Company: automotive, 1st tier supplier	CEO	September 23, 2008, East London	In person	Recording, transcription
Firstpro Engineering	Company: automotive, 1st tier supplier	Quality Management and Human Resources Manager	September 23, 2008, East London	In person	Recording, transcription
Ford Foundation China	NGO	Representative	February 18, 2008	Phone	Recording
Ford Motor Company South Africa	Company: automotive, OEM	Quality Systems Engineer	September 30, 2008, Sylverton, South Africa	In person	Recording, transcription
Ford Motor Company South Africa	Company: automotive, OEM	Manager: Employee Wellness and Occupational Health	September 14, 2007, Sylverton, South Africa, and September 19, 2008, Cape Town	In person	Recording, transcription
Ford Motor Company South Africa; National Association of Automobile Manufacturers of South Africa (NAAMSA)	Company: automotive, OEM and association	Manager, Environmental and Safety Engineering, Chairperson of NAAMSA Fuel and Emission Committee	February 20, 2007, Sylverton, South Africa	In person	Recording, transcription
Foreign Trade Association, AVE-Sector Model	Business association: textile	Director	April 13, 2007, Cologne	In person	Recording

Organization name	Organization type	Function/position	Time and place	Form	Documentation
Foschini Group	Company: retailer, textile industry	Senior HR Manager: Corporate Social Investments and Employee Wellness	September 16, 2008, Cape Town	In person	Recording, transcription
Foschini Group	Company: retailer, textile industry	Risk Manager	September 16, 2008, Cape Town	In person	Recording, transcription
Foschini Group	Company: retailer, textile industry	Group Logistics and Sourcing Director	September 16, 2008, Cape Town	In person	Recording, transcription
Frame Textile Group	Company: textile industry	Group Human Resources Director	October 1, 2007, Durban	In person	Recording, transcription
General Motors South Africa	Company: automotive, OEM	Benefits Coordinator	February 23, 2007, Struvendale, South Africa	In person	Recording, transcription
German Technical Cooperation Agency (GTZ)	Development Agency	Programmbüro Sozial- und Ökostandards	April 11, 2007, at GTZ Headquarters, Eschborn	In person	Notes
German Technical Cooperation Agency (GTZ) and Business Social Compliance Initiative (BSCI) China	Government Agency and Association: CSR, textile industry	Sino-German Corporate Social Responsibility Project Technical Advisor, BSCI Roundtable China	April 17, 2008, Beijing	In person	Recording

Organization	Type	Position	Date/Location	Method	Record
German Technical Cooperation Agency (GTZ), Pretoria	Development agency	Country Director	February 19, 2007, Pretoria	In person	Recording, notes
German Technical Cooperation Agency (GTZ)	Expert, researcher	Researcher, PhD student	Meetings throughout April 2008, Hangzhou and Beijing	In person	Notes
German Technical Cooperation Agency (GTZ)	Expert, researcher	Scientific Researcher China Wind Power Research and Training Project (CWPP)	Meetings in April 2008, Beijing	In person	Notes
Global Compact Germany and German Technical Cooperation Agency (GTZ)	Public–private partnership and development agency	Executive Director Centre for Cooperation with the Private Sector/PPP, Coordinator Global Compact Germany German Industry Private Sector/PPP	April 25, 2007, Berlin	In person	Recording, notes
Global Compact Germany and German Technical Cooperation Agency (GTZ)	Public–private partnership and development agency	Manager Centre for Cooperation with the Private Sector/PPP, Coordinator Global Compact Germany	April 25, 2007, Berlin	In person	Recording, notes
Global Public Policy Institute (GPPI)	Company: consultancy	Director	April 27, 2007, Berlin	In person	Notes

Organization name	Organization type	Function/position	Time and place	Form	Documentation
Hangzhou Dadi Garments Co., Ltd.	Company: textile industry	Foreign Trader Manager	April 5–6, 2008, Tonglu	In person	Recording, notes, visual inspection
Hangzhou Futan Knitting Co., Ltd. (Futan)	Company: textile industry	General Manager	April 10, 2008, Hengcun	In person	Notes, visual observation
IBM Global Services China	Company: 1st tier supplier to automotive and textile industry	Project Manager Corporate Citizenship and Corporate Affairs	April 15, 2008, Beijing	In person	Recording, notes
International Labour Organization (ILO) Workplace Education Program, China	International organization, public–private partnership	Chief Technical Advisor	April 17, 2008, Beijing	In person	Recording, notes
International Trimmings and Labels	Company: textile industry	Invoicing Supervisor	September 17, 2008, Cape Town	In person	Recording, transcription
International Trimmings and Labels	Company: textile industry	Quality Management Representative	September 17, 2008, Cape Town	In person	Recording, transcription
International Trimmings and Labels	Company: textile industry	Nursing Sister, Occupational Health	September 17, 2008, Cape Town	In person	Recording, transcription
Interplex Industries Inc.	Company: 1st tier supplier to automotive industry	Global Account Program Engineering Manager	April 2008, Hangzhou	In person	Notes
iTrainee (International Graduate Recruitment) and Polymax Group Company Ltd.	Companies: textile (import-export and textile production), human resources consultancy	Account Manager	April 22, 2008, Ningbo	In person	Notes

Organization	Type/Description	Role	Date, Location	Mode	Documentation
Jordan and Co., South Africa	Company: textile industry, 1st tier supplier to retailers, retailer of Asics, former supplier of Nike and Adidas	Managing Director, CEO	September 20, 2007, Cape Town	In person	Recording, transcription
Konrad-Adenauer-Stiftung (KAS)	NGO, Think Tank	Head of Division Southeast Europe and Coordinator Rule of Law	July 2008, Berlin	In person	Notes
Levi's	Company: textile brand	Marketing Director	October 2, 2008, Cape Town	In person	Recording, transcription
Lloyd Textile Trading Limited	Company: textile export and production	Consultant Sourcing and Production	April 11, 2008, Hangzhou	In person	Protocol
LP Apparel, Inc. and LP Apparel Group	Companies: textile, production and exports	President	April 11, 2008, Hangzhou	In person	Notes, protocol
Massmart	Company: retailer, textile industry	Group Corporate Affairs Executive	September 29, 2008, Johannesburg	In person	Recording, transcription
MDC International (HK) Ltd., Hangzhou Office	Company: import-export and production	General Manager	On many occasions throughout April 2008, Hangzhou	In person	Recording, notes
Migra Textiles	Company: textile	Director Dyehouse Division	September 17, 2008, Cape Town	In person	Recording, transcription
Migra Textiles	Company: textile	Director	September 17, 2008, Cape Town	In person	Recording, transcription
Monviso (part of Seardel Group Trading)	Company: textile and sportswear	Human Resources Manager	September 16, 2008, Cape Town	In person	Recording, transcription
Monviso (part of Seardel Group Trading)	Company: textile and sportswear	Sales Executive	September 16, 2008, Cape Town	In person	Recording, transcription

Organization name	Organization type	Function/position	Time and place	Form	Documentation
Monviso (part of Seardel Group Trading)	Company, textile, clothing	Production Executive	September 16, 2008, Cape Town	In person	Recording, transcription
Monviso (part of Seardel Group Trading)	Company: textile and sportswear	CEO	September 16, 2008, Cape Town	In person	Recording, transcription
National Association of Automobile Manufacturers of South Africa (NAAMSA)	Association: OEM and 1st tier suppliers	CEO	February 13, 2007, Pretoria	In person	Recording, transcription
National Association of Automotive Component and Allied Manufacturers (NAACAM)	Association: automotive suppliers and component manufacturers	Executive Director	September 29, 2008, Johannesburg	In person	Recording, transcription
National Cleaner Production Centre (NCPC)	Government agency, environment	Head of Regional Office Cape Town	March 27, 2007, Cape Town	In person	Recording, transcription
National Energy Regulator of South Africa (NERSA)	Government agency	Executive Manager Hydrocarbons Division	June 1, 2008, Florence	In person	Notes
The National Labor Committee (NLC)	NGO	Campaigner	March 4, 2008, New York City	In person	Notes, protocol
The National Labor Committee (NLC)	NGO	Director	March 4, 2008, New York City	In person	Notes, protocol
National Union for Metal and Steel of South Africa (NUMSA), Robert Bosch South Africa	Union, company: 1st tier supplier automotive	NUMSA, Employee, Peer Educator HIV/AIDS	September 19, 2007, Brits, South Africa	In person	Recording, transcription

Organization	Role	Date and location	Mode	Documentation
Nike South Africa	Corporate Responsibility Specialist	October 1, 2008, Midrand, South Africa	In person	Recording, transcription
Nike South Africa	Procurement and Sourcing Manager	October 2, 2008, Cape Town	In person	Recording, transcription
Nissan South Africa	Employee Wellness	February 14, 2007, Rosslyn, South Africa	In person	Recording, transcription
Nissan South Africa	CSR Manager	February 14, 2007, Rosslyn, South Africa	In person	Recording, transcription
Nissan South Africa	Senior Manager Strategic Projects, Corporate Affairs and Communication	February 14, 2007, Rosslyn, South Africa	In person	Recording, transcription
Nissan South Africa	Manager: Integrated Systems	February 14, 2007, Rosslyn, South Africa	In person	Recording, transcription
Not affiliated to an organization	Activist	On many occasions throughout April 2008, Hanzhou/Tonglu and Shanghai	In person	Notes
NTS Ltd. and Steilmann	Product Manager	April 8, 2008, Shanghai	In person	Recording, notes
Paltex	Managing Director	September 13, 2007, Garankuwa, South Africa	In person	Recording, transcription

Company: textile and sportswear brand

Company: textile and sportswear brand

Company: automotive, OEM

Company: automotive, OEM

Company: automotive, OEM

Company: automotive, OEM

Human rights activist, artist

Company, textiles, retailer, clothing

Company: textile industry

Organization name	Organization type	Function/position	Time and place	Form	Documentation
Polymax Group Company Ltd.	Company: textile industry import-export and production, clothing	Vice President, Human Resources and Development, Administrative Director	April 22, 2008, Ningbo	In person	Recording, notes
Polymax Group Company Ltd., former OTTO Sourcing Manager, China	Company: textile production and export	President	April 22, 2008, Ningbo	In person	Notes
Port Elizabeth Regional Chamber of Commerce and Industry (PERCCI)	Chamber of Commerce	CEO	September 26, 2007, Port Elizabeth, South Africa	In person	Recording, transcription
Robert Bosch, South Africa	Company: 1st tier supplier, automotive	Sourcing and Logistics, Head Auditor of Robert Bosch SA	September 19, 2007, Brits, South Africa	In person	Recording, transcription
Robert Bosch, South Africa	Company: 1st tier supplier, automotive	Environmental Engineering and Development Manager	September 19, 2007, Brits, South Africa	In person	Recording, transcription
Robert Bosch, South Africa	Company: 1st tier supplier, automotive	Peer Educator, HIV/AIDS Workplace Program	September 19, 2007, Brits, South Africa	In person	Recording, transcription
Robert Bosch, South Africa	Company: 1st tier supplier, automotive	Human Resources Director	September 19, 2007, Brits, South Africa and September 19, 2008, Cape Town	In person	Recording, transcription

SANS Fibre	Company: textile industry	Manager	March 30, 2007, Cape Town	In person	Recording, transcription
SANS Fibre	Company, textile industry	Union Representative	March 30, 2007	In person	Recording, transcription
SANS Fibre	Company: textile industry	Sales Manager	March 30, 2007, Cape Town	In person	Recording, transcription
SANS Fibre	Company: textile industry	General Manager	March 30, 2007, Cape Town	In person	Recording, transcription
Schaeffler Group South Africa (LUK, INA, FAG)	Company: 1st tier automotive supplier	Human Resources Manager	September 22, 2008, Port Elizabeth	In person	Recording, transcription
Schaeffler Group South Africa (LUK, INA, FAG)	Company: 1st tier automotive supplier	Key Accounts Manager, Export Sales Co-ordinator	September 22, 2008, Port Elizabeth	In person	Recording, transcription
Schaeffler Group South Africa (LUK, INA, FAG)	Company: 1st tier automotive supplier	Manager: Metallurgy and Surface Treatment and Kaizen Co-ordinator	September 22, 2008, Port Elizabeth	In person	Recording, transcription
Schaeffler Group South Africa (LUK, INA, FAG)	Company: 1st tier automotive supplier	Managing Director, President Automotive Division	September 22, 2008, Port Elizabeth	In person	Recording, transcription
SEQUA (Foundation for Economic Development and Vocational Training)	Development agency	Program Coordinator Public–Private Partnerships (PPP)	April 13, 2007, Bonn	In person	Notes, recording
Shaoxing Dhawoo Textile (part of Dhawoo Mode)	Company: textile industry	Former Manager, Foreign Trade Assistant, Human Resources	April 9, 2008, Shanghai	In person	Recording, notes

Organization name	Organization type	Function/position	Time and place	Form	Documentation
Shatterprufe	Company: 1st tier automotive supplier	Product Engineering and Corporate Quality Assurance Manager	September 22, 2008, Port Elizabeth	In person	Recording, transcription
Skadden, ARPS, Slate, Meagher, and Flom	Law firm, activist, CSR expert	Registered Foreign Lawyer (New York)	April 15, 2008, Beijing	In person	Recording, notes
Social Accountability International (SAI)	NGO/association, consultancy	Training Program South and Middle America	March 6, 2008, New York City	In person	Recording, notes
Social Accountability International (SAI)	NGO/association, consultancy	Manager of Corporate Programs and Training	March 6, 2008, New York City	In person	Recording, notes
Social Accountability International (SAI)	NGO/association, consultancy	Director of Corporate Programs and Training	March 6, 2008, New York City	In person	Recording, notes
Social Accountability International (SAI)	NGO/association, consultancy	Program Assistant	March 6, 2008, New York City	In person	Notes
Social Accountability International (SAI)	NGO/association, consultancy	SAI China Workplace Program Manager	April 15, 2008, Beijing	In person	Recording, notes
South Africa Medical Research Council, Centre for Health Policy, and School of Public Health University of Witswatersrand	Expert, university, national institute	Researcher, HIV, Health, and Development	September 19, 2008, Cape Town	In person	Recording, transcription
South African Business Coalition on HIV/AIDS (SABCOHA)	Association: HIV/AIDS	CEO	March 19, 2007, Johannesburg	In person	Recording, transcription

Organization	Type	Role	Date and place	Mode	Documentation
South African Bureau of Standards (SABS)	Government agency	Manager: Systems and Service Standards	September 12, 2007, Pretoria	In person	Recording, transcription
South African Bureau of Standards (SABS)	Private, for-profit part of SABS, certification organization and consultancy	Environmental Management Systems Certifier	September 12, 2007, Pretoria	In person	Recording, transcription
Southern African Clothing and Textile Workers' Union (SACTWU), SANS Fibre	Union: textile	Regional Trainer HIV-AIDS for SACTWU	March 30, 2007, Cape Town	In person	Recording, transcription
Tchibo	Company: discounter, textile	Senior Manager Corporate Responsibility	August 15, 2008, Hamburg	In person	Recording, notes
Tchibo-GTZ-China Project	Public–private partnership	Program Office Administrator CSR	April 11, 2008, Hangzhou	In person	Recording, transcription
Team Puma	Company: textile industry	HIV/AIDS and Occupational Health Manager	April 2, 2007, Cape Town	In person	Recording, transcription
Team Puma	Company: textile industry	Project Developing Manager	April 2, 2007, Cape Town	In person	Recording, transcription
TEXFED	Association, textile	Executive Director	March 21, 2007, Pretoria	In person	Recording, transcription
UN Global Compact Regional Learning Forum, Southern Africa	Public–private partnership	Director	February 16, 2007, Pretoria	In person	Recording, transcription
UN Global Compact Regional Learning Forum, Southern Africa	Public–private partnership	Co-director	February 16, 2007, Pretoria and September 18, 2007, Johannesburg	In person	Recording, transcription

Organization name	Organization type	Function/position	Time and place	Form	Documentation
University of Cape Town	Expert on automotive industry and market liberalization	Associate Professor	September 17, 2007, Cape Town	In person	Notes
University of Cape Town	Expert	Environmental Evaluation Unit	September 19, 2008, Cape Town	In person	Recording, transcription
University of Kwazulu-Natal	Expert	Professor, Expert: Textile Industry	March 29, 2007	In person	Recording, transcription
University of Pretoria	Expert, policy advisor	Advisor to New Partnerships for Africa's Development (NEPAD) and Professor at University of Pretoria, Faculty of Health Sciences, Expert: HIV/AIDS in South Africa	September 13, 2007, Bramley, South Africa	In person	Recording, transcription
Vacuform	Company: 1st tier automotive supplier	Managing Director	October 1, 2008, Rosslyn, South Africa	In person	Recording, transcription
VW South Africa	Company: automotive, OEM	Manager: Occupational Health, Employee Wellness and HIV/AIDS	September 25, 2007, Uitenhage, South Africa	In person	Recording, transcription
VW South Africa	Company: automotive, OEM	Occupational Health and Safety Specialist	September 25, 2007, Uitenhage, South Africa	In person	Recording, transcription

Organization	Type	Position	Date, Location	Format	Record
VW South Africa, former Department of Environmental Affairs of Gauteng, Department of Environmental Affairs of the Municipality of Johannesburg and of the International Association for impact Assessment of South Africa (IAIASA)	Company: automotive, OEM; government agencies, international organization	Environmental Controller Manufacturing Planning, former Environmental Officer and Member of association for Impact Assessments	September 25, 2007, Uitenhage, South Africa	In person	Recording, transcription
Welform Precision, Ltd.	Company: 1st tier automotive supplier	Managing Director Asia Operations	On many occasions throughout April 2008, Hangzhou	In person	Notes
Western Cape Department of Health	Government agency	Chief Director Health Programs	September 17, 2008, Cape Town	In person	Recording, transcription
Wonderful Earth (Far East) Ltd.	Company: textile, import-export, and production	CEO	April 8, 2008, Shanghai	In person	Recording, notes
Woolworths South Africa	Company: retailer, textiles	HIV/AIDS Manager and Medical Practitioner, Occupational Health Nurse	September 21, 2007, Cape Town	In person	Notes
Woolworths South Africa	Company: retailer, textiles	Corporate Social Investment Specialist	September 21, 2007, Cape Town	In person	Notes
Woolworths South Africa	Company: retailer, textiles	Good Business Journey Manager	September 21, 2007, Cape Town	In person	Notes
Worker Rights Consortium (WRC)	NGO	Assistant Director for Policy Communications	March 11, 2008, Washington, DC	In person	Notes

Organization name	Organization type	Function/position	Time and place	Form	Documentation
World Environment Center (WEC)	NGO/business association	Director of Global Corporate Programs	March 10, 2008, Washington, DC	In person	Recording, notes
World Watch Institute, China Watch	NGO	China Program Manager	March 11, 2008, Washington, DC	In person	Notes, protocol
World Wide Fund for Nature (WWF) China	NGO	Director Scientific Development and International Policy Program and Government Interaction	February 4, 2008	Phone	Recording, notes
World Wide Fund for Nature (WWF) South Africa	NGO	Trade and Investor Advisor, Director Automotive Desk	September 29, 2008, Johannesburg	In person	Recording, transcription
Worldwide Responsible Accredited Production (WRAP), Social Responsibility Committee of the American Apparel and Footwear Association	Business Association: CSR	Vice Chairman, President and CEO	February 8, 2008	Phone	Recording, transcription

Index